SOCIOLOGY

SOCIOLOGY

A Biographical Approach

PETER L. BERGER

&

BRIGITTE BERGER

Drawings by Robert Binks

BASIC BOOKS, INC.

PUBLISHERS

NEW YORK   LONDON

SECOND PRINTING
© 1972 by Peter and Brigitte Berger
Library of Congress Catalog Number 74–185617
SBN 465-06346-2
Manufactured in the United States of America
DESIGNED BY THE INKWELL STUDIO

Preface

This book is designed to serve as a textbook for introductory sociology courses in undergraduate colleges. We hope that it is readable enough to be of interest also to some who are not enrolled in such courses.

Sociology textbooks have multiplied like the sands of the sea. It makes sense, therefore, to indicate here the major characteristics of our book:

We have given the book the subtitle "A Biographical Approach." What we mean by this is that we have organized the material, as far as possible, in a sequence that corresponds to the stages of social experience in the biography of individuals. We think that this is more helpful to the beginning student than the usual organization of material in terms of a sociologist's preconceived notions about the structures of society. Clearly, this biographical organization could not be applied mechanically all through the book. While it dictated that the family would be discussed early in the book and old age toward the end, it is debatable whether, say, the discussion of power should precede or succeed that of deviance. Nor does this matter. What we have tried to do with the biographical organization, as well as with the entire presentation, is to consistently relate the analysis of large institutional structures to the concrete, everyday experience of individuals as they live their lives in society.

Throughout the book, we have emphasized concepts and basic perspectives rather than the presentation of data. The accumulation of data in most areas of sociology is enormous and growing at a rapid pace. To give an overview of this vast mass of information in an introductory course is not only very difficult but, we think, defeats the purpose of such a course. It seems to us that this purpose ought to be the communication of an underlying sociological perspective, of an understanding of how sociology essentially goes about its business. If the student has acquired a basic "kit" of concepts, he can subsequently apply this himself to whatever data may come to his attention—whether in other courses, in his reading or, for that matter, in his own social experience. Naturally it has been necessary to introduce data of all descriptions, but this was always done with the aforementioned purpose in mind. For example, when we have presented data on the American class system, this was not done in order to give a comprehensive panorama of everything sociologists have to say about this subject, but rather to illustrate how sociologists go about their business in this particular area of social life.

It may be said, then, that our approach emphasizes "theory" in sociology, in the sense of the conceptual architecture by which sociologists try to make sense of their findings. We have not, however, dealt with theory in a separate chapter. We have felt that, in an introductory text, it was better to introduce all theoretical problems in immediate connection with sociologists' efforts to interpret actual social experience. It is customary in most undergraduate curricula to confront students first with the concrete empirical applications of sociology, and only later (often in an advanced course for majors) with the various traditions of sociological theory. We agree with this procedure in terms of course sequences, but this is no reason for avoiding the theoretical approach in the introductory course itself.

Most of the data we have introduced are about contemporary American society. This "ethnocentrism" is methodological rather than ideological. We are certainly not suggesting that American society is the only important one to look at, or that sociology cannot or has not dealt effectively with other societies. Rather, we felt that, for American students, data about their own society would more effectively illustrate the sociological approach in general than data about unfamiliar or even exotic societies. We recognize that this is an arguable pedagogical position, but, be this as it may, this is the direction we have taken in this book.

We have felt that an introductory textbook is not the proper place to push our particular point of view in sociology. Rather, we have tried to give a picture of a broad consensus in the field. Wherever such consensus is lacking, we have tried, as fairly as we could, to present the divergent viewpoints and to show the implications of each, without trying to arbitrate or judge between them. Our own point of view may broadly be described as "humanistic," that is, as a conception of sociology as belonging essentially to the humanities. This conception of the field stands in the tradition of classical European (particularly German and French) sociological theory. In our case, the conception has been strongly influenced by the phenomenological approach to sociology, especially as it is found in the work of Alfred Schutz. We have elsewhere written in defense of this point of view. Here, we have tried to avoid such partisanship to the best of our ability. This is an introduction to sociology as generally understood by American sociologists, *not* an introduction to "humanistic," "phenomenological" or "Schutzian" sociology. The one place where we have deliberately introduced a Schutzian perspective (where we have done it inadvertently, we may be sure that critics will point it out) is in our discussion of the relationship of everyday social life to the institutional order. This, though, was done not with partisan intent but for the aforementioned purpose of making the sociological material "alive" for the student.

We have, separately, written two other books with an undergraduate audience in mind. Neither of these is an introductory textbook, but we should say how, in our understanding, the present book relates to them. The first is Peter Berger, *Invitation to Sociology* (Garden City, N.Y., Doubleday-Anchor, 1963). This is an informal exposition of a "humanistic" approach to sociology. It has been widely used as supplementary reading in introductory courses and, for some, may serve the same purpose here. The other is Brigitte Berger, *Societies in Change* (New York, Basic Books, 1971). This is a textbook in comparative sociology, with special emphasis on social change. It may be consulted by those readers who are frustrated by the "ethnocentrism" of the illustrations in the present book.

While broadcasting commercials on behalf of our diversified line of literary products, we will take the liberty of mentioning yet one more book—Peter Berger and Thomas Luckmann, *The Social Construction of Reality* (Garden City, N.Y., Doubleday-Anchor, 1967). For better or for worse, this will give anyone who is sufficiently curious an idea of the implications for sociological theory of a Schutzian approach. However much we may want to sell our own books, we would not really recommend this one for a beginning student.

Finally, there are some personal acknowledgments to be made. Above all we want to thank William Gum, our editor at Basic Books, for his unflagging enthusiasm and encouragement during the writing of this book. We want also to thank Maria Carvainis and Loretta Li, of Basic Books, for their patience and efficiency in making various technical arrangements; James Ecks for imaginative work on the instructor's manual, Daniel Pinard for research assistance and Susan Woolfson for secretarial services that are most inadequately described by this term.

Peter L. Berger   *Brigitte Berger*
RUTGERS UNIVERSITY   LONG ISLAND UNIVERSITY

Contents

SOCIOLOGY

Chapter 1

THE
EXPERIENCE
OF
SOCIETY

THERE IS THE STORY of the drunk and the garbage can. It seems that this drunk was sitting on the sidewalk in front of a garbage can. Earnestly and with great effort he attempted to embrace it. Finally, after several failures, the drunk succeeded in bringing his hands together around the garbage can. He grinned in triumph, but then a troubled expression settled on his face as he whispered to himself: "I'm surrounded!"

Society is our experience with other people around us. This experience is with us practically from the moment we are born. It serves as the context of everything else we experience, including our experience of the natural world and of ourselves, because these other experiences are also mediated and modified for us by other people: our mothers first call us by name and explain to us the difference between a tree and a telegraph pole. Indeed, whether we are still children or have grown up to be alleged adults, an overwhelming proportion of our thoughts, anxieties, hopes, and projects revolve around other people, be they individuals or groups. We keep on reaching out to others and, happily or disturbingly, all those others keep on surrounding us. Society is a lifelong experience, and it is also one of our most fundamental experiences; and it is these things long before we start reflecting about it in any deliberate way. Certainly, our experience of society antedates any acquaintance with a discipline called sociology, and it would remain a central fact of our lives even if we avoided such acquaintance completely.

BASIC VARIETIES OF EXPERIENCE

Our experience of society is not all of one piece. On the contrary, it is immensely variegated. Sociology, of course, purports to be an intellectual discipline that seeks to understand our experience of society, and, as we shall see, one of its foremost tasks is to do some justice to the immense variety of this experience. But there are two differentiations in our experience with other people that are basic and that may serve as the starting point of our thinking about society: some of our encounters with others are *big surprises;* some have become *routine events.* And some others we encounter as *individuals in face-to-face situations;* but some others again we confront as *agents of remote, anonymous groupings.*

BIG SURPRISES   We may confidently assume that when Adam and Eve first caught sight of each other, they were startled out of their wits. The first smiles of a baby still have such a character of surprising freshness, a kind of morning-dew of experience. Indeed, our early childhood experiences retain such a powerful place in our memory because, then, the world was still filled with so many astonishing surprises. It seems in retrospect that, then, a large number of our encounters with other people were startlingly new, unique, rich with significance. This quality in our experience with others diminishes steadily as we grow older. More and more, we meet others in situations that have become thoroughly routine and, as a rule, hold no surprises to speak of. Compare your recollections of your first day in school with your experience of the college class in which this textbook is being used. Then, however much you may have been prepared for the experience by your parents or by older children, you very probably went through that day in the consciousness of living through a historic occasion. You were tight with expectation, closely watching the teacher and the other children, registering everything that went on and (very importantly) keeping a firm watchfulness on your own behavior in the situation. Unless you are now in a very unusual class indeed, it is safe to guess that none of this applies to your present experience. You have been in other college classes before and, even if you don't know the details of what will go on in this one, you have a reasonable certainty that none of it will astound you. Not only do you have a general expectation as to what the others in the situation will do, but you are quite relaxed about your own responses. Indeed, you are by now "sophisticated" about the whole business of the educational process—and "sophistication" means precisely that experiences that used to be big surprises can now be handled as routine events.

CAN ADULTS BE SURPRISED?

To be sure, you may still be surprised as an adult—who knows, maybe even in a sociology class. You might fall in love. Somebody might throw a rock through the window. Or the professor, in a desperate effort to capture your attention, might take his pants off. While such surprises are always possible, they are rather improbable; what is more important, they are not part of your own or the others' expectations, and therefore will not govern your or their behavior in the situation. On the contrary, everyone's behavior will be governed by the notion that what is going on is a routine example of the process called college education. And, incidentally, it would be very difficult for the professor to teach anything over a period of time if this notion did *not* prevail, for the simple reason that the students' attention would be so much riveted to the astonishing goings-on in the classroom that little would be left over for the material being taught. Even the professor who takes off his pants in order to break the routine will find, upon doing it the third time (assuming that the dean of women has not intervened in the meantime), that his students will have become quite relaxed about *that* too. Startled exclamations ("look what he's doing!") will have given way to sober acknowledgment ("there he goes again"). In other words, the big surprise itself will have been *routinized*.

ROUTINE EVENTS AND STRUCTURES

For better or worse, our experience of society is very largely an experience of *routines*.[1] We may regret this, because it robs life of excitement. We may also console ourselves by reflecting that it is only because most of our experience is ordinary that we have any energy left over for the extraordinary things that

[1] The terms "routine" and "routinization" are derived from the classical German sociologist Max Weber (1864–1920). In German, the original terms are *Alltag* and *Veralltaeglichung*—literally, "the everyday" and the process by which something is *made to be* everyday.

do happen from time to time. In any case, regrettable or reassuring, the routine character of most of our experience with others is a necessary condition for society as an ongoing enterprise. No body of knowledge could be taught in a classroom in which each moment was as exciting as Adam's first rendezvous with Eve. Similarly, no continuous transactions of *any* sort could go on between people who, each time they met, would have to redefine all the terms of their relationships and all the rules of their dealings with each other. If such a society were possible (which it is not), life would perhaps be very exciting, but it would also be very difficult indeed. At best, everyone would be exhausted all the time; at worst, everyone would go out of his mind.

The insight into the routine, and necessarily routine, character of society has a very important implication: because most of our experience with other people consists of routines, this experience becomes discernible as a fabric that endures over a period of time—or, as sociologists like to say, society consists of *structures*.[2] This term has acquired a number of highly technical meanings in sociology, but for our immediate purpose we can take it as referring to something quite simple—namely, the networks of recurring patterns in which people behave in routine situations. Some of these networks are imposed upon the immediate transactions between individuals; others cover large numbers of people, some of whom have never met face-to-face, but who are related to each other in complex, often invisible, but nonetheless very real ways. For example, a classroom has a structure, in the sense that there is an ongoing pattern in the manner in which the individuals deal with each other each time they meet in this situation. But what goes on in this particular classroom is part of much larger structures—not only that of the college in question but, finally, of the educational establishment as a vast system of indirect relations between numerous individuals, most of whom remain unknown to each other personally.

[2] The term "structure" has been widely used by sociologists. It has become very technical in the usage of the so-called structural-functional school in American sociology, of which Talcott Parsons and Robert Merton have been the most distinguished representatives. The term is used here much more loosely.

MEETING INDIVIDUALS AND REPRESENTA-TIVES: IS THE TEACHER AN INDIVIDUAL?

This brings us to the second basic differentiation in our experience of society—that between face-to-face encounters and relations with others in the absence of such encounters.[3] The face-to-face situation is, of course, the original and most important case in our experience with other people. It is in such situations, in early childhood, that we first learn to relate to others. Throughout life, it is in face-to-face encounters with others that we carry on most of our business with the rest of mankind—including, crucially, the business of being recognized as a distinct and (if we are lucky) cherished person. Whatever meaning life has for us is, in the main, discovered, maintained, threatened or re-created in face-to-face relations with other people.

Put differently, the world in which we live is, above all, constituted by meanings that are attached to others whom we recurringly encounter face-to-face. However, quite early in life we discover that this fairly small world of our immediate experience is surrounded on all sides by much larger, often quite complicated or even incomprehensible patterns of relations between people. The process of growing up consists, in part, of the progressive discovery of these wider worlds that both border upon and (as we find out later) are the foundations of the little world that we experience directly. Furthermore, we then discover that many of the individuals whom we meet face-to-face are, quite apart from their unique qualities as individuals, agents or representatives of the structures of this wider world. Thus the teacher in school will undoubtedly be experienced as a unique individual (with good, bad or indifferent qualities, from the child's point of view); at the same time, though, she will be experienced *as a teacher,* as a specimen of the large category of peo-

[3] The analysis of the progression from face-to-face encounters with concrete individuals to anonymous relations with others beyond such encounters is derived from Alfred Schutz (see the suggested readings for this chapter).

ple called teachers, and thus as an agent of vast, behind-the-scenes structures called the school system, or education, or even "society" as an abstract entity. As soon as this happens, the child learns two things—first, to relate to people *anonymously,* that is, as typical figures in addition to their concrete individuality; and second, to locate himself and his limited experience in broad contexts shared with innumerable others who are and remain unseen.

MICRO-WORLD AND MACRO-WORLD

We can put this by saying that, in our experience of society, we simultaneously inhabit different worlds. First of all, crucially and continuously, we inhabit the *micro-world* of our immediate experience with others in face-to-face relations. Beyond that, with varying degrees of significance and continuity, we inhabit a *macro-world* consisting of much larger structures and involving us in relations with others that are mostly abstract, anonymous and remote. Both worlds are essential to our experience of society, and (with the exception of early childhood, when the micro-world is all we know) each world depends upon the other for its meaning to us. The micro-world and what goes on in it only makes full sense if it is understood against the background of the macro-world that envelops it; conversely, the macro-world has little reality for us unless it is repeatedly represented in the face-to-face encounters of the micro-world. Thus the transactions in the college classroom derive most of their sense from their being experience as part of the enveloping process of education; conversely, education would remain a vague idea with little reality to it in our own minds, unless it became part of our immediate experience with others in face-to-face situations. In our experience, then, micro-world and macro-world ongoingly interpenetrate each other. The sociologist, if he is to understand this experience, must constantly be aware of the two-fold manifestation of the phenomenon known as society, the micro-scopic as well as the macro-scopic one.

EVERYDAY LIFE
AND INSTITU-
TIONS

The same insight can be put in slightly different terms: Our experience of society is, first of all, an experience of other people in *everyday life*.[4] By the latter is meant, quite simply, the fabric of familiar routines within which we act and about which we think most of our waking hours. This sector of our experience is the most real to us, it is our habitual and ordinary habitat. The others, who are its co-inhabitants with us, are distinct individuals with whom we deal face-to-face at least at recurring intervals. At the risk of evoking irrelevant science-fiction associations, we may call this world of everyday life our "home world." Occasionally we leave it—by venturing or being thrown into some hitherto unknown sector of society, by having its routines interrupted by extra-ordinary events, or by escaping the sphere of social experience altogether (as in dreams or hallucinations). Normally, we return from these excursions into the non-everyday with a measure of relief; indeed, normally we experience these re-entries into the world of our everyday life as "coming home to reality." Needless to say, this does not necessarily mean that we *like* the world of our everyday life; all the same, for whatever this is worth, it is "home."

This world of the familiar is not only enveloped by another, larger world that is, at least in part, *un*familiar; the familiar world of everyday life is constantly invaded by processes that originate beyond its boundaries. What is more, it is to a great extent *organized* by these processes. Take an everyday situation such as prevails in a college classroom. Very possibly, sooner or later, something happens that will unleash emotions of rage in one of the individuals present against another. It is even possible that this rage releases positively homicidal inclinations. Nevertheless, it is very unlikely (one may hope) that these inclinations will be followed. Instead of homicide, what is likely to take place is a merely verbal act of ag-

---

[4] The concept of everyday life is a central element in Schutz's sociology.

gression, perhaps a healthy fistfight, in many cases nothing at all as the violent impulses are silently suppressed. Needless to say, such management of aggressiveness is part of the familiar fabric of everyday life. All the same, it has its origins beyond the world of the individual's immediate experience and it refers to the structures of this larger world, while at the same time it serves to organize what goes on in the little world of everyday life. In other words, everyday life is crisscrossed by patterns that *regulate* the behavior of its inhabitants with each other and that, at the same time, relate this behavior to much larger contexts of meaning (such as, in our instance, canons of acceptable etiquette, the moral order and the sanctions of law). These regulatory patterns are what are commonly called *institutions*.[5] Everyday life takes place within the enveloping context of an institutional order; it is intersected at different points by specific institutions that, as it were, reach into it, and its routines themselves consist of institutionalized behavior, that is, of behavior that is patterned and regulated in established ways. Again, it is important to understand the reciprocal relationship of these two aspects of our experience of society: everyday life can only be understood against the background of the specific institutions that penetrate it and of the overall institutional order within which it is located. Conversely, specific institutions and the institutional order as a whole are real only insofar as they are represented by people and by events that are immediately experienced in everyday life.

[5] The term "institution" is used here very much as most contemporary sociologists use it. Compare the following, rather authoritative definition by Shmuel Eisenstadt: "Social institutions are usually conceived of as the basic focuses of social organization, common to all societies and dealing with some of the basic universal problems of ordered social life. Three basic aspects of institutions are emphasized. First, the patterns of behavior which are regulated by institutions ('institutionalized') deal with some perennial, basic problems of any society. Second, institutions involve the regulation of behavior of individuals in society according to some definite, continuous, and organized patterns. Finally, these patterns involve a definite normative ordering and regulation; that is, regulation is upheld by norms and by sanctions which are legitimized by these norms." (Article on "Social Institutions," *International Encyclopedia of the Social Sciences*, Vol. 14 [New York, Macmillan, 1968], p. 409).

KNOWING MYSELF
AND KNOWING
SOCIOLOGY

Our biography is very largely the story of our experience with society. To be sure, there are biographical moments that take us out of society, from, say, the solitary ecstasy of se-

cret dreams of glory, or the very private anguish of a nocturnal toothache, to the final solitariness of dying. But when we stop to reflect upon our biography to date, most of our recollections refer to other people—as individuals, in groups, and as encountered in institutions. We have social biographies. Indeed, the time span of our biography is only a segment of the larger time span of the society in which it occurs—in other words, biography is located within history. Conversely, our knowledge of society is biographically acquired; we *grow into* a steadily expanding circle of social and institutional relationships. If we think of the institutional order as a map, we can envisage our biography as a trajectory across it. The same biography can be subdivided into a series of specific *careers* within this or that institutional sector.[6] Each such career has an established and generally understood sequence of positions, which we ordinarily run through more or less according to schedule. Thus our career in the educational sector may run from nursery-school toddler to doctoral candidate, in the sexual sector from eager experimenter to frustrated observer, in the occupational sector from promising young man to certified failure, and so forth. Thus we live not only in a social order of space, but of time as well. As we live our lives, we perform a journey through society (extensive or restricted, as circumstances determine). And if we stop to look back upon our lives, we will probably conclude that the stages of this journey make up most of what it has all been about. To approach the intellectual inquiry into our experience of society by way of biographical sequences is, therefore, not just a convenient

[6] The term "career" has been developed in the so-called symbolic-interactionist school of American sociology, and has been used successfully, for instance, to describe the stages run through by an aspiring juvenile delinquent or by a hospital patient. For a vivid description of the latter case, see Julius Roth, *Timetables* (Indianapolis, Bobbs-Merrill paperback, 1963).

means of ordering what sociologists have to offer by way of interpretations and materials, but rather follows logically from the
inner structure of this experience.

READINGS

The key ideas of this chapter are derived from Alfred Schutz (1899–1959), an
Austrian philosopher and sociologist who spent the closing years of his life in
America. Schutz is not easy reading for the beginner, but those who would like
to try might begin either with one of Schutz's theoretical essays or with one of
his more vivid case studies. For a case of the former, important for the considerations of this chapter, read Alfred Schutz, "On Multiple Realities," *Collected Papers,* Vol. I (The Hague, Nijhoff, 1962), pp. 207–259. For one of the latter, see
Alfred Schutz, "Don Quixote and the Problem of Reality," *Collected Papers,* Vol.
II (The Hague, Nijhoff, 1964), pp. 135–158.

For a general statement of the perspective of sociology as related to the concrete life experience of the individual, see Peter L. Berger, *Invitation to
Sociology—A Humanistic Perspective* (Garden City, N.Y., Doubleday-Anchor,
1963).

Chapter 2

THE
DISCIPLINE
OF
SOCIOLOGY

THE BASIC ELEMENTS in the experience of society we have looked at in the previous chapter have about them a certain degree of timelessness. The ancient Egyptians, say, also lived in a micro-world, also were "surrounded" by a macro-world, also had institutions that ordered their lives and that preserved them from what we have called big surprises. Insofar as man is a social being, it is inconceivable that man should ever live outside society, and living in society inevitably entails some of the elements that we have discussed. One result of this is that we can understand, to a very great extent, the life of people in ancient Egypt because, however different this life may have been in many respects, nevertheless it was a life in society, essentially similar to our own.

WHY IS SOCIOLOGY A NEW STUDY?

Yet the ancient Egyptians did not develop a discipline called sociology, or anything remotely like it. And, indeed, they had no concept corresponding to our concept of society. Not only the discipline of sociology but the very notion that something like society exists is a very recent business. There are many reasons, but the principal one is this: sociology is an intellectual response to the peculiar crisis of modern Western society. If one is to understand what sociology is and what it does, one must understand the nature of this response.

There are people who derive pleasure from reflecting about their situation and about any number of other things. This is not true of most people. Generally speaking, people only stop to reflect when, for one reason or another, the routine of their lives has been interrupted by something they consider to be a problem. Most thinking is a form of problem-solving. Presumably this goes back to the very simple and fundamental fact that thinking hurts, is painful. In any case, most people only have recourse to this terrible form of activity when they have to. One might add that if this were not the case it would be just about impossible to get anything done. Thinking is not only painful but it takes a lot of time. This is well expressed in the story of the bearded man who could no longer sleep after a friend had asked him whether, while sleeping, he kept his beard inside or outside the blanket. For most people, therefore, reflection, especially systematic reflection, is a relatively rare occasion. This is true of social experience as much as of any other. People have always lived in society. But people only begin to reflect about society when the latter, for whatever reasons, has become a problem to them. This can happen either as a result of some accident in their individual biography or as a result of large-scale events in the society in which they live. Thus, society and its institutions can become just as much of a problem to the individual who finally discovers that he cannot stand his wife as to the individual whose country is plunged into war. In either case, the smooth flow of his routine experience of society will have been interrupted, almost inevitably he will be forced to think at least about certain aspects of that experience, and if he is so inclined temperamentally, he might eventually be led to ask some rather far-reaching questions about society as such.

OUR ROUTINE EXPERIENCE: A TAKEN-FOR-GRANTED WORLD

Such occasions for reflection are relatively rare both in the lives of individuals and in the history of societies. Most of the time, both individuals and numbers of individuals living together in societies live in a world that is taken for granted.[1] This means that the fundamental structures in which social experience takes place are not questioned but are lived through as seemingly natural and self-evident conditions of life. This taken-for-granted quality pertains both to the micro-world and to the macro-world. For example, the social experience of a college classroom is taken for granted as a familiar routine, and it is very unlikely that the participants in that situation will begin to reflect about it unless something happens to interrupt the routine. Such an interruption could occur if one or more of the participants suddenly disrupted or ignored the accus-

---

[1] The term "world-taken-for-granted" was coined by Alfred Schutz.

tomed procedures for such situations. But similarly, the large context of institutions, which serves as the background for the classroom situation, will also remain unquestioned most of the time. Most people will take it for granted that there is such a thing as higher education, that it has a purpose, and that the way this institution is conducted makes sense. What we are witnessing today in many countries is that this taken-for-granted assumption about higher education is being massively questioned—precisely because things have gone wrong in a rather monumental way, because the institution in question has no longer been able to perform its taken-for-granted tasks in society and *therefore* has become a problem about which one must think. To protect this taken-for-granted quality, society usually has available a whole set of explanations, justifications, promises and threats to be applied in those instances when somebody *does* raise a question.

SHORING-UP THE STRUCTURES: LEGITIMATIONS

These devices to maintain the taken-for-granted quality of society are called *legitimations*.[2] The latter range from very simple statements that such-and-such is the way things are done to moral, philosophical and religious systems of explanation. Thus, the person who asks why education should take place in a classroom rather than outside under a tree may simply be answered to the effect that this is the way that things are done in America. On the other hand, the person who questions the validity of the entire system of higher education may be given answers that involve such highly abstract principles as culture, progress, development or the well-being of American society.

Through most of human history, the principal legitimations for the maintenance of society have been provided by religion. The mechanism by which such religious legitimation operates is essentially simple. The structures and institutions of society are interpreted as being part and parcel of the basic order of the universe.

[2] The term "legitimations" was used by Max Weber, though in a slightly more restricted sense than here.

In this way, the routines of social experience are linked directly to the very nature of things as willed by the gods. In ancient Egypt this notion was expressed by the term *ma'at*. There is no exact translation of the term. Essentially, it means "right order." This right order extends from the world of the gods to the world of men, embracing both in one all-enveloping meaning. The gods act in accordance with *ma'at* in the way they run the universe. To be in conformity with *ma'at* is to be in proper communion with the gods. But the notion of *ma'at* also embraces the institutional arrangements of Egyptian society. The king is the principal embodiment of *ma'at* in the world of men. But all proper ways of doing things, as enjoined by the institutions of society, are extensions of the same *ma'at*. Thus, to be a loyal subject, a good father or a productive peasant are not only morally approved ways of living in society but expressions of the underlying order of things which link the individual to the entire universe. Similar religious legitimations of society are characteristic of all primitive or archaic civilizations. To a considerable extent, this linkage between society and cosmos still prevailed in the Christian Middle Ages.

THREATS TO THE TAKEN-FOR-GRANTED: A SOURCE OF SOCIOLOGY

The peculiar crisis of modern society began with the disintegration of this medieval unity, that is, with the disintegration of Christendom. The progressive weakening of the religious underpinnings of society had set in with the beginning of what we call modern history and has created an ever-deepening crisis of legitimation. The challenge to the religious legitimations of society was extended to the political sphere and, finally, to every sector of the institutional system. The threats to the taken-for-granted quality of social experience have thus become progressively more frequent and more radical.

When the taken-for-granted quality of a society is weakened, that society as a whole or sections of it become a problem, and consequently, people begin to think about social matters. Any number of biographical accidents can produce such a situation in the life of an individual. More important, however, are those cases in which these accidents refer not only to individual biography but to the history of entire societies or groups. Foreign invasion, war, civil strife or massive contact with an alien culture—all of these can be occasions for the weakening in the taken-for-granted quality of the basic structures and institutions of a society. In such instances, people from all levels of the society may begin to question its basic assumptions and perhaps to have new ideas about the way in which men ought to live together. Such situations, in other words, are fertile ground for the development of sociological thought or comparable forms of reflection. Another interesting case is that of group marginality—that is, a situation in which a particular group is excluded from full participation in the life of the society. Exploited classes, groups of resident strangers or groups of people with highly deviant practices or beliefs have always provided a social context conducive to reflections about society. The very important place of Jews in the history of modern Western social thought is an illustration of the effect of marginality on the perception of society.

SOCIAL SHOCKS AND THE HISTORY OF SOCIAL THOUGHT

All of this is nothing new. Examples of such shocks to the taken-for-granted quality of social experience can be found from time to time all the way back to antiquity. There even exists a poem dating from the period of turmoil following the end of the Old Kingdom in ancient Egypt (and this dates it well over 2000 years B.C.), in which the poet bemoans the upheaval of all things that used to be the accustomed way in his society and then is led by all this to ask some very fundamental questions about the meaning of human life. A very famous example from classical antiquity is Thucydides, whose bitter experiences of the defeat of Athens in the Peloponnesian War led him to a searching inquiry into the meaning of history and social order, the depth and scope of which have led some people to suggest that Thucydides is the true father of modern sociology. The Islamic Middle Ages provide an illustration of the fertility of marginality for social thought in the figure of Ibn-Khaldun, who spent most of the productive years of his life as a political exile wandering from one country to another, and who transformed his personal experience of strangeness into one of the most important works of social thought of pre-modern times. With the break-up of the medieval world in the West, such experiences multiplied and accelerated. And there is quite a number of thinkers in early modern history to whom the title of father of sociology might plausibly be assigned. One may mention here such figures as Francis Bacon, Erasmus, Machiavelli or Montaigne.

Crises in history used to take a long time to develop. If the crisis in modern man's experience of society can be said to begin with the disintegration of Christendom, it reached its climax with the French Revolution. For a rather short time, the absolute state and its institutions had seemed to fill the gap left by the disintegration of the medieval order. The splendid trappings of the absolute monarchy, especially in France, the hierarchical system of estates and the legitimations provided by the doctrine of the divine right of kings provided a new taken-for-granted order in which human life could be lived. The great thinkers of the Enlightenment, particularly in France and England, had cast increasing doubt on the validity and legitimacy of this order. But it was the Revolution of 1789 that shattered this order in a massive upheaval of monumental proportions. The execution of the King served as the bloody and dramatic ratification of this historic act of destruction. The French Revolution and its consequences inaugurated a period of crisis in which man's social experience was increasingly questioned, reflected upon and perceived in startling new perspectives. In a very real sense, the French Revolution has never stopped. Philosophically, politically and economically, it represents the beginning of a crisis which we still experience today. Its intellectual repercussions make up most of what we call the history of social thought since then. The discipline of sociology is one of these intellectual repercussions.

THE BEGINNINGS OF SOCIOLOGY: AUGUSTE COMTE

Sociology, as a discipline of that name, arose in the nineteenth century, first in France and then, rather independently, in Germany and in America. It developed strongly especially in these three countries. After an earlier period, it is possible to speak of a classical age of sociology. The dates of this would be roughly between 1890 and 1930, when most of the fundamental work in the field was done. A great part of what has happened since in sociology has been by way of elaboration and following up the insights provided by the great writers of the classical period. We will now look briefly at this history.

The name "sociology" was invented by Auguste Comte (1798–1857). Comte was primarily a philosopher, who founded the school of philosophy called positivism. His ambitions, both for his philosophy and for the new discipline of sociology that was a part of it, were very high. Comte wanted no less than to produce a rational religion for humanity that would repudiate both traditional religion and the ideology of the French Revolution. Essentially, Comte was a conservative. He was shocked by the turmoil that the Revolution had produced and by its tumultuous consequences for France and other countries. He was a strong believer in what nowadays would be called law and order. Indeed, the basic purpose of sociology was to be to discover the laws of social order and thus the means to maintain such order. On the other hand, in many ways Comte was himself a child of the Enlightenment. He was opposed to the Christian church, which he regarded as a retarding force in the history of man. He was an ardent believer in progress, and even more so in science, for which he had exorbitant expectations.

In his early years Comte had been associated with Henri de Saint-Simon, a rather eccentric French thinker of this period, who had started something like a secular church. The Saint-Simonians regarded themselves as a kind of priestly order that would be the guardian of a new faith of progress and rationality for mankind.

Among other somewhat bizarre characteristics, they wore a uniform, the jacket of which had buttons going down the back, which no one could either close or open without help from someone else. The idea here was to demonstrate (in a somewhat painful way, one might say) that human beings are dependent on each other. Comte later quarreled with Saint-Simon, and each of them denounced the other for allegedly having stolen his ideas. But the quasi-religious fervor of the Saint-Simonians continued to be expressed in Comte's later work. Sociology was to be a kind of new theology, stripped of the latter's supernatural trappings. Sociology was to be the new queen of the sciences, integrating man's theoretical knowledge and also serving as a guidebook to his practical actions to reform and reorder the world. In a phrase that has become very famous, Comte characterized the purpose of science as being "to know in order to predict in order to control." This, incidentally, has remained the positivist ideal to this day, not only in sociology but in other sciences as well.

Not much of the specific content of Comte's sociology survived into the classical period, and he occurs very little in contemporary sociology, except as an occasional footnote that no one reads. Indeed, a few years ago an irreverent student attended a meeting of the American Sociological Association with a nametag that simply read "A. Comte, Founder," and no one raised an eyebrow. Nevertheless, there are some ideas of Comte's that, in a sort of subterranean way, have continued to influence sociology after him.

COMTE'S CONTRIBUTIONS: STAGES OF MAN; "STATICS AND DYNAMICS"

Two of his notions, particularly, should be mentioned. One is the notion that human history has proceeded in three stages which he called the theological, the metaphysical and the positive. The first of these stages was supposed to be the age in which man was ruled by religious delusions, the second in which these delusions had become somewhat secularized and transformed into philosophical positions, and the third being the age of science or, as Comte would say, positive science, which has just begun and which is supposed to be an age of great enlightenment and freedom from illusion. Very few people after Comte took these specific stages very seriously, but the notion that there is a more or less inevitable progression of steps in the development of man and, indeed, of his society is an idea which has proven very durable. Another influential notion of Comte's has been his division of the subject matter of sociology into what he called statics and dynamics—the first dealing with more or less stable structures remaining the same over periods of time, the second dealing with the forces of change, conflict and turbulence in society. In a number of disguises this notion, too, has survived in present-day sociology. But even the redemptive, not to say messianic, conception that Comte had of sociology has reasserted itself from time to time, especially in France and in America. There have been rather few attempts to sell the idea that sociology should be the new queen of sciences. Early in this century, however, a number of people on the faculty of Brown University in Providence, Rhode Island, submitted a memorandum to the president of that institution, suggesting that the entire university should be reorganized under the department of sociology. Needless to say, this memorandum did not meet with an enthusiastic response. All the same, even today we find individuals who somehow expect sociology as a discipline to produce the authoritative answers to all the problems that plague society. In view of the fact that such exorbitant expectations of sociology are bound to be severely disappointed, it is fortunate that there are relatively few people that harbor them.

ÉMILE DURKHEIM: HOW IS SOCIAL ORDER POSSIBLE?

If we now turn to the classical period of sociology in France, the pre-eminent figure by far is Émile Durkheim (1858–1917). For a period of about twenty years, Durkheim occupied the chair of sociology at the Sorbonne which had been specially created for him. He not only shaped French sociology in a decisive way during this period, but was a very important figure in French intellectual and even political life, far beyond the limits of the discipline of sociology. He actively participated in the major intellectual and political crises of France during that period. This was a period of considerable political turmoil, that of the Third Republic in which France was clearly divided into two political camps, the Left and the Right. The former represented the ongoing faith in the ideals of the Revolution, the latter the continuing conservative resistance to it.

Durkheim was very clearly identified with the Left, though it must be emphasized that at that time this did not as yet have the socialist connotation which this term would have today—Left meant republican, progressive, anti-clerical. The conflict came to a head during Durkheim's lifetime during the famous Dreyfus affair, which seemed to split France right down the middle. Durkheim, as a Jew (he was a descendant of a long line of Alsatian rabbis), felt this conflict even more sharply than did others. When the conflict ended with a clear victory for the Left, ratified in the separation of church and state of 1905, Durkheim became an important figure in government circles as well as in academic ones. When, after 1905, religious instruction was banished from the government schools, Durkheim was called upon to form a commission which was to investigate the following question: How was one to instruct children in morality in the absence of traditional religious instruction? Durkheim strongly felt that sociology would have an important answer to this question, and indeed succeeded in establishing sociology as an important discipline in the curriculum. In other words, sociology became a kind of secular catechism (not too dissimilar from what, in American secondary school education, is known as civics). It is not difficult here to see the continuation of the Comtean concern. Sociology, to be sure, was conceived of as a science, but it was also more than a science: it was part of a secular, humanistic creed which, it was believed, would have direct and important consequences for morality and politics.

FROM
MECHANICAL TO
ORGANIC
SOLIDARITY

Durkheim's period in French history was marked by pervasive disharmony and disorder. His practical and political activities were directly concerned with coping with this disorder. His basic theoretical concern can be directly related to these biographical roots. It can be formulated very simply: How is social order possible? The attempt to answer this question runs like a red thread through Durkheim's entire work. It is the main theme of his first important work, *The Division of Labor*. In this book Durkheim applies his sociological perspective to history. Sociologically, he is in a position to say that every human society requires solidarity—that is, a feeling among people that they belong together. But, historically, it is possible to find very different sorts of solidarity. Durkheim distinguishes between two major types, which he calls mechanical and organic solidarity. Mechanical solidarity, which is typical of primitive and ancient societies, is one in which people belong together in a total way, somewhat comparable to the solidarity that still prevails today in many families. Organic solidarity, which is typical of modern societies, is a much more complicated type in which the basic form of relationship is not a simple feeling of belonging together but a complex web of contractual relationships. A society held together by mechanical solidarity is built on faith and fellow-feeling; a society based on organic solidarity, on the other hand, is held together by law and reason. Durkheim was concerned not only with differentiating these two types of social order but with tracing the development of organic solidarity as a fundamental feature of the modern world. There was a strong bias in favor of this type of society, which Durkheim viewed as a product of progress.[3]

[3] Émile Durkheim, *The Division of Labor in Society* (New York, Free Press, 1964), available in paperback.

"SOCIAL FACTS ARE THINGS" AND "COLLECTIVE CONSCIOUSNESS"

Durkheim's most influential work was *The Rules of Sociological Method*.[4] This slim and elegantly written book contained both Durkheim's basic ideas about the discipline of sociology and a program for the future work of the discipline. During the earlier period of his work, Durkheim was engaged in an ongoing fight with representatives of other academic disciplines (such as philosophy and psychology), who denied either the validity or the autonomy of sociology. Durkheim, of course, strongly stressed both. In the *Rules* he tried to show that society had a reality of its own which could not be reduced to psychological facts. As he put it, society was "a reality sui generis." This distinctive character of social reality is manifested by the fact that one cannot wish that reality away. Society resists our thoughts and wishes because it has an objectivity which, though not the same, is comparable to the objectivity of nature. Durkheim expressed this in one of his most famous sentences: "Social facts are things." It is characteristic of a "thing" that it exists outside ourselves, that it is capable of resisting us and that we cannot find out what it is by looking into our own minds. Also in the *Rules* Durkheim first discussed what later was to become a major theme of his work, namely, that society is formed by a combination of the consciousnesses of individuals—a combination which he later was to call collective consciousness. In other words, at the foundation of society there are thoughts, ideas, constructs of the mind.

A dramatic application of Durkheim's insistence on the autonomous reality of society was his study of *Suicide*.[5] In the study, Durkheim was concerned with the social causes of suicide. It was particularly dramatic because suicide appears to be one of the most

[4] Émile Durkheim, *The Rules of Sociological Method* (New York, Free Press, 1950), available in paperback.

[5] Émile Durkheim, *Suicide* (New York, Free Press, 1951), available in paperback.

uniquely individual acts that men are capable of. Nevertheless, Durkheim showed, by the use of copious statistical data, that a person's social background was decisive in determining the likelihood of suicide. Thus, a most unique individual event turns out to be determined by collective and highly abstract factors. For example, Durkheim was able to show that there was more suicide in the cities than in the countryside, more suicide among Protestants than among Catholics, more suicide among divorcees or widows than among married women. In each case, Durkheim argued, the discrepancy is to be explained by a difference in social ties or solidarity. In connection with these findings, Durkheim coined one of his most influential concepts, that of *anomie*. Literally, the word, which is derived from Greek, means disorder or normlessness; what Durkheim meant by it was a state, either of individuals or of groups, in which there is a lack of solidarity or social ties. In the context of his study of suicide, Durkheim was able to show, in the most dramatic way possible, that such solidarity is literally necessary for life and that being deprived of it is an almost unbearable condition for human beings.

The crowning work of Durkheim was his book entitled *The Elementary Forms of the Religious Life,*[6] which was published shortly before his death. This work is one of the classics in the sociology of religion, and argues in great detail that religion is fundamentally a social phenomenon, that is, that religion reflects the society in which it exists. In a more profound way, however, the same book actually shows that society is essentially a religious phenomenon— in the sense that it is, in the final analysis, based upon the ultimate values held by its members. Sociology here, once more, is placed in the immediate vicinity of philosophy. The vision of society it finally produces is one of a group of human beings banded together around common beliefs and values.

[6] Émile Durkheim, *The Elementary Forms of the Religious Life* (New York, Free Press, 1954), available in paperback.

THE DURKHEIM SCHOOL

Durkheim was not only a very influential figure by himself, but became the founder of a very important school. This school, commonly referred to as the Durkheim School, dominated the social sciences in France for a period of about thirty years. During this period, sociology in France meant Durkheimian sociology. In quite a number of other disciplines concerned with man, it was students of Durkheim who produced important and influential works. This was especially true of ethnology (what, in America today, we would call cultural anthropology), history, linguistics, psychology and law. Over more than a quarter century, this community of scholars, in constant communication with each other and animated by an essentially common frame of reference, produced a truly remarkable body of knowledge about human events. This accumulation of information and insights is far from exhausted even today. The Durkheim School, however, did not survive beyond the 1930's. There are several reasons for this, such as the fact that many of its representatives were Jews and were cruelly decimated during the Nazi Occupation of France during World War II. But the basic reason is probably connected with the close linkage between Durkheimian sociology and the political faith with which it was so closely tied. The rationalism and optimism of Durkheim's republican creed did not survive the anguish of the Second World War. After the liberation of France, Durkheimian sociology did not make a comeback. Most of French sociology was either taken over by Marxists or came under heavy influence from abroad, especially from the United States. The work of Durkheim and his school nevertheless remains as one of the greatest accomplishments in the history of the discipline.

GERMAN
RESPONSES TO
THE FRENCH
REVOLUTION

Sociology in Germany had a very different history, though it also, if somewhat less directly, was linked to the intellectual repercussions of the French Revolution. The connection here was not direct but by means of the general problem of history, which was the major preoccupation of German thought during the nineteenth century—especially as represented in the towering figures of Hegel and Marx. For Hegel, the French Revolution posed the problem of history in a dramatic and inescapable manner. And throughout his life, despite the increasing conservatism of his older years, Hegel felt that the Revolution had been an important and fundamentally positive event in the advance of the human spirit. He expressed this for many years in a quasi-religious way by always lighting a candle on Bastille Day. It was Marx, however, who much more directly made the Revolution a central concern for the sciences of man. For Marx, the French Revolution was only a preamble to the great proletarian revolution that was to come and that was to inaugurate a new age of humanity. But it was the great example of the French Revolution that led Marx to develop many of his basic conceptions —such as those of class and class struggle, of the pre-eminence of economic factors in history, and of the dynamics of revolution as such. Much of German sociological thought during the classical period consisted of an ongoing attempt to *refute* Marx. In fact, the very notion of the discipline of sociology became an alternative to the "science of socialism" as propounded by Marx's followers. As in France, then, the original impetus for sociology in Germany was anti-revolutionary and conservative in spirit. It should be emphasized that this did not mean at all that the final consequences and implications of the discipline were also to be of this kind.

MAX WEBER: MODERNITY, CAPITALISM AND THE ROLE OF IDEAS IN HISTORY

Just as in France, sociology in Germany during the classical period is dominated by one gigantic figure —Max Weber (1864–1920). Except for the last years of his life, Weber was much less directly involved in the political struggles of his day than Durkheim. He much more conformed to the ideal of detachment of the German academician. Even academically he was, during his own lifetime, less of a success than Durkheim had been. Nevertheless, he exerted a tremendous influence on many of his contemporaries, an influence which increased rather than decreased after his death. Weber's fundamental intellectual problem, at least at first sight, looks more circumscribed than Durkheim's. His problem was that of the origins of capitalism. Weber was convinced of two things —one, of the very peculiar character of the modern world, and, two, of the pre-eminent role of capitalism in having produced this modern world. The question about the origins of capitalism was thus, for Weber, a question about the foundations of the modern world. There was, however, a further and more fundamental dimension to this question, which only becomes apparent when we understand Weber in confrontation with Marx. Beyond the question about the origins of capitalism, Weber was concerned with the role of ideas in history. Marx had emphasized the pre-eminence of economic factors in history and, more specifically, the dependence of human consciousness upon what he called the economic substructure of social life. In an oversimplification that did violence to the sophistication of Marx's own system of thought, many of his followers converted these ideas into a system of rigid and one-sided economic determinism. It was this that Weber was concerned to refute. He sought to do this in the most dramatic way possible, namely, by showing how economic processes themselves are in turn dependent upon what goes on in the minds of men, more specifically on values and beliefs.

"THE PROTESTANT ETHIC": "INNER-WORLDLY ASCETICISM"

The germinal work in this enterprise of Weber's was *The Protestant Ethic and the Spirit of Capitalism.*[7] This book, which succeeded in creating a controversy among scholars that has gone on for over half a century now, tried to establish a causal connection between the origins of capitalism and certain aspects of the Protestant religion.

The key concept in Weber's argument was what he called "inner-worldly asceticism." This, according to Weber, was one of the major effects of Protestantism on the history of Western societies, although in many respects this happened unintentionally. Inner-worldly asceticism was a transformation of religious discipline from being concerned with the other world to the affairs of this one. The Lutheran Reformation gave it its first impetus by changing the notion of vocation from a purely religious to a secular one; Luther stressed that any lawful occupation in the world was as pleasing to God as the profession of a priest, a monk or a nun. But it was only in the Calvinist Reformation and its consequences that, according to Weber, Protestant inner-worldly asceticism came to maturity. Calvinism insisted that all of life, including man's economic activity, should be subjected to a rigid religiously motivated discipline. In a very ingenious explanation, Weber linked this with the psychological consequences of the Calvinist doctrine of predestination: although nothing could have been further from Calvin's own mind, his later followers began to look upon worldly success as some sort of proof that they were among the elect (that is, among that relatively small number that God had predestined for salvation). In any case, it was Calvinism that gave the most decisive and durable legitimation to economic activity and, more specifically, to economic activity that involved discipline, hard work and saving. Such an ethic of self-denial, Weber argued, was very important for the development of

[7] Max Weber, *The Protestant Ethic and the Spirit of Capitalism* (New York, Scribner's, 1930), available in paperback.

attitudes and practices conducive to capitalist enterprise. Weber then went on to argue that it was indeed in those countries that were most directly and powerfully influenced by Calvinism that modern capitalism arose in its most characteristic forms. Weber's theory, whether right or wrong, has completely transformed our historical perspective on the origins of the modern world. Beyond that, it has offered one of the most persuasive arguments against the Marxist interpretation of history.

THE *ABSENCE* OF INNER-WORLDLY ASCETICISM

Following *The Protestant Ethic and the Spirit of Capitalism,* Weber started a vast work in the comparative sociology of religion.[8] This covered investigations into the religions of India, China and the ancient Middle East. At the time of Weber's death he was working on the sociology of Islam. In retrospect, the amount of learning that went into this enterprise is staggering. Some of the specific studies in the sociology of religion undertaken by Weber have had a profound effect on scholarship in these areas —for example his study of the relationship of intellectuals to the salvation religions of India, his study of the Chinese bureaucracy and his interpretation of prophecy in ancient Israel. But while Weber went off in many directions in the course of his work, he always returned to what was his major concern, namely, the relationship of intellectual and economic processes in history. Having, to his own satisfaction, established the relationship of religion to capitalism in the West, he used the entire history of man's religion as a gigantic laboratory to verify his original thesis. Over and over again, his major point in his studies of ancient and non-Western religions was the absence of inner-worldly asceticism.

[8] Max Weber, *The Religion of India* (New York, Free Press, 1958); *The Religion of China* (New York, Free Press, 1958); *Ancient Judaism* (New York, Free Press, 1952)—all three available in paperback.

"ELECTIVE AFFINITIES" BETWEEN IDEAS AND GROUPS

It should be emphasized that Weber did not at all wish to substitute a religious or ideational determinism for the economic determinism of the Marxists. On the contrary, he always stressed the interrelation of these various factors. The key concept which he used in this connection was that of *elective affinity,* by which he meant the process by which certain ideas and certain social groups as it were "seek each other out" in history. Thus, for example, Weber did not argue either that Confucianism produced a Chinese bureaucratic system or, for that matter, that it was simply a reflection of the latter. Rather, he maintained, that whatever might have been the original motives of Confucius and his immediate followers, Confucianism turned out to be a religious and ethical system that was peculiarly suited to the needs of this particular class of people in China (the class which he called the "bureaucratic literati"). It was as if this group and these ideas elected each other, chose each other, because of the natural affinity between them.

In some respects Weber was much less of a theoretician or methodologist than Durkheim. Yet his contributions both to theory and to methodology in sociology have been very great indeed. These contributions, however, were not his major interest; rather they were the by-product of his work on substantive problems of sociology, especially of the sociology of religion. All the same, his largest work is a systematic treatise in sociological theory entitled *Economy and Society.*[9] This developed in great detail some concepts of sociology that have remained in use to this day. The same work also contains some very important analyses, for example, Weber's inquiry into the nature of bureaucracy.

Unlike Durkheim, Weber did not become the founder of a school.

[9] Max Weber, *Economy and Society* (New York, Bedminster Press, 1968). A useful selection from this was previously published under the title of *From Max Weber,* edited by Hans Gerth and C. Wright Mills (New York, Oxford, 1958), in paperback.

Perhaps to some extent this was due to differences in personality between the two men. It was also, to a large extent, the result of differences in the academic systems of Germany and France. While in France academic and intellectual life has been very much centralized, this has not been the case in Germany. Despite his enormous influence, Weber remained essentially a figure standing by himself. The same is true of other important writers in German sociology during the classical period.

GEORG SIMMEL: DYADS, TRIADS AND THE ROLE OF THE STRANGER

Next to Weber, probably the most important of these was Georg Simmel (1868–1918). Simmel's work in sociology was only part of a much larger work concerned with philosophy and intellectual history.[10] Indeed, most of Simmel's contribution to sociology is contained in one, albeit quite voluminous, work which, in turn, was a collection of essays on a number of different subjects. Nevertheless, Simmel's influence has been very great and still continues today. Simmel was interested in developing what he himself called "a formal sociology." By that he meant propositions about the nature of social reality which would be very general and which could be filled with varying historical content. For example, in an essay which has become very famous, Simmel investigated the influence of numbers upon social relationships, coining the terms "dyad" and "triad" to designate, respectively, human groups consisting of two and three members. Simmel analyzed in great detail what the differences between these groups were. He was very careful to formulate these analyses in such a way that they could apply to groups engaged in every conceivable sort of relationship. For another example, in what is probably his most famous essay, Simmel analyzed the role of the stranger in human society, again doing so in such a way that the analysis could apply to greatly different situations.

[10] Kurt Wolff (ed.), *The Sociology of Georg Simmel* (New York, Free Press, 1950), available in paperback.

VILFREDO PARETO: A SYSTEMATIC STUDY OF IDEOLOGICAL STRUGGLE

Before turning to American developments in the discipline, mention should be made of one isolated and somewhat eccentric figure in European sociology who nevertheless has been one of great importance. This is the Italian sociologist Vilfredo Pareto (1848–1923). Originally an economist, in which capacity he also made some enduring contributions to economic theory, Pareto turned to sociology in the later stages of his career because he was convinced that the assumptions of rational behavior that underlay economics did not go very far in explaining human behavior. Pareto produced one gigantic work of sociological theory, which in English is entitled *The Mind and Society*.[11] A sprawling book, full of fascinating historical illustrations of all kinds, this work presents an original approach to sociological thought. In some respects like Marx, Pareto viewed society as primarily an arena of struggle and of deceit. Thus the main areas of social life that interested him were politics and ideas and the relationship between those two. He tried to show in great detail how much of social life was only possible because of systematic illusions and myths that served the interests of specific groups. But unlike Marx, Pareto had no recipes to offer for the cure of society. An aristocrat by background and a cynic by inclination, he was satisfied to view the follies of mankind in an attitude of sardonic detachment. Pareto's sociology constitutes one of the most elaborate systems produced in the history of the discipline, and it has influenced a number of other sociologists in different countries—though there are very few, indeed, who would identify with the system as a whole.

[11] Vilfredo Pareto, *The Mind and Society* (New York, Dover, 1963).

AMERICAN SOCIOLOGY: SOLVING PRACTICAL PROBLEMS

Sociology in America developed under distinct circumstances that were very different from those in Europe. The social experience out of which American sociology came had very little to do with the political and ideological controversies that stimulated sociology in France and Germany. Rather, it was the experience of the problems of an immigrant society caught in the turmoil of rapid industrialization and the growth of cities. From the beginning, American sociology had a very strong practical interest. But that was characterized not so much by politics as by social reform and social work. This practical, reformist trend in American sociology has proven to be very persistent. In the beginning, there were strong theoretical influences from Europe, but soon quite distinctive American traits developed.

Again, unlike the situation in Europe, it is not possible in America to point to one or even several overtowering figures during the classical period of sociology. There were a number of individuals who were influential in the development of the discipline; some of them founded schools, others did not. Two important figures of the earlier period were William Graham Sumner (1840–1910) and Thorstein Veblen (1857–1929).

WILLIAM GRAHAM SUMNER: MORES AND ETHNOCENTRISM

Sumner had been influenced by the English philosopher, Herbert Spencer, and was part of the broad intellectual movement that has been called Social Darwinism. Like others in this movement, Sumner tried to draw out the implications of biological evolution for society. He became very popular during his lifetime, partly, no doubt, because his notions of sociology corresponded very much to what many people in American society believed anyway. Specifically, Sumner believed that society followed its own evolutionary laws and that the state and the law could not, and should not, do very much about these. This notion was very congenial to an age that still believed in the virtues of untrammeled capitalism and that was highly suspicious of the interference of government in economic affairs. Sumner's most influential work was entitled *Folkways*.[12] It had great influence in American sociology for many years. Some of its concepts, like those of *mores* (customs that have become part of a society's morality) and *ethnocentrism* (a view of the world determined by one's own group membership), have become part of general usage.

THORSTEIN VEBLEN: "DEBUNKING"

If Sumner might today be described as an establishmentarian sociologist, Veblen was by temperament a rebel. The son of Norwegian farmers in the Middle West, he did not learn English until he started going to school. All his life he considered himself marginal to American society, and he was in active rebellion against all of its values, from capitalism to sexual morality. Veblen's work is one of the most consistent embodiments of the debunking theme in sociology. His most famous work is *The Theory of the Leisure Class*,[13] which is a venomous portrait of the life-style of the upper classes in America and elsewhere. Veblen (who, incidentally, was hardly influenced at all by Marxism or other European traditions of radicalism) may be regarded as the founder of an indigenous American tradition of radical or critical sociology; that is, sociology that regards as its mission the critique of the status quo in society.

---

[12] William Sumner, *Folkways* (New York, Dover, 1906), available in paperback.

[13] Thorstein Veblen, *The Theory of the Leisure Class* (New York, Macmillan, 1899), available in paperback.

THE EMPIRICISTS: THOMAS, ZNANIECKI AND PARK

However, it was only after World War I that American sociology took on the distinctive character which, in the main, it has retained until today. The turning point came as American sociologists, with great determination and in great numbers, turned to empirical investigations, many of them leaving theoretical considerations behind as an impractical and essentially useless activity. This new period in American sociology can be conveniently dated from 1919, when the first volume of a very influential empirical study came out, W. I. Thomas's and Florian Znaniecki's *The Polish Peasant in Europe and America*.[14] This was an extensive investigation, stretching over a period of years, of the culture and life of Polish immigrants in America, at the same time looking into the background of their home culture. The theme and the method of the *Polish Peasant* were indicative of this new atmosphere in the field in America. Both Thomas and Znaniecki were professors at the University of Chicago, and it was that institution which, in the 1920's and into the early 1930's, was without question the center of almost everything that was vital and innovative in American sociology. The term "Chicago School" has been used to designate a whole group of sociologists working at Chicago during this period. Their major interest was in the city, and in the works of men like Robert Park and Louis Wirth they laid the foundations of what was to become the special field of urban sociology. They emphasized field work, that is, going out and collecting data rather than sitting in a study and spinning out theories. As Park kept advising his students: "Get your hands dirty with research!" The Chicago sociologists also had a special affinity for social phenomena that were deviant or far-out in some way. Thus they produced a string of monographs on various colorful corners of urban life, such as the worlds of skid row or of crime. The Chicago School was also the beginning of what

[14] W. I. Thomas and Florian Znaniecki, *The Polish Peasant in Europe and America* (Chicago, University of Chicago Press, 1919–1921).

was later to be called the sociology of disorganization or of deviance.

GEORGE HERBERT MEAD'S "ROLE THEORY" AND "SYMBOLIC INTERACTIONISM"

A very important figure connected with the Chicago School was George Herbert Mead (1863–1931). The relationship between Mead and the Chicago School of sociology was curious. Mead was in no way a sociologist; he was a professor of philosophy at the University of Chicago almost all his life, never considered himself anything else but a philosopher and, indeed, produced work of considerable technical complexity in philosophy. Nevertheless, his influence on American philosophy has remained very slight while his influence on American sociology and social psychology has been enormous. Another curious fact about Mead is that the work which was to prove most influential was not published until after his death. That was the book entitled *Mind, Self and Society*.[15] In this work, Mead analyzed in great detail how the human self is created by social processes, stressing that it is impossible to understand man except as he can be understood in his social context. A key concept in Mead's social philosophy is that of *role* (which we will discuss in the next chapter), and Mead's writings on this subject have become the foundations of what was later called "role theory" in American sociology, social psychology and cultural anthropology. Mead's influence has remained very strong to this day, and he is generally regarded as the most influential figure in the school of sociology and social psychology which today is called symbolic interactionism.

[15] George Herbert Mead, *Mind, Self and Society* (Chicago, University of Chicago Press, 1934), available in paperback.

TALCOTT
PARSONS AND
ROBERT MERTON:
"STRUCTURAL-
FUNCTIONALISM"

In the period between the two world wars, American sociology grew steadily and attained a recognized and respected place in the academic establishment. It was during this period that American sociologists devoted great attention to the development of empirical research methods and statistical techniques. In these areas, American sociology gained a lead which to date has remained unchallengeable. Interest in theory diminished at this time. American sociologists began to derive pride from their professional self-image as "hard-nosed empiricists." It was only in the 1940's that a strong interest in sociological theory re-emerged in America. This has very largely been the achievement of two men: Talcott Parsons of Harvard University, and Robert Merton of Columbia University.[16] Although there are considerable differences in the work of these two men, both together can be taken as the founders of the school of theory known as structural-functionalism. This is an approach to society (originally used by cultural anthropologists in England) which views the latter as an ongoing system, each part of which functions in one way or another in relation to all the others. Findings about society can then be analyzed as either being functional or dysfunctional in terms of maintaining the social system. Structural-functionalism probably became the dominant form of sociological theory in America in the 1950's, and has only begun to decline in influence in the very recent past.

[16] Talcott Parsons, *The Social System* (New York, Free Press, 1951); Robert Merton, *Social Theory and Social Structure* (New York, Free Press, 1957), both available in paperback.

THE SOCIOLOGICAL ESTABLISHMENT: RADICAL CRITICS AND NEW BEGINNINGS

In the years following World War II, there existed in America something that could properly be called a sociological establishment, that is, a very respected and settled academic field. Its ethos and major strength were derived from its empirical work, using increasingly sophisticated methods. The rise of computers further contributed to the latter. Internationally, there was no question about the pre-eminence of American sociology. The works of American sociologists were avidly read and translated in other parts of the world, including Europe, and it was understood to be part of the proper training of a sociologist to study at least for a few years in America. Indeed, the relationship of America to sociology in those years was not too dissimilar from that of Germany to philosophy in the nineteenth century.

Recently there have been some changes in this situation. In America itself there has been rising dissatisfaction with the sociological establishment. In the very recent past it has been sharply, sometimes unfairly, attacked by radical critics on the Left. But there has also been a much wider feeling of dissatisfaction with its approach and atmosphere, and doubts about the usefulness of its findings. At the time of writing, American sociology is in a state of considerable flux, and it is hard to predict just where the field will be going. At the same time, compared especially to the 1950's, this is a period of vigorous discussion and self-examination which may well result in a real vitalization of the discipline. After the initial postwar dependence on American sociology, there have also been new beginnings in Western Europe, especially in Germany and France. Marxist regimes in Eastern Europe have, in recent years, shown a new tolerance toward sociology, which they had previously denounced as being nothing but bourgeois ideology. As a result there has been a modest, but nevertheless interesting, development of sociology in some of these countries, including the So-

viet Union. Internationally too, the situation of sociology is very
fluid and full of intriguing new possibilities.

Needless to say, this outline of the history of the discipline has
been very sketchy. The main point we have been trying to make is
that sociology must always be traced back to the fundamental experiences of the society within which it originated. More than almost any other discipline, sociology reflects the social conditions
under which it emerges and is produced. A sociologist is in society,
and while society is the object of his inquiries, it also determines in
large measure the directions which these inquiries will take.

R E A D I N G S

It is suggested that the student read, in their entirety, one or more of the
following classical books of sociology. Each represents a distinctive style of sociological thought. All are available in paperback editions:

Durkheim, Émile, *The Rules of Sociological Method* (New York, Free Press,
1950).

Sumner, William, *Folkways* (New York, Dover, 1906).

Veblen, Thorstein, *The Theory of the Leisure Class* (New York, Macmillan,
1899).

Weber, Max, *The Protestant Ethic and the Spirit of Capitalism* (New York,
Scribner's, 1930).

Chapter 3

BECOMING A MEMBER OF SOCIETY— SOCIALIZATION

BEING AN INFANT: NON-SOCIAL AND SOCIAL COMPONENTS

For better or for worse, all of us begin by being born. The first condition we experience is the condition of being an infant. When we begin to analyze what this condition entails, we obviously come up against a number of things that have nothing to do with society. First of all, being an infant entails a certain relationship to one's own body. One experiences hunger, pleasure, physical comfort or discomfort and so forth. In the condition of being an infant one is assaulted in numerous ways by the physical environment. One experiences light and darkness, heat and cold; objects of all sorts impinge upon one's attention. One is warmed by the rays of the sun, one is intrigued by the smoothness of a surface or, if one is unlucky, one may be rained upon or bitten by a flea. Being born means to enter into a world with a seemingly infinite richness of experience. A good deal of this experience is not social. Needless to say, an infant at the time does not make such distinctions. It is only in retrospect that it is possible to differentiate the social and the non-social components of his experience. Having made this distinction, however, it is possible to say that the experience of society also begins at birth. The world of the infant is populated by other people. Very soon he is able to distinguish between them, and some of them become of overwhelming significance for him. From the beginning, the infant not only interacts with his own body and with his physical environment, but with other human beings. The biography of the individual, from the moment of birth, is the story of his relations with others.

More than that, the non-social components of the infant's experience are mediated and modified by others, that is, by his social experience. The sensation of hunger in his stomach can only be assuaged by the actions of others. Most of the time, physical comfort or discomfort is brought about by the actions or omissions of others. The object with the pleasurably smooth surface was probably placed within the infant's grasp by somebody. And very likely, if he is rained upon, it is because somebody left him outside without cover. In this way, social experience, while it can be distinguished from other elements in the infant's experience, is not in an isolated category. Almost every aspect of the infant's world involves other human beings. His experience of others is crucial for *all* experience. It is others who create the patterns through which the world is experienced. It is only through these patterns that the organism is able to establish a stable relationship with the outside world—not only the social world but the world of physical environment as well. But these same patterns also penetrate the organism; that is, they interfere with the way it functions. Thus it is others who set the patterns by which the infant's craving for food is satisfied. But in doing so, these others also interfere with the infant's organism itself. The most obvious illustration of this is the timetable of feedings. If the child is fed at certain times, and at certain times only, the organism is forced to adjust to this pattern. In making this adjustment, its functioning changes. What happens in the end is not only that the infant is fed at certain times but that he is hungry at those times. Graphically, society not only imposes its patterns upon the infant's behavior but reaches inside him to organize the functions of his stomach. The same observation pertains to elimination, to sleeping and to other physiological processes that are endemic to the organism.

TO FEED OR NOT TO FEED: A QUESTION OF SOCIAL LOCATION

Some of these socially imposed patterns may be due to the individual peculiarities of the adults who deal with the infant. For example, a mother may feed her infant whenever he cries, regardless of schedule, because she has very sensitive eardrums or because she loves him so much that she cannot bear to think that he might be in discomfort for any length of time. More commonly, however, the decision of whether to feed the infant whenever he cries, or whether to impose a fixed timetable upon him, is not a peculiar decision of the mother as an individual but is a much broader pattern of the society in which the mother lives and which she has learned as the proper one for the problem at hand.

This has a very important implication: in his relations with others, the child experiences a tightly circumscribed micro-world. Only much later does he become aware of the fact that this micro-world has as its background an infinitely vaster macro-world. Perhaps, in retrospect, one envies the infant for this ignorance. Nevertheless, this invisible macro-world, unknown to him, has shaped and predefined almost everything he experiences in his micro-world. If his mother switches from a rigid feeding schedule to a new regime of feeding him whenever he cries, it will of course not occur to the infant to credit anybody but her for this pleasurable change in his circumstances. What he does not know is that the mother acted upon the advice of some expert who reflects the notions currently in vogue in, say, the American college-educated upper middle class. In the final analysis, then, it is not so much the mother as that invisible collective entity that has (in this case pleasurably) invaded the infant's physiological system. There is a further implication, however. Namely, if the infant's mother had belonged to another class, such as the non-college-educated working class, the infant would still be screaming for his food to no avail. In other words, the micro-worlds of the infant's experience differ from each other according to which macro-worlds they are imbedded in. Infancy is experienced relative to its overall location in society. The same principle of relativity pertains to later childhood, adolescence or any other biographical stage.

Feeding practices may be taken as an important case in point. A large number of variations in this are, of course, possible—feeding the infant on a regular schedule as against so-called demand feeding, breast feeding as against bottle feeding, different timetables for weaning and so on. Not only are there great differences between societies in this but also between classes within the same society. For example, in America bottle feeding was first pioneered by middle-class mothers. It then rather rapidly spread to other classes. Later, it was once more middle-class mothers who led a reaction against it in favor of breast feeding. Quite literally, therefore, the income level of an infant's parents decided whether, when hungry, he would be presented with his mother's breast or with a bottle.[1]

---

[1] John and Elizabeth Newson, *Patterns of Infant Care* (Baltimore, Penguin Books, 1965), pp. 176ff.

Between societies, the differences in this area are truly remarkable. In the middle-class family in Western society, before the spread of various notions concerning demand feeding by experts in the field, there was a rigid, almost industrial regime of feeding schedules. The infant was fed at certain hours and at those hours only. In between he was allowed to cry. This practice was variously justified either in terms of practicality or its alleged contribution to the infant's health. By contrast, we may look at the feeding practices of the Gusii in Kenya.[2]

Among the Gusii there are no feeding schedules at all. The mother nurses the infant whenever he cries. At night the mother sleeps naked under a blanket with the child in her arms. As far as feasible, the infant has continuous and instant access to his mother's breast.

When the mother is working, she either carries the infant tied to her back, or he is carried alongside her by someone else. On these occasions also, when the infant starts to cry, he is fed as quickly as possible. The general rule is that the infant is not allowed to cry for more than five minutes before he is fed. Compared with most feeding patterns in Western society, this strikes one as very "permissive" indeed.

There are, however, other aspects of Gusii feeding practices that impress one in a rather different way. Thus, beginning a few days after birth, the infant is fed a gruel as a supplement to his mother's milk. It appears from the data that the infant does not take to this gruel with much enthusiasm. This does not help him any; he is fed by force. This forced feeding is done in the rather unpleasant manner of the mother holding the infant's nose. When, in order to breathe, the infant then opens his mouth, the gruel is poured into it. Also, while other individuals may do so, the infant's mother shows very little affection, and actually rarely fondles the infant. Probably this is done so as to avoid jealousy from onlookers, but it means in practice that the infant experiences more affection from other people than from his own mother. Thus, there are other aspects of Gusii child-rearing at this early stage which, when compared with Western patterns, impress us as quite harsh. On the other

[2] Beatrice Whiting (ed.), *Six Cultures—Studies in Child Rearing* (New York, Wiley, 1963), pp. 139ff.

hand, when it comes to weaning, the Gusiis again show a very high degree of "permissiveness" as compared with Western societies. Thus, while in Western societies the very great majority of children is changed from the breast to the bottle before the age of six months, Gusii children are weaned up to the age of twenty-two months.

TOILET TRAINING: THE BUSH OR "INSPIRATION" Toilet training is another area of the infant's behavior in which, in a very obvious way, social patterns are imposed upon the very physiological functioning of the organism. Generally speaking, there are rather few problems in this area in primitive societies. The general rule is that as soon as children can walk they follow the adults into the bush or into some other area designated by the community as appropriate for elimination. There is especially little problem in warm climates where little or no clothing is worn by small children. Thus, among the Gusii, toilet training consists of the relatively simple matter of getting the child to defecate outside the house. This, on the average, is usually done around twenty-five months of age, and usually takes about one month to accomplish. There seems to be little concern over urination. Since small children wear no lower garments, there is no problem of soiling clothes. Children are taught modesty in eliminating functions, but apparently this is learned in a process of simple imitation without threats or sanctions.[3]

By contrast, toilet training is a very great preoccupation in Western societies. (It seems likely that if Freud had been a Gusii, it would never have occurred to him to give toilet training such an important place in his theory of child development.) If one compares, say, American society with that of the Gusii, it is not difficult to see why toilet training should be more of a problem in the former. There is, after all, the multiplicity of clothing worn by children, the complexity of housing arrangements, not to mention the general unavailability of bush. Thus, the tribulations, successes and

---

[3] Whiting, *ibid.*, pp. 154ff.

failures of toilet training are a frequent topic of conversation among American mothers. In a recent study of a community in New England,[4] the observers found an amazing range of punitive measures inflicted on children who did not respond to toilet training as they were supposed to. These measures ranged from rubbing the infant's nose in his own feces, to the use of suppositories or enemas to get the infant used to regularity. (Actually, from one-fourth to one-third of the mothers interviewed reported use of the latter measures.) It seems that small children cordially dislike enemas, and the threat of their use was usually enough to "inspire" the child to defecate when his mother wanted him to.

If a Gusii sociologist, however, concluded from this material that American toilet-training practices are particularly rigid, he would be mistaken in generalizing from this to the way Americans treat their children in other areas of behavior. For example, Americans take for granted that children want to be very much in motion, and by and large this is tolerated even in the lower grades of school. Frenchmen, by contrast, have a very different view of this matter.[5] In a recent study of French child-rearing practices, an American observer was amazed at the way in which French children are taken to play in a park dressed in elegant clothes and somehow manage not to get dirty. American children, of course, manage to get themselves absolutely covered with dirt within no time at all in comparable situations. The explanation of the difference lies in the relative immobility of French children. The American observer noticed this in French children between two and three years of age, and was amazed by their capacity to remain absolutely still for long periods of time. The same study tells of the case of a French child sent by his teacher to see a school psychologist for no other reason than because the child would not sit still in class. The French schoolteacher, completely unused to such behavior, concluded that the child must be ill. In other words, a degree of motor activity taken for granted in an American school was looked upon as evidence for some sort of pathology in France.

[4] *Ibid.*, pp. 944ff.
[5] Margaret Mead and Martha Wolfenstein (eds.), *Childhood in Contemporary Cultures* (Chicago, Phoenix Books, 1955), pp. 106ff.

SOCIALIZATION: RELATIVE PATTERNS EXPERIENCED AS ABSOLUTE

The process through which an individual learns to be a member of society is called *socialization*. There are a number of aspects to this. All the processes just discussed are aspects of socialization. In this sense, socialization is the imposition of social patterns on behavior. And, as we have tried to show, these patterns even interfere with the physiological processes of the organism. It follows that, in the biography of every individual, socialization, and especially early socialization, is a tremendously powerful and important fact. From the point of view of the outside observer, the patterns that are imposed in socialization are highly relative, as we have seen. They depend not only upon the individual peculiarities of the adults who are in charge of the child but also upon the various social groupings to which these adults belong. Thus, the patterns of a child's behavior depend not only upon whether he is a Gusii or an American but also whether he is a middle-class or working-class American. From the point of view of the child, however, these same patterns are experienced in a very absolute way. Indeed, there are reasons to think that if this were not so, the child would become disturbed and socialization could not proceed.

The absoluteness with which societies' patterns confront the child is based on two very simple facts—the great power of the adults in the situation, and the ignorance of the child of alternative patterns. Psychologists differ in their view as to whether the child experiences the adults at this stage of life as being very much under his control (because they are generally so responsive to his needs) or whether he feels continually threatened by them (because he is so dependent upon them). However this may be, there can be no question that, objectively speaking, adults have overwhelming power in the situation. The child can, of course, resist them, but the probable outcome of any conflict is a victory on the part of the adults. It is they who control most of the rewards that he craves and most of the sanctions that he fears. Indeed, the simple fact that most children are eventually socialized affords simple proof of this proposition. At the same time, it is obvious that the small child is ignorant of any alternatives to the patterns that are being imposed upon him. The adults confront him with a world—for him, it is *the* world. It is only much later that he discovers that there are alternatives to this particular world, that his parents' world is relative in space and time, and that quite different patterns are possible. Only then does the individual become aware of the relativity of social patterns and of social worlds—in the extreme case, he might even follow up this insight by becoming a sociologist.

INITIATING A CHILD: *THE* WORLD BECOMES *HIS* WORLD

There is, thus, a way of looking at socialization from what one might call the "policeman's point of view"; that is, socialization can be viewed primarily as the imposition of controls from without, supported by some system of rewards and punishments. There is another, if you will, more benign way of looking at the same phenomenon, namely, one can look upon socialization as a process of initiation in which the child is permitted to develop and expand into a world available to him. In this aspect, socialization is an essential part of the process of becoming fully human and realizing the full potential of the individual. Socialization is a process of initiation into a social world, its forms of interaction and its many meanings. The social world of his parents first confronts the child as an external, vastly powerful and mysterious reality. In the course of socialization, that world becomes comprehensible. The child enters it, becomes capable of participating in it. It becomes *his* world.

LANGUAGE, THINKING, REFLECTION AND "TALKING BACK"

The primary vehicle of socialization, especially in this second aspect, is language. We will return to language in somewhat greater detail a little later on. At this point we would only stress how essential language is for socialization and, indeed, for any continuing participation in a society. It is in acquiring language that a child learns to convey and retain socially recognized meaning. He begins to be able to think abstractly, which means that his mind becomes able to move beyond the immediate situation. It is also through the acquisition of language that the child becomes capable of reflection. Past experience is reflected upon and integrated into a growing, coherent view of reality. Present experience is ongoingly interpreted in terms of this view, and future experience can not only be imagined but planned for. It is through this growing reflection that the child becomes conscious of himself as a self—in the literal sense of re-flection, that is, of the child's attention *turning back* from the outside world to himself.

It is very easy, and, of course, up to a point correct, to think of socialization as a shaping or molding process. Indeed, the child is shaped by society, molded in such a way that he can be a recognized and participant member of it. But it is also important not to see this as a one-sided process. The child, even the very young infant, is not a passive victim of socialization. He resists it, participates in it, collaborates with it in varying degrees. Socialization is a reciprocal process in the sense that not only the socialized but the socializers are affected by it. This can be observed fairly easily in everyday life. Usually parents succeed to a greater or lesser degree in shaping their children in accordance with the overall patterns established by society and desired by themselves. But the parents also are changed by the experience. The child's capacity for reciprocity, that is, his capacity to act on his own upon the world and the other people inhabiting it increases in direct relation to his capacity to use language. Quite literally, the child then starts to *talk back* to the adults.

In the same vein, it is important to recognize that there are limits to socialization. These limits are given in the child's organism. Given an average intelligence, it is possible to take an infant from any part of the world and socialize him into becoming a member of American society. Any normal child can learn English. Any normal child can learn the values and patterns for living that are attached to the English language in America. Probably every normal child could also learn a system of musical notation. But clearly every normal child could *not* be developed into a musical genius. Unless the potential for this were already given in the organism, any efforts at socialization in this direction would come up against hard and impregnable resistance. The present state of scientific knowledge (especially in the area of human biology) does not permit us to describe the precise limits of socialization. All the same, it is very important to be aware that these limits exist.

TAKING THE ATTITUDE OF AND TAKING THE ROLE OF THE OTHER

What are the mechanisms by which socialization proceeds? The fundamental mechanism is a process of interacting and identifying with others. A crucial step is when the child learns (in Mead's phrase) *to take the attitude of the other*.[6] This means that the child not only learns to recognize a certain attitude in someone else, and to understand its meaning, but that he learns to take it himself. For example, the child observes his mother taking an attitude of anger on certain occasions—say, on occasions where he soils himself. The attitude of anger not only is expressed by various gestures and words but also conveys a particular meaning, namely, that it is wrong to soil oneself. The child will first imitate the external expressions of this attitude, both verbally and nonverbally. It is in this process of interaction and identification that the meaning of this attitude is appropriated by the child.

This particular phase of socialization will be successfully accomplished when the child has learned to take the same attitude toward himself, even in the absence of his mother. Thus, children can be observed "playing mother" to themselves when they are alone—for example, by rebuking themselves for infractions of the rules of toilet training, sometimes by acting out a complete little skit in imitation of similar previous performances on the part of the mother. Eventually, it is no longer necessary to go through the skit. The attitude has become firmly imbedded in the child's consciousness, and he can refer to it silently and without acting it out. Similarly,

[6] These and the following concepts were coined by George Herbert Mead. See our recommendations for readings for this chapter.

the child learns *to take the role of the other*. For the present purpose, we can simply understand a role as an attitude that has become fixed in a consistent and reiterated pattern of conduct. Thus, there are not only a variety of attitudes which the mother takes toward the child, but there is an overall pattern of conduct which can be called the "mother role." A child not only learns to take on specific attitudes but to take on these roles. Playing is a very important part of this learning process. Everyone, of course, has watched children playing at being their parents, at being older brothers or sisters, and then later at being policemen, cowboys or Indians. Such playing is not only important for the particular roles that it involves but for teaching the child to play *any* role. It doesn't matter, therefore, that this particular child will never be either cowboy or Indian. But, in playing the role, a reiterated pattern of conduct is learned in the first place. *The point is not to become an Indian, but rather to learn how to play roles.*

SOCIALIZATION: FROM "SIGNIFICANT OTHERS" TO "GENERALIZED OTHER"

Beyond this general teaching function of "playing at" roles, the same process may also communicate social meanings that are "for real." How American children play the role of policeman will greatly depend on what this role means in their immediate social milieu. To a white suburban child the policeman means a figure of authority and reassurance, someone to turn to in the case of trouble. To a black child of the inner city, the same role very likely implies hostility and danger, a threat rather than reassurance, someone to run away from rather than to. We may also assume that playing the roles of cowboy and Indian has very different meanings indeed in white suburbia or on an Indian reservation.

Socialization thus proceeds in a continuous interaction with others. But not all the others encountered by the child are equally important in this process. Some are clearly of central importance. In the case of most children, these are the parents and whatever brothers and sisters might be around. In some cases there are added to this group such figures as grandparents, close friends of the parents and domestic servants. There are other people who stay in the background and whose place in the process of socialization could best be described as one in which background noise is provided. These are all sorts of casual contacts, ranging from the mailman to the neighbor whom one only sees occasionally. If one thinks of socialization as a kind of drama, one could think of it in terms of ancient Greek theater, in which case some of the participants may be compared to the major protagonists of a play while others function as a chorus.

The major protagonists in the drama of socialization Mead called *significant others*. These are the people with whom the child interacts most frequently, to whom he has an important emotional relationship, and whose attitudes and roles are the crucial ones in his situation. Obviously, it is very important for what happens to the child just who or what these significant others are. By this we mean not only their individual particularities or eccentricities but their location in the larger society. In the earlier phases of socialization, whatever attitudes or roles are taken by the child, it is from the significant others that they are taken. In a very real sense they *are* the child's social world. As socialization proceeds, however, the child begins to understand that these particular attitudes and roles refer to a much more general reality. For example, the child then begins to understand that it is not only his mother who is angry when he soils himself but that that anger is shared by every other significant adult that he knows, and, indeed, by the adult world in general. It is at this point that the child learns to relate not only to specific significant others but to a *generalized other* (another Meadian term) which represents society at large. This step can be easily seen in terms of language. In the earlier phase, it is as if the child says to himself (in many cases he will actually do so), "Mommy doesn't want me to soil myself." After the discovery of the generalized other, it becomes a statement such as this: "One does not soil oneself." The particular attitudes have now become universal. The specific commands and prohibitions of individual others have become general norms. This step is a very crucial one in the process of socialization.

INTERNALIZATION, CONSCIENCE AND SELF-DISCOVERY

It will now make sense that one of the terms used to describe socialization, and sometimes used almost interchangeably with it, is that of *internalization*. What is meant by this is that the social world, with its multitude of meanings, becomes internalized in the child's own consciousness. What previously was experienced as something outside himself can now become experienced within himself as well. In a complicated process of reciprocity and reflection, a certain symmetry is established between the inner world of the individual and the outer social world within which he is being socialized. The phenomenon we usually call conscience illustrates this most clearly. Conscience, after all, is essentially the internalization (or, rather, the internalized presence) of moral commands and prohibitions that previously came from the outside. It all began when somewhere in the course of socialization a significant other said, "Do this," or "Don't do that." As socialization proceeded, the child identified with these statements of morality. In identifying with them, he internalized them. Somewhere along the line, he said to himself, "Do this," or "Don't do that,"—probably in much the same manner that his mother or some other significant person first said them to him. Then these statements became silently absorbed into his own mind. The voices have become inner voices. And finally it is the individual's own conscience that is speaking to him.

Once more it is possible to look upon this in different ways. One can look at internalization from what we previously called the "policeman's point of view," and it will be correct to do so. As the example of conscience clearly illustrates, internalization has something to do with controlling the individual's conduct. It makes it possible for such controls to be continuous and economical. It would be terribly expensive for society, and probably impossible, to constantly surround the individual with other people who will say, "Do this," and "Don't do that." When these injunctions have become internalized within the individual's own consciousness, only occasional reinforcements from the outside are necessary. Most of the time, most individuals will control themselves. But this is only one way of looking at the phenomenon. Internalization not only controls the individual but opens up the world for him. Internalization not only allows the individual to participate in the outside social world but it also enables him to have a rich inner life of his own. *Only by internalizing the voices of others can we speak to ourselves. If no one had significantly addressed us from the outside, there would be silence within ourselves as well. It is only through others that we can come to discover ourselves.* Even more specifically, it is only through significant others that we can develop a significant relationship to ourselves. This, among other reasons, is why it is so important to choose one's parents with some care.

"HE'S ONLY A CHILD"— BIOLOGICAL GROWTH AND BIOGRAPHICAL STAGES

There is, of course, a certain parallelism between the biological processes of growth and socialization. If nothing else, the growth of the organism sets limits to socialization. Thus, it would be futile if a society wanted to teach language to a child one month old or calculus to a child aged two years. However, it would be a great mistake to think that the biographical stages of life, as defined by society, are directly based on the stages of biological growth. This is so with regard to all stages of biography, from birth to death, but it is also true of childhood. There are many different ways of structuring childhood not only in terms of its duration but in terms of its characteristics. It is no doubt possible for the biologist to provide a definition of childhood in terms of the degree of development of the organism; and the psychologist can give a corresponding definition in terms of the development of the mind. Within these biological and psychological limits, however, the sociologist must insist that childhood itself is a matter of social construction. This means that society has great leeway in deciding what childhood is to be.

Childhood, as we understand and know it today, is a creation of the modern world, especially of the bourgeoisie.[7] It is only very recently in Western history that childhood has come to be conceived of as a special and highly protected age. This modern structure of childhood is not only expressed in innumerable beliefs and values regarding children (for example, the notion that children are somehow "innocent") but also in our legislation. Thus, it is today a just about universal assumption in modern societies that children are not subject to the ordinary provisions of criminal law. It was not so very long ago that children were simply looked upon as little adults. This was very clearly expressed by the manner in which they were dressed. As recently as the eighteenth century, as we can see by looking at paintings from this period, children walked around with their parents dressed in identical fashion—except, of course, in smaller sizes. As childhood came to be understood and organized as a very special phase of life, distinct from adulthood, children began to be dressed in special ways.

A case in point is the modern belief in the "innocence" of children, that is, the belief that children ought to be protected from certain aspects of life. For fascinating comparative reading, we may look at the diary kept by the royal physician during the childhood of Louis XIII of France at the beginning of the seventeenth century.[8] His nanny played with his penis when Louis was less than one year old. Everyone thought that this was great fun. Soon afterward, the little prince made a point of always exhibiting his penis amid general merriment. He also asked everyone to kiss it. This ribald attention to the child's genital parts continued for several years and involved not only frivolous maids and the like but also his mother, the Queen. At the age of four the Prince was taken to his mother's bed by a lady of the court and told, "Monsieur, this is where you were made." Only after he reached about seven years of age did the notion arise that he ought to have a certain degree of modesty about this part of his body. One may add that Louis XIII was married at the age of fourteen, by which time, as one commentator remarks wryly, he had nothing left to learn.

[7] Philippe Ariès, *Centuries of Childhood* (New York, Knopf, 1962).
[8] *Ibid.*, pp. 100ff.

DIFFERENT
WORLDS OF
CHILDHOOD

A classical case of the different worlds of childhood, known to almost everyone, is the contrast between Athens and Sparta in this respect.[9] The Athenians were very much concerned that their young men should grow up into well-rounded individuals, as capable in poetry and philosophy as in the arts of war. Athenian education reflected this ideal. The world of the Athenian child (at least the male child) was a world of ongoing competition, not only physically but mentally and aesthetically. By contrast, Spartan education stressed only the development of discipline, obedience and physical prowess—that is, the virtues of the soldier. Compared with Athenian practices, the way in which the Spartans raised their children was overwhelmingly harsh if not downright brutal. The practice of letting children go hungry, forcing them to steal their own food, was only one of many expressions of this conception of childhood. Needless to say, it was much more agreeable to be a little boy in Athens than in Sparta. But this is not the major sociological point. Rather the point is that Spartan socialization produced very different kinds of individuals from socialization in Athens. Spartan society, which glorified the military aspect of life over any other, wanted such individuals, and in terms of these goals the Spartan system of child-rearing made perfect sense.

The kind of childhood which was developed in the modern West is, today, rapidly spreading throughout the world. There are many reasons for this. One of them is the dramatic decline in infant mortality and children's diseases which has been one of the truly revolutionary consequences of modern medicine. As a result, childhood has become a safer and happier phase of life than it has ever been before, and this has encouraged the spread of the Western conception of childhood as a specially valuable and to-be-protected stage of life. Compared with previous periods of history in the West and elsewhere, socialization today has taken on unique qualities of gentleness and concern for all the needs of the child. It is very likely

[9] Compare, for example, H. I. Marrou, *A History of Education in Antiquity* (New York, Mentor Books, 1956).

that the spread of this conception of socialization and the structure of childhood that goes with it are having very important effects on society, even in the political sphere.

MEETING OURSELVES: THE MEADIAN CONCEPTS OF "I" AND "ME"

So far we have emphasized the way in which socialization introduces the child into a particular social world. Equally important is the way in which socialization introduces the child to himself. Just as society has constructed a world into which the child can be initiated, so society also constructs specific types of self. Not only is the child socialized into a particular world but he is socialized into a particular self. What takes place within the child's consciousness in this process has been expressed by the Meadian concepts of the *I* and the *me*.[10] We have already mentioned as an interesting consequence of socialization that a child can speak to himself. The *I* and the *me* are the partners in precisely this kind of conversation. The *I* represents the ongoing spontaneous awareness of self that all of us have. The *me*, by contrast, represents that part of the self that has been shaped or molded by society.

These two aspects of the self can enter into conversation with each other. For example, a little boy growing up in American society is taught certain things that supposedly are appropriate to little boys, such as fortitude in the face of pain. Suppose he bangs his knee and it starts to bleed. The *I* is registering the pain and, we might imagine, wants to scream its head off. The *me*, on the other hand, has learned that good little boys are supposed to be brave. It is the *me* that makes our little boy bite his lip and bear the pain. Or suppose that the little boy has grown a little older and has a very attractive teacher in school. The *I* registers the attraction and wants nothing more than to grab the teacher and make love to her. The *me*, however, has appropriated the social norm that such things are simply not done. It is not difficult to imagine a silent inner conver-

---

[10] These concepts are also taken from Mead.

sation between these two aspects of the self, the one saying, "Go ahead and get her," the other warning, "Stop; this is wrong." Socialization, then, in a very important way, shapes a part of the self. It cannot shape the self in its entirety. There is always something spontaneous, something uncontrollable, which sometimes erupts in unforeseen ways. It is that spontaneous part of the self that *confronts* the socialized part of the self.

APPROPRIATING AN IDENTITY: BEING ASSIGNED OR SUBSCRIBING

The socialized part of the self is commonly called *identity*.[11] Every society may be viewed as holding a repertoire of identities—little boy, little girl, father, mother, policeman, professor, thief, archbishop, general and so forth. By a kind of invisible lottery, these identities are assigned to different individuals. Some of them are assigned from birth, such as little boy or little girl. Others are assigned later in life, such as clever little boy or pretty little girl (or, conversely, stupid little boy or ugly little girl). Other identities are put up, as it were, for subscription, and individuals may obtain them by deliberate effort, such as policeman or archbishop. But whether an identity is assigned or achieved, in each case it is appropriated by the individual through a process of interaction with others. It is others who identify him in a specific way. Only if an identity is confirmed by others is it possible for that identity to be real to the individual holding it. In other words, identity is the product of an interplay of identification and self-identification. This is even true of identities that are deliberately constructed by an individual.

For example, there are individuals in our society who are identified as male who would prefer to be female. They may do any number of things, all the way to surgery, in order to reconstruct themselves in terms of the desired new identity. The essential goal which they must achieve, however, is to get at least some others to

---

[11] It is not quite clear who first used the concept of identity in this sense. Its popularity in recent years is largely due to the work of Erik Erikson, who may be described as a sociologically inclined psychoanalyst. See his *Childhood and Society* (New York, Norton, 1950).

accept that new identity, that is, to identify them in these terms. It is impossible to be anything or anybody for very long all by oneself. Others have to tell us who we are, others have to confirm our identity. There are, indeed, cases where individuals hold on to an identity that no one else in the world recognizes as real. We call such individuals psychotics. They are marginal cases of great interest, but their analysis cannot concern us here.

DIFFERENT SOCIETIES, DIFFERENT IDENTITIES: AMERICAN AND SOVIET SOCIALIZATION

If the relationship between socialization and identity is understood, then it will be clear how it comes about that entire social groups or societies can be characterized in terms of specific identities. Americans, for instance, can be recognized not only in terms of certain patterns of conduct but also in terms of certain characteristics that many of them have in common—that is, in terms of a specifically American identity. Numerous studies have shown how certain basic American values, such as autonomy, individual achievement and seriousness about one's career, are introduced into the socialization process from the beginning, especially in the case of boys.[12] Even the games which American children play reflect these values, for example in their emphasis on individual competition. There are severe penalties for failure to live up to these values and to the identity which they intend. These penalties range from being made fun of by other children to being a failure in the occupational world.

By contrast, Soviet society has emphasized discipline, loyalty and cooperation with others for collective achievement. It is these values which have been emphasized in Soviet child-rearing and educational practices. The goal here, of course, has been to produce an identity that is suitable to the Soviet ideal of socialist society. The

[12] This is an influential (well-merited) study of life in a Canadian suburban community, with special emphasis on family and childhood patterns: J. R. Seeley, R. A. Sim and E. W. Loosley, *Crestwood Heights* (New York, Basic Books, 1956), pp. 118ff.

Soviet child thus grows up in a situation in which he is much more firmly controlled than his American contemporary, but in which he is also more protected against unsettling necessities to make choices of his own. As a result, as has been observed by some American investigators, Soviet children show a much greater serenity than American children of the same age.[13] One may leave aside the question whether the Soviet claim to have produced the "new socialist man" is justified. What is clear, however, is that Soviet society, for better or for worse, has set up such socialization processes as are conducive to a specific type of identity which is in accordance with the ideals and needs of that society.

SECONDARY SOCIALIZATION: ENTERING NEW WORLDS

In talking about education, we have already implied that socialization does not come to an end at the point where an individual child becomes a full participant in society. Indeed, one may say that socialization never comes to an end. In a normal biography, what happens simply is that the intensity and scope of socialization diminish after early childhood. Sociologists distinguish between *primary* and *secondary socialization*. By primary socialization is meant the original process by which a child becomes a participant member of a society. By secondary socialization are meant all later processes by which an individual is inducted into a specific social world. For example, every training in an occupation involves processes of secondary socialization. In some cases, these processes are relatively superficial. For example, no profound changes in the identity of an individual are required to train him to be a certified public accountant. This is not the case, however, if an individual is to be trained to be a priest or to be a professional revolutionary. There are instances of secondary socialization of this kind that resemble in intensity what goes on in the socialization of early childhood. Secondary socialization is also involved in such widely different experiences as improving one's general social position, changing

[13] David and Vera Mace, *The Soviet Family* (Garden City, N.Y., Dolphin Books, 1964), pp. 264ff.

one's place of residence, adapting to a chronic illness or being accepted by a new circle of friends.

RELATIONS TO INDIVIDUALS AND THE SOCIAL UNIVERSE

All processes of socialization take place in face-to-face interaction with other people. In other words, socialization always involves changes in the micro-world of the individual. At the same time, most processes of socialization, both primary and secondary, relate the individual to complex structures of the macro-world. The attitudes which the individual learns in socialization usually refer to broad systems of meaning and of values that extend far beyond his immediate situation. For example, habits of neatness and cleanliness are not only eccentric notions of a particular set of parents but are values of great importance in a broad middle-class world. Similarly, roles learned in socialization refer to vast institutions that may not be readily visible within the individual's micro-world. Thus, learning the role of being a brave little boy is not only conducive to approval by one's parents and playmates but will have significance to the individual as he makes his career in a much broader world of institutions, ranging from the college football field to the military. Socialization links micro-world and macro-world. First, socialization enables the individual to relate to specific individual others; subsequently, it enables him to relate to an entire social universe. For better or for worse, being human entails having such a relationship on a lifelong basis.

READINGS

The conceptual approach of this chapter is based on George Herbert Mead, especially his *Mind, Self and Society* (Chicago, University of Chicago Press, 1934). Mead is not an easy author to read for the beginning student. For the latter, we would recommend Anselm Strauss (ed.), *George Herbert Mead on Social Psychology* (Chicago, Phoenix Books, 1964), which contains selections from Mead's work and a useful introduction by the editor. One of the best books for an understanding of the different worlds of childhood is Philippe Ariès, *Centuries of Childhood* (New York, Knopf, 1962), available in paperback.

Chapter 4

WHAT IS AN INSTITUTION? THE CASE OF LANGUAGE

WE HAVE PREVIOUSLY DEFINED institutions as regulatory patterns, that is, as programs imposed by society upon the conduct of individuals. Probably this definition did not arouse resistance on the part of the reader, since, while different from it, the definition does not seem to offend directly against the common usage of this term. In common usage the term means organizations that somehow "contain" people—such as *a* hospital, *a* prison, or, for that matter, *a* university. Or it refers to the large societal entities that are seen as hovering almost like metaphysical beings over the life of the individual—like "the state," "the economy" or "the educational system." Thus, if the reader were asked to name an institution, he would very probably come up with one of these cases. He would be right, too. This common usage, however, is too one-sided. More precisely, it associates the term too closely with those societal entities that are recognized and codified by the law. Perhaps this is an example of the influence of lawyers on the way we think. Be this as it may, for our purpose here it is important to show that the meaning of institutions in the perspective of sociology is *not* quite this. For this reason, we want to take a moment, or a short chapter, to show that language is an institution.

Indeed, we would argue further that language is very probably *the* fundamental institution of society, as well as being the first institution encountered by the individual biographically. It is fundamental, because all other institutions, whatever their various purposes and characteristics, build upon the underlying regulatory pattern of language. The state, the economy and the educational system, whatever else they may be, depend upon a linguistic edifice of classification, concepts and imperatives for individuals' actions—that is, they depend on a world of meanings that was constructed by means of language and can only be kept going by language.

Also, language is the first institution encountered by the individual. This statement may surprise. Probably, if asked about the first institution the child experiences, the reader will think of the family. Again, in a way, he is right. For the great majority of children primary socialization takes place in the context of a particular family, which in turn is a case in point of the broad institution of kinship in that particular society. And, of course, the family is a very important institution; we will discuss this in the next chapter. *But the child is unaware of this.* What he, in fact, experiences is his parents, brothers and sisters, and whatever other relatives may be around at that time. Only later does he become aware that these particular individuals, and what they do, are a case in point of the much larger social reality known as "the family." Presumably, this insight occurs as the child begins to compare himself with other children— something that hardly happens in infancy. Language, on the other hand, impinges on the child very early in its macro-social aspects. From a very early stage on, language *points to* broader realities that lie beyond the micro-world of the child's immediate experience. It is through language that the child first becomes aware of a vast world "out there," a world that is mediated by the adults who surround him but which vastly transcends them.

LANGUAGE: THE OBJECTIFICATION OF REALITY

First of all, of course, it is the child's micro-world itself that is structured by language. Language *objectifies* reality—that is, the incessant flux of experience is firmed up, stabilized, into discrete, identifiable objects. This is true of material objects. The world becomes organized in terms of trees, tables and telephones. The organization goes beyond the act of naming, of course; it also involves the meaningful relations between all these objects. The table is pushed under the tree if one wants to climb up on it, and the telephone, perhaps, summons the doctor if one falls off. Language also structures, by objectification and by establishing meaningful relations, the human environment of the child. It populates reality with distinct beings, ranging from Mommy (in most cases a sort of presiding goddess, whose throne stands in the center of an expanding universe) to the bad-little-boy who throws tantrums next door. And it is by means of language that the fact becomes established that Mommy knows best, but that bad-little-boys will be punished; and, incidentally, it is only through the power of language that such propositions can retain their established plausibility even if experience offers little or no proof.

Very importantly, it is by means of language that roles become stabilized in the experience of the child. We have already talked of roles in connection with the child's learning to take the role of the other—a crucial step in the socialization process. The child learns to recognize roles as recurring patterns in the conduct of others— the experience that we have previously described with the phrase "here he goes again." [1] This recognition becomes a permanent fixture in the child's mind, and thus in his interaction with others, by means of language. It is language that specifies, in a repeatable way, just *what* it is that the other is at again—"Here he goes with the punishing-father bit again," "Here she goes again putting on her company-is-coming face" and so on. Indeed, only by means of such linguistic fixation (that is, giving to the action of the other a fixed meaning, which can be repeatedly attached to each case of such action) can the child learn to take the role of the other. In other words, language is the bridge from "Here *he* goes again," to "Watch out, here *I* come."

LANGUAGE: THE INTERPRETATION AND JUSTIFICATION OF REALITY

The micro-world of the child is structured in terms of roles. Many of these roles, however, extend into the wider reaches of the macro-world, or, to use the reverse image, are extensions of that macro-world into the immediate situation of the child. *Roles represent institutions.* [2] As father goes through his punishing bit once more, we may assume that this performance is accompanied by a good deal of verbiage. As he punishes, he talks. What is he talking about? Some of

---

[1] The definition of role used here is quite conventional by now, not only in sociology but in the social sciences generally. Compare the following definition by Ralph Turner: "In . . . most . . . usages, the following elements appear in the definition of role: it provides a comprehensive *pattern* for behavior and attitudes; it constitutes a *strategy* for coping with a recurrent type of situation; it is *socially identified,* more or less clearly, as an entity; it is subject to being played recognizably by *different individuals;* and it supplies a major basis for *identifying* and *placing* persons in society." (Article on "Role: Sociological Aspects," *International Encyclopedia of the Social Sciences,* Vol. 13 [New York, Macmillan, 1968], p. 552).

[2] We are here combining the concept of role with that of representation, as coined by Durkheim.

the talking may just be a way of giving vent to his own annoyance or anger. But, in most cases, much of the talking is a running commentary on the offending act and the punishment it so richly deserves. The talking *interprets* and *justifies* the punishment. Inevitably, it does this in a way that goes beyond the father's own immediate reactions. The punishment is put in a vast context of manners and morals; in the extreme case, even the divinity may be invoked as a penal authority. Leaving aside the theological dimension (about which, regrettably, sociology has nothing to say), the explanations of manners and morals relate the little drama in the micro-world to a whole system of macro-scopic institutions. The punishing father now represents this system (say, good behavior and morality as such); when he is at it again, that is, when he repeats the performance in a recognizable role, then that role represents the institutions of the moral system.

Language thus confronts the child as an all-encompassing reality. Almost everything else that he experiences as real is structured on the basis of this underlying reality—filtered through it, organized by it, expanded by it or, conversely, banished through it into oblivion—for that which cannot be talked about has a very tenuous hold on memory. This is true of *all* experience, but it is especially true of the experience of others and of the social world.

BASIC CHARACTERISTICS OF AN INSTITUTION: EXTERNALITY

What, then, are some of the essential characteristics of an institution? We will try to clarify these, using the case of language.[3] And we would make a further suggestion: in the future, if the reader comes across a statement about institutions, what they are or how they operate or how they change, a good rule of thumb will be to ask first how that statement looks when applied to language. Needless to say, there are institutions that are very different from language—think, for

[3] These characteristics of an institution closely follow Durkheim's description of social facts.

instance, of the state. All the same, if such a general statement, even if appropriately modified to cover a different institutional case, makes no sense at all when applied to language, then there is a good chance that something is badly wrong with the statement.

Institutions are experienced as having external reality; that is, an institution is something outside the individual, something real in a way (one might say, in a "hard" way) different from the reality of the individual's thoughts, feelings or fantasies. In this characteristic, an institution resembles other entities of outside reality—even trees, tables and telephones, all of which are *out there* whether the individual likes it or not. He cannot wish a tree away—nor an institution. Language is experienced in this way. To be sure, when someone is speaking, he is, as it were, "throwing out" something that was previously "inside" himself—not just the sounds of which language is made up but the meanings that language is intended to convey. Yet this "throwing out" (a more elegant term for this is "externalization") is in terms of something that is not the idiosyncratic creation of the speaker. He is, let us say, speaking *English.* The English language, though, was not created in the depths of his particular consciousness. It was out there long before this moment at which he is using it. It is *as* something out there that he experiences it, as well as the other he is speaking to, and both of them experienced the English language as such an outside reality when they first learned it.

BASIC CHARACTERISTICS OF AN INSTITUTION: OBJECTIVITY

Institutions are experienced as possessing objectivity. This is really repeating the previous statement in a slightly different form. Something is objectively real when everyone (or nearly everyone) agrees that it is actually there, and that it is there in a certain way. The last point is important. There is *correct* English and *incorrect* English—and this remains so, *objectively* so, even if an individual should think that the rules determining this are the height of folly and that he would have a much better, more rational way of organizing the language. Most of the time, of course, the individual gives little thought to this; he accepts the language as he accepts other objective facts in his experience. The objectivity of one's first language is particularly powerful. Jean Piaget, the Swiss child psychologist, tells the story somewhere of a small child who was asked whether the sun could be called anything else except "sun." "No," replied the child. How did he know this, the child was asked. The question puzzled him for a moment. Then he pointed to the sun and said, "Well, look at it."

BASIC CHARACTERISTICS OF AN INSTITUTION: COERCIVENESS

Institutions have coercive power. To some extent, this quality is already implied by the preceding two: the fundamental power of an institution over the individual is precisely that it is objectively there and that he cannot wish it away. It may happen, though, that he overlooks the fact, or forgets it—or, even worse, that he would like to change the whole arrangement. It is at those points that the coercive power of the institution is very likely to show itself in quite crude forms. In an enlightened middle-class home, and at an age when everyone agrees that such slips are to be expected, the young child is mainly treated to gentle persuasion when he offends against the canons of correct English. This gentle power may extend to the progressive school. It will hardly extend to the child's peers in that school. They are likely to treat offenses against their own code of proper English (which, needless to say, is not quite the same as that of the schoolteacher) with brutal ridicule and possibly with physical persecution. The adult faces persecution on every side if he should continue such defiance. The working-class youth may lose his girl because he refuses to speak "nice"—as he may lose his promotion. Webster's dictionary and Fowler's *Modern English Usage* stand guard at every rung of the status ladder. But pity the middle-class youth who *continues* to speak "nice" in the army! As to the middle-aged professor, who tries to ingratiate himself with the young by speaking "their language" and who, of course, is always at least two years behind in the latter's rapidly shifting orthodoxies, *his* encounter with the coercive power of language reaches the pathos of Sophoclean tragedy.

To recognize the power of institutions is *not* to say that they cannot be changed. Indeed, they change all the time—and *must* so change, because they are nothing but the inevitably tenuous products of innumerable individuals "throwing out" meanings into the world. Thus, if everyone in America stopped speaking English tomorrow, the English language as an institutional reality in America would abruptly cease to exist. In other words, the objective existence of the language depends on the ongoing speech of many individuals who, in speaking, are expressing their subjective intentions, meanings and motives.[4] It is clear that this kind of objectivity, unlike the objectivity of the facts of nature, can never be a static one. It is always changing, is in dynamic flux, sometimes goes through violent convolutions. But *for the individual* it is not easy to bring about deliberate change. If he is by himself, in most cases, his chances of succeeding in such an enterprise are minimal. Let the reader imagine himself in the role of grammatical reformer or of innovator of vocabulary. He may have some success in his immediate micro-world. Indeed, he probably had some such success as a young child: his family may have adopted a couple of his more outrageous baby-talk creations as part of the family's ingroup language. As an adult, the individual may have similar mini-victories as he speaks with his wife or his circle of close friends. But, unless he is a recognized "great writer" or statesman, or unless he goes to incredible efforts to organize masses of people around his banner of linguistic revolution (one may think here of the revival of classical Hebrew in modern Zionism or of the less successful effort to do the same for Gaelic in Ireland), his impact on the language of his macro-world will probably be close to nil on the day he leaves this vale of words.

[4] The differentiation between language and speech is derived from Ferdinand de Saussure, a linguist greatly influenced by Durkheim.

BASIC CHARACTERISTICS OF AN INSTITUTION: MORAL AUTHORITY

Institutions have moral authority. Institutions do not simply maintain themselves by coercive power. They claim the right to legitimacy—that is, they reserve to themselves the right not only to hit the offender over the head but to reprimand him morally. Institutions, of course, vary in the degree of moral loftiness as-cribed to them. This variation is usually expressed in the degree of punishment inflicted on the offender. The state, in the extreme case, may kill him; the suburban community may just snub his wife at the country club. In both cases, the act of punishing is accompanied by a sense of indignant righteousness. The moral authority of language will only rarely express itself in physical violence (though, for instance, there are situations in modern Israel where the non-Hebrew speaker may become physically uncomfortable). It does express itself in the successful stimulation of shame and sometimes even guilt in the offender. The foreign child who keeps on making mistakes in English, the poor immigrant carrying the burden of his accent, the soldier who cannot overcome his ingrained habits of linguistic politeness, the avant-garde intellectual whose erroneous jargon shows that he is not "with it" after all—these individuals suffer from more than external reprisals; like it or not, one must concede to them the dignity of moral suffering.

BASIC CHARACTERISTICS OF AN INSTITUTION: HISTORICITY

Institutions have the quality of historicity. Institutions are not only facts but historical facts; they *have* a history. In almost all cases experienced by the individual, the institution was there before he was born and it will be there after he is dead. The meanings embodied in the institution were accumulated there over a long time, by innumerable individuals whose names and faces can never be retrieved from the past. Thus the speaker of contemporary American English is reiterating, without knowing it, the verbalized experiences of generations of dead people—Norman conquerors, Saxon serfs, ecclesiastical scribes, Elizabethan lawyers, not to speak of Puritans, frontiersmen, Chicago gangsters and jazz musicians of more recent times.

Language (and, indeed, the world of institutions generally) may be seen as a broad stream flowing through time. Those who sail on it for a while, or who live alongside it, keep throwing objects into it. Most of these sink to the bottom or dissolve right away. Some coagulate in such a way that they are carried along, for a longer or shorter period. Only a few make it all the way downstream, to the point where this particular stream, as all others, ends in the ocean of oblivion that is the termination of any empirical history.

An Austrian writer, Karl Kraus, has called language the house in which the human spirit lives. Language provides the lifelong context of our experience of others, of self, of the world. Even when we imagine worlds beyond this one, we are constrained to put our intimations or hopes in terms of language. Language is *the* social institution above all others. It provides the most powerful hold that society has over us.

READINGS

This chapter has the character of an excursus. No additional reading is necessary here. But the reader might be advised to turn to accounts of the child's experience of language, if he wants to pursue these considerations further. The classical scientific accounts of this are by Jean Piaget, especially in his *Language and Thought in the Child* (London, Routledge and Kegan Paul, 1926). One of the most beautiful accounts of a child's discovery of language (in this instance doubly poignant, because of the terrible handicaps of this particular child) may be found in Helen Keller's autobiography, *The Story of My Life* (New York, Doubleday, Page & Co., 1903), especially in the appendix that contains the account of Miss Sullivan, the author's teacher.

Chapter 5

THE
FAMILY

THE FAMILY AS THE WORLD

The child does not at first experience the family as such, as we have shown earlier. That is, the child is not aware of the family as a specific institution within the larger society. The family is, for the child, an entire world of people and meanings of very great significance for him. In the beginning, of course, it is the only world. Seen from the outside or in retrospect, the family contains the most significant others in the early part of an individual's biography. In our society, in most cases, the family contains *all* the most significant others at that stage of life. In terms of what we have said earlier about socialization, it will be evident that the family, both in its overall societal form and in the particular modification of that form as it is experienced by an individual, is a fundamentally important institution. For almost everyone, the family is, as it were, the *home port* from which the individual starts out on his lifelong journey through society. What happened to him at this point of departure will significantly affect the later phases of the journey.

Already at that early stage, of course, the outside observer can look upon the family as the individual's micro-world. As far as the child himself is concerned, however, it is only later that he himself experiences the family in this way. As the child becomes aware of the large structures that loom in the background of his everyday life, he begins to see his own family as the circumscribed vantage point from which he views and relates to these larger structures. The family also, however, provides him with his major linkage to the macro-world. It does so not only because it is a channel of information about the latter, but because the attitudes and roles expressed within the family (notably by its adults) represent various structures of the macro-world.

THE FAMILY AS A PLACE OF WAITING

As the child grows up he comes to realize increasingly that the family is the place in which he *waits* for the larger world. It is, after all, in the macro-world that he will make his way in the future. Depending upon circumstances, this future graduation will be looked upon with anxiety or with eager anticipation. If the latter is the case (in our society, very often at the stage of adolescence), the family will be viewed as an irritating barrier between the individual and the supposedly worthwhile and fulfilling experiences that await him in the macro-world. The perspective of most adults on this situation is typically quite different. For them the family is a *refuge* from the macro-world; it is the place to which they can retreat from the latter's tensions, frustrations and anxieties. For most adults in our society, the family is—at least in expectation—the most important locale of their private life, and thus the locale of highly significant expectations for self-fulfillment and emotional satisfaction.

What do we mean as sociologists when we say "family"? What *is* the family? For many people who have remained uncontaminated by sociology, this question may seem quite absurd. They would answer that of course everybody knows what the family is. Up to a point they would be quite correct; everybody in a society—or almost everybody—knows what the family is in the sense that he is very familiar (significantly, this word derives from "family") with it and knows how to act within its settings. In other words, the family is an essential component of almost everyone's taken-for-granted world. It is all the more necessary to gain some distance from this taken-for-granted perspective if one is to understand what the institution is all about. Indeed, despite this familiarity, most individuals (social scientists are no exception) would have a hard time coming up with a definition of the family. Familiarity breeds not so much contempt as blindness. We find it easier to give a physical description of a stranger just met than of parents or spouses. Sociology tries to introduce a sufficient element of artificial strangeness into what is most familiar to us in order that we may be able to describe the familiar in clearer ways.

As we have already indicated in our discussion of socialization, there are vast variations between societies in the form and functioning of the family. Despite this relativity, though, the family is one of the most pervasive institutions of man. We know of no human society that has not had the family in some form. What is more, the family, in a very direct way, relates to the biological constitution of man. It combines biological and social functions in a more direct way than any other institution.

BASIC HUMAN ACTIVITIES

Very many different definitions of the family have been proposed by social scientists, and not much purpose would be served by going through them here. Almost everyone agrees, however, that three basic human activities are affected by the family as an institution. These three activities are sexuality, procreation and primary socialization. It is through the structures of the family (or, as cultural anthropologists prefer to say, of kinship) that human sexual relations are patterned. The family provides a typology of others in terms of their degree of relationship to the individual, and it is this typology which determines the permissible partners for sexual relations. The incest taboo, which, in itself, could be described as one of the most ancient and powerful institutions in human history, is the most important expression of this function of the family. In view of the very great strength of sexuality as a motive of human conduct, it is clear that this institutional patterning is of great importance for any human society. The biological fact which underlies the patterning of procreation is the duration of human pregnancy and of the helplessness of the infant after birth. Not only is the mother relatively incapacitated during the period of pregnancy, but the human infant is completely helpless at birth and would die unless social arrangements are made for its care and protection. The family as an institution has provided patterns of conduct surrounding the biological process of procreation and allowing it to proceed with greatly diminished danger. Fi-

nally, in almost all human societies, the family has provided the locale for primary socialization—locale meaning here that it is
within the family that the child's major significant others are first
encountered.[1]

SECONDARY FUNCTIONS: THE LEGAL

An immense variety of other meanings and activities have accumulated around these fundamental
functions of the family. These so to
speak secondary functions of the
family are not only greatly different in different societies but also
have undergone great changes within the same society. The typology of others which everywhere serves as the moral scheme by
which sexuality is patterned has provided different systems of no-
menclature with far-reaching legal implications. It is the family that
generally provides the individual with a name and determines his
basic legal standing. This not only makes it possible to reckon the
individual's descent (which has far-reaching economic as well as
legal implications) but also provides the basic means by which individuals can be identified and located in the social order.

Even in the development of Western societies there have been
vast changes in the exact character of the legal provisions governing the family. At one extreme we find the family in ancient Rome
(even more patriarchal than ancient Israel), in which the father occupied a position of absolute legal power, extending even to the
power over life and death of every member of the family. At the
other extreme we find contemporary family law, not only in America but in other Western societies, which has increasingly emphasized the independent rights of every member of the family, including the children. Indeed, modern Western law has developed
far-reaching provisions to protect the individual *from* his own family (as, for instance, the legal protection available to children

[1] See, for instance, E. Adamson Hoebel, *Man in the Primitive World* (New
York, McGraw-Hill, 1958), pp. 281ff; Mischa Titiev, *Introduction to Cultural
Anthropology* (New York, Holt, 1959), pp. 261ff. Some of the fundamental work
done by cultural anthropology in this area has been the achievement of Margaret
Mead. See, for instance, her *Male and Female* (New York, Morrow, 1955).

against their parents). What is more, the state concerns itself with the individual directly, regardless of family status (aid to dependent children, in this country, is a case in point).

SECONDARY FUNCTIONS: THE ECONOMIC

Similarly, a vast array of economic arrangements have developed around the basic function of protecting the process of procreation and of infancy. In most human societies, the family household (though it may be very differently defined in terms of size and constituency) is regarded as a basic economic unit. There are great differences, however, in the way in which this unit relates to the larger economy. Again, in most human societies, primary socialization is taken care of within the family, but the relationship of this to the broader educational processes required in society will be very different from case to case. Thus there are many societies in which the family is, in effect, the only educational institution in existence. In other societies, again, there may be an entire network of educational institutions outside the family, competing or collaborating with it in the training of children.

Sociologists use the term *conjugal nuclear family* to refer to the type of family that now prevails in Western societies. What is meant by the term is quite simple, namely, a family which, in effect, consists only of a married couple and its children. This family type represents a considerable shrinkage both in the scope and the functioning of the institution. In terms of scope, it has reduced the participant members to what could well be described as an irreducible minimum. Grandparents, maiden aunts, cousins and their children —not to speak of remoter kin—have virtually disappeared from the scene, at least as far as the household is concerned. What is more, the children themselves normally leave the household once they themselves are grown up.

The conjugal nuclear family also represents a considerable shrinkage in functions as compared with earlier forms of the family in Western societies. We have already mentioned the great changes in the legal definition of the family. There has been a fundamental change in its economic functions, which can most simply be described as a shift from production to consumption. In earlier times, the family as a unit participated in the productive processes of the economy. This was true of the farmer, of the craftsman and of the shopkeeper. This productive role of the family has virtually disappeared in contemporary society. What the family does as an economic unit is not to produce but to consume, and it is as a consuming unit that it relates to the economy in an important way. There has been a dramatic shrinkage in the educational function of the family. To be sure, it is still basically in charge of primary socialization. But the vast network of independent educational institutions has not only taken away the educational functions of the family after the children reach school age but increasingly has penetrated into earlier and earlier phases of childhood, through kindergartens, nursery schools, day care centers and the like.

MORE FUNCTIONS: FULFILLMENT AND THE PRIVATE SPHERE

To think only of a shrinkage of functions, however, would give a distorted picture of the place of the family in modern society. As the family has lost certain functions it has gained others.[2] These new functions are basically concerned with the private needs, expectations and fulfillments of the individual. In a way which would have been quite surprising even to our grandparents, the family today is widely expected to provide fundamental personal fulfillment and satisfactions to all its members. Morally this has meant a great shift in emphasis from duties and responsibilities to rights and gratifications in the area of family life.

Modern society has probably, for the first time in history, created an area of social activity that we commonly refer to as *private life,* and that sociologists have called the *private sphere.*[3] This is

[2] The discussion of the concomitant losses and gains of functions of the modern family is derived from Talcott Parsons. See Talcott Parsons, Robert Bales *et al., Family, Socialization and Interaction Process* (New York, Free Press, 1955).

[3] The concept of the private sphere has been developed in recent years primarily by German sociologists.

an area of social life that is quite strictly segregated from the great public institutions, notably the economy and the state. It contains much more than the family; for example, it contains the whole world of private associations ranging from religious cults to groups formed around a particular hobby through which individuals manage to fill their leisure time. However, without any question, the family is the most important institution of the private sphere. This social location of the family in the institutional order is at the opposite pole from the place it occupies in primitive or archaic societies. There the typical situation is that the family occupies the central place in the institutional order. Indeed, the major functions carried out today by the economy and the state are there carried out by the institutions of kinship. Thus, in these societies, there is no clear segregation between the family and the totality of the institutions in the society. It is precisely this segregation, however, which characterizes the family in our society.

Thus there has been a massive shift in the overall social position of the family. One important aspect of this has been a greatly different relationship between micro-world and macro-world. In premodern societies, these two existed in a kind of continuum. The roles played in the family extended directly into the macro-world. Thus the individual growing up in the family would simultaneously grow into the roles assigned to him within the family and in the society at large. Today, in modern society, the barriers between the micro-world of the family and the macro-world of the society at large are very sharp and clear. As a result of this, the individual, between birth and maturity, crosses a number of sharply defined social thresholds. Very frequently these crossings have the consequence that he is estranged from the family in which he began his career in society.

TECHNOLOGICAL CHANGE: THE INDUSTRIAL REVOLUTION

The emergence of the contemporary conjugal nuclear family has been the consequence of gigantic transformations in technology, in the economy and in the demographic structure of society. Parallel to these there has been a profound shift in the realm of attitudes and values. No historical change of such dimension can be traced to a single cause. However, if one were to ask about the single most important factor in bringing about these far-reaching changes in the character of the family, one would have to point to the industrial revolution and to that modern technology which both caused it and was tremendously accelerated by it.

It was modern technological production which forced the family out of its ancient productive role. In modern industry it is no longer possible to have the family household perform a productive function, nor can the family be transposed to those locales where industrial production takes place. A way of illustrating this would be to imagine what a modern factory would be like if the families of the workers were permitted to carry on their normal activities on the premises—such as women cooking or mending clothes, children playing with their toys and perhaps grandmother playing with the household pet. For similar although not quite identical reasons, the family was banished from the realm of modern bureaucracy, and thus from the great bulk of administrative and white-collar work which has grown phenomenally in modern society. The same is true of modern armies. As recently as in the Thirty Years' War armies consisted not only of fighting troops but of hordes of their dependents—women and children, camp followers of every description and legal standing. The modernization of warfare, which set in seriously in the eighteenth century, meant, among other things, the separation of military organization from the family life of its members. And, of course, modern armies are themselves highly bureaucratized. Through modern technology and its twin phenomenon, modern bureaucracy, the family was banished from the sphere of productive work.

As we have already remarked, its place of banishment was that private sphere which, a unique creation of modern society, became increasingly the area in which individuals sought fulfillment in their personal lives. In this private sphere children could be raised in an atmosphere detached from the serious and often desperate tensions of the world of work. It is perhaps not surprising that this sphere of private fulfillment became increasingly dominated by children.

DEMOGRAPHIC AND ECONOMIC CHANGE

The shattering demographic revolution of modern times may also be traced back to the industrial revolution because it was technology, and more specifically medical technology, which made it possible. Advances in the field of medicine have brought about an increase in the life-span of all individuals and, most important, a drastic reduction in infant mortality. At the same time, there has been a marked decline in the birth rate, which was already noticed in demographic studies in France at the end of the eighteenth century and in the United States at the start of the nineteenth century. The decline in the birth rate has clear economic implications. As the family became transformed from a productive to a consuming unit, children ceased to be an economic asset and became an economic liability. On a farm, let us say, children can be economically useful; in an urban apartment, in the family of someone like a certified public accountant, the only thing that children do *economically* is to produce costs. But it was, once more, modern medical technology which made it increasingly possible to translate these economic considerations into effective, practical steps to have fewer children. The overall effect of these demographic processes is that children in modern societies are more scarce while, at the same time, they may be expected to live longer.

The reduction in infant mortality has been one of the most dramatic transformations of the modern world. In the United States, for example, between 1910 and 1969, infant mortality was reduced almost five-fold. During the same period the birth rate was reduced almost by half; that is, only about half the number of children were born in 1969 as compared with 1910, but their chance of survival

beyond infancy was five times better. It is these demographic facts
that must be taken into account if one is to grasp the significance of
the new structures of childhood that we mentioned previously. In
this situation, once more, modern technology becomes an aid in the
realization of certain values. Technology has transformed the
household. This is particularly relevant for the housewife-mother.
Although the technical innovations in the household have not made
great changes in the amount of time spent by mothers in the care of
children, they have greatly changed the way in which different activities are performed within that time-span. This was put dramatically by an advertisement for disposable diapers: "You simply
throw them away instead of toiling over them. You now have more
time to spend *with* your baby."

NEW ATTITUDES AND EXPECTATIONS

New values and attitudes concerning
sexuality, love and family have developed side by side with these
transformations in the structure of
family life. It would almost certainly
be a mistake to see these non-material factors as being either the
simple cause or the simple result of the technological and demographic developments just discussed. The relationship between material development and ideas in society is much more complex than
that. Very probably the best way to think of this relationship is as
one of reciprocity or mutual influence. As we have seen, Max Weber
used the term "elective affinity" to describe such a relationship. By
this he meant that certain ideas and certain material developments
in history have a particular affinity for each other so they, as it
were, "seek each other out." A good illustration of this is the development of the modern Western conception of love between the
sexes. Its origins are well known and long antedate the beginnings
of modern industrial society. More precisely, these origins must be
sought in the cult of chivalry as it developed at the height of the
Middle Ages and was carried from one end of Europe to another
by the troubadours or wandering minstrels. In a slow development
extending over several centuries, this way of looking at the relation-

ship between men and women penetrated to other classes of society. It finally penetrated to the bourgeoisie. Clearly, then, this new idea of love was not a product of the industrial revolution. At the same time, it could by no conceivable argument be seen as one of the latter's causes. What happened, rather, was that as the bourgeoisie began to develop a particular structure of family life as a result of its relation to the new economy, these ideas about love found a peculiarly fertile ground. Very similar statements can be made about other values affecting modern family life.

The modern conjugal nuclear family has been charged with emotional and moral expectations of a very high order. Husband and wife are supposed to love each other, and do so permanently. Parents are supposed to devote great attention to the welfare of their children. Both adults and children in the family are supposed to crucially define themselves and find personal fulfillment in the activities going on within the family circle. It is perhaps not surprising that, in view of these very high expectations, the contemporary family has been very unstable. The separation from productive work has greatly added to this instability; to put it crudely, a man will be much less disposed to get rid of a wife who is contributing to his work than of one who is simply adding to his costs. Conversely, as women entered the labor force in growing numbers, a wife earning a salary herself is more easily disposed to get rid of a husband who has become a burden to the family or a hindrance to her own career.

Another factor of this instability has been the reduction in the scope of the family: there are far fewer people around to give cohesion and continuity to what goes on within the family circle. Thus the development of the modern family has not only been accompanied by a steady rise in separation and divorce rates but almost every individual family faces a peculiar crisis at the time its children leave the home. We have already mentioned the fact that older people have no real place in the modern family. This fact becomes all the more serious in its social implications when one reflects that, with the dramatic rise of life expectancy in modern societies, there are so many old people around. Thus the life expectancy of the average American in 1920 was fifty-four years; in 1967 it had risen to seventy years.

THE EXTENDED AND CONJUGAL NUCLEAR FAMILY

The modern family is built around the relationship between the two marriage partners. A contrasting type is the *extended family,* which is based on a much larger and more complex set of relationships. The modern family, both as a social type and as a collection of values, has been one of the most successful exports of the Western world. It has rapidly advanced in Asia and Africa, and is today well on its way to becoming a universal phenomenon.[4] The conjugal nuclear family, both in fact and in principle, is radically destructive of older family traditions in almost every human society. Its values emphasize the worth of the individual as against those of his groups. Each individual is to be evaluated in his own terms, not through those of his groups. And it is as an individual that he, or she, has intrinsic rights.

One of the most important consequences of these values, of course, has been the assertion (an increasingly successful assertion) of the right of everyone, man or woman, to choose his or her marriage partner. The basis upon which this choice is to be made is supposed to be love, understood as an emotional thunderstorm, both unpredictable and democratic, cutting across all traditional lines separating people from each other. This is not exactly what happens in practice. On the contrary, it has been exhaustively shown that people marry by and large within certain social lines. In American society this is mainly in terms of class lines, although racial, ethnic, religious and geographic lines are also very important. Love, then, may be a thunderstorm, but it seems to be rather careful where it hits at any given moment. Nevertheless, the *ideal* of the conjugal nuclear family entails a revolution in values. People rarely live up to their ideals in history, but the very fact that these ideals exist makes a profound difference for what in fact is happening.

The values of the conjugal nuclear family are directly related to

[4] See William Goode, *World Revolution and Family Patterns* (New York, Free Press, 1963); M. F. Nimkoff (ed.), *Comparative Family Systems* (Boston, Houghton Mifflin, 1965).

various statistical characteristics. There has been a long-lasting trend, observable in America and in other Western societies, toward earlier marriages and toward a decrease in the age difference between marriage partners. The age of marriage, of both men and women, has been steadily declining in the United States—quite strikingly so during the last quarter century. The same is true of age difference between marriage partners. The remarkable growth in student marriages in recent decades has been a dramatic illustration of both trends. It is not hard to see how the companionship in such marriages would undermine the old authority of the husband: "I have known him since we were freshmen in college. What does he know that I don't know?!" To some extent, to be sure, these trends may be related to the growing affluence of society. But they are also to be related to the conjugal ideology, in which material considerations are supposed to be less and less important for the decision to marry. The only thing that is supposed to matter is the profound emotional relationship between the marriage partners, and this, of course, can happen at any age and is not dependent on the material accomplishments of either.

MARRIAGE, DIVORCE AND REMARRIAGE

All of this indicates how important marriage still is to most people today—despite the fact that its definition has greatly changed. A concomitant rise in divorce statistics (the divorce rate has more than tripled since fifty years ago in the United States) has sometimes been taken as a counter-indicator to the last statement. This, we would argue, is a very basic misunderstanding of the meaning of divorce. Much more interesting than the divorce rates by themselves are the rates for remarriage, which have also been steadily rising, especially so among individuals who marry for the first time and get divorced at an early age. Not only are the divorce rates not an argument against the continuing importance of marriage but, rather, provide evidence for the peculiar value which is placed on marriage (and, consequently, on family life in general) in modern society. The great majority of individuals do not divorce because they are tired of marriage as an institution but because the particular partner of this particular marriage did not meet their expectations. Most of them are willing to try again. In other words, divorce is not caused by people having low expectations of marriage but, on the contrary, by their having very high expectations indeed. The values of the conjugal nuclear family, detached as they are from most other material interests—at least in principle—greatly encourage the notion that if a particular marriage does not live up to its expectations, everyone concerned has the right to dissolve it and try again.

It is safe to say that the burden of these changes has fallen more heavily on women than on men. Girls are under strong social pressure (from their parents, especially their mothers, as well as from peers) to marry at an early age. Such early marriages are commonly entered into with little awareness of the realities of family life on the part of *either* partner (who are *both* very young). The arrival of the first child is often a rather rough initiation into these realities—for obvious reasons rougher on the wife than the husband. The burden of reconciling the domestic imprisonment imposed by childcare with aspirations of personal and occupational independence falls very one-sidedly on the women in this situation. A later crisis, however, is endemic to the same basic demographic trends. Not only do women marry young, and marry equally young men, but they have their children at an early age. The average middle-class American woman gives birth to her *last* child before she is thirty. Assuming that the earlier crises are successfully overcome by the marriage partners, the children will be a center of concern for both parents for several years—but not equally so. It is the woman, *not* the man, who is likely to say, "My family is my career." Yet these children, like their parents, are under social pressure to leave the parental household as early as possible—first to school, then into marriages of their own. At that point, what happens to the woman who made the above statement? Her "career," of course, is shattered—usually when she is in her forties, with decades of her life still ahead of her. Conversely, the husband finds himself in a newly empty house, with a frustrated and (not without reason) resentful wife, and the temptation is strong to search for greener, and younger, pastures elsewhere.

FAMILIES WITH DIFFERENT INCOMES: *THE URBAN VILLAGERS* AND *CRESTWOOD HEIGHTS*

But while it is correct to see the conjugal nuclear family as the prevailing type in Western societies (and increasingly victorious in other societies as well), it would be a mistake to see this as a uniform and undifferentiated phenomenon. On the contrary, even within American society itself there are broad differences in family structure and family life, particularly as between different classes of the population. We will, a little later, discuss at some length the phenomena of class in modern society (or, as sociologists often speak of this, the phenomena of stratification). We do not at this point have to go into the details of this, and for our purposes it would be quite sufficient if the reader thinks of class at this point simply in terms of income—that is, as one goes up in the class system, one moves from lower-income to upper-income strata. In terms of family life, it is interesting to compare what have, in effect, become two classical studies of social life in North America: the study by Herbert Gans, *The Urban Villagers* (a study of white, working-class people in the West End of Boston), and the study by John Seeley and his collaborators, *Crestwood Heights* (a study of an upper-middle-class suburban community in Toronto). Both Gans and Seeley were primarily interested in family life, and a comparison of their findings is very fruitful for an understanding of the family in contemporary society.[5]

[5] Herbert Gans, *The Urban Villagers* (New York, Free Press, 1962); J. R. Seeley, R. A. Sim and E. W. Loosley, *Crestwood Heights* (New York, Basic Books, 1956). It should be pointed out, though, that Gans studied a heavily Jewish group. It is possible that this ethnic difference, along with class, is a factor in the findings.

ADULT-CENTERED AND CHILD-CENTERED FAMILIES The working-class family, as described by Gans, is an adult-centered family. Needless to say, this in no way means that working-class people love their children less than upper-middle-class parents. It rather means that they have different ideas about the rights of adults and children within the family. In the West End family, the child is expected to develop from being a baby to becoming an adult without overly great participation of the parents in the process. The little girl is expected, quite early, to help her mother in the raising of smaller children. She becomes a kind of little mother. Or, as she helps in the performance of household chores, she becomes a kind of little housewife. The little boy, on the other hand, is quite early given the same freedom that his father has to come and go as he pleases. He is expected to live his childhood increasingly without the supervision of his parents. Thus the children quite early create for themselves a world that is separate from that of their parents and in which the latter take very little part. As Gans puts it:

> Parent-child relationships are segregated almost as much as male-female ones. The child will report on his peer-group activities at home, but they are of relatively little interest to parents in an adult-centered family. If the child performs well at school, parents will praise him for it, but they are unlikely to attend his performance in a school program or a baseball game in person. *This is his life, not theirs.*[6]

Quite logically, as Gans observed, many children in this setting behave very differently at home from the way they behave on the street with their peers. The same child very often is very energetic and even boisterous on the street and becomes quite passive or even sullen at home. Quite clearly, the place where such a child primarily expresses himself is on the street and not within the family.

Childhood in Crestwood Heights is an altogether different story.

[6] Gans, *op. cit.*, p. 57. Italics ours.

Children dominate the home. Children are encouraged to express themselves as much as possible within the family, and the adults make every effort to pay close and continuous attention to what the children are doing. Great efforts will be made to entertain and educate the child. Normally, he will be encouraged to bring his friends home. Mothers will organize parties for their children, or take them out for special events in the community. Unlike the children studied by Gans, Seeley's upper-middle-class kids are not expected to do any work around the home. Of course usually there are fewer children around anyway, so that the problem of taking care of younger brothers and sisters is much smaller in scope. Interestingly enough, when children in Crestwood Heights are asked to do this or that chore on behalf of the household, the parents regard it as perfectly normal that they should pay their children a special allowance for such work.

HUSBANDS AND WIVES: THE DIVISION OF LABOR

While in most human societies there is a division of labor between the sexes, this division is very sharp in the working-class family. The wife is supposed to be in charge of the home and of the children, insofar as their activities are supervised at all. The husband is expected to be the breadwinner, and definitely not expected to participate in any way in the running of the household or the day-to-day rearing of children. Very often the mother administers discipline problems herself, although in particularly serious cases the father may be called upon to come in when he returns home from work. By contrast, the typical Crestwood Heights family is supposed to be a place of intense exchange between all its members and, indeed, a refuge for them from the rest of the world. The family is a place where the father is supposed to relax in the company of his wife and children after a hard day of work, a place where children are encouraged to discuss their own problems, and where everyone shares as much as possible in the activities of the group. While it is still true, of course, that it is the wife who does most of the work around the home, it is regarded as normal that the husband will help her as far as he is able. While the wife is expected to "realize herself" as a woman (both as a wife and as a mother) within the family, the husband also looks upon the family in terms of self-realization.

This is quite different from the notions prevailing in the working-class family where the husband is expected to realize himself as a man primarily outside the circle of his home. But while the Crestwood Heights family emphasizes the common values and activities of all its members, at the same time very strong emphasis is placed upon their individual rights and aspirations. Both father and mother will have their own circles of friends, some of them not shared with the marriage partner. The children will, if at all possible, be given their own rooms, which will be considered their province, to be administered by them as they wish. It will be both their right and their responsibility to decorate and to keep these rooms clean. Individual eccentricities and aspirations are encouraged and respected unless they are too wildly deviant from the overall norms of the community (and sometimes even then). The children, at an early age, are given a monetary allowance in order to learn how to administer money responsibly. Independence in all things is encouraged.

DISCIPLINING THE CHILD: TWO APPROACHES

The difference between these two types of family becomes very clear in the matter of authority and discipline. The way of disciplining children in the West End is primarily by means of punishment and reward. The assumption is that children need continuous discipline if they are not to run wild. There is both physical and verbal punishment. Especially the mothers slap their children quite frequently, tell them what to do and not to do, and often enough present them with the ultimate threat, which is that the father will be told when he comes home. All of this is not supposed to, and in fact does not, interfere with the affection that exists between parents and children. Punishment is not rejection. At the same time, there is very little general theory as to how children should be raised or for what purpose. Methods of child-rearing, both as far as discipline is concerned and in other matters, are based on short-term traditions or simply developed spontaneously by the parents. Except for certain broad moral expectations, there are no very clear goals for which the children are disciplined.

The situation is very different in Crestwood Heights. In this class there is a strong prejudice against "punitive" or "authoritarian" methods in dealing with children. The family is supposed to be "democratic." As a result of this, there is considerable uncertainty as to how children should be treated. Mothers worry simultaneously over "over-domination" and "over-indulgence." Not only are individuals uncertain about this, but they quarrel with each other —this, of course, is particularly the case between parents. It is generally agreed that children require a consistent pattern, but no one really knows what this is supposed to be. Quite naturally, therefore, parents in this type of upper-middle-class family frequently turn to experts for advice. These experts may be people such as psychiatrists, educational experts, counselors and the like, or they may be books or other media of communication. Generally speaking, parents avoid direct confrontations in which it would be necessary to take positions of authority. The overall ideal is that the parents should be the "friends" of their children. It is not difficult to see that on such occasions when the parents do want to establish their adult authority, this effort does not look very credible to the children. There continues to be physical punishment, but parents feel guilty about it and try to hide it. Generally, more subtle, psychological pressures are involved. In other words, the child is not forced, but coaxed, into cooperation. Precisely because the means of discipline are psychological rather than physical, the threat of rejection in this type of family is much greater. In other words, the upper-middle-class child has more reason to fear that his parents are threatening to withdraw love from him than is the case with the working-class child whose parents physically beat him. As Seeley and his co-workers rather unpleasantly put it: "Both father and mother apply steady and sometimes relentless pressure. The most striking feature of this kind of control lies in the ability of the parents to use a minimum of violence and to economize psychological pressure in securing obedience." [7]

OTHER TYPES OF FAMILIES

In the preceding we have compared the family types that are found in upper-middle-class and working-class milieus in modern American society. These are by no means the only types to be found. There is a distinct family structure in the upper class. One of its characteristics is a strong emphasis on extended kinship so that, in a way, it represents a counterpoint to the conjugal nuclear family within Western society.[8] A quite different family type, again, exists in the groups below the working class as described by Gans. These are the groups who comprise what Oscar Lewis has aptly named "the culture of poverty." As Lewis has demonstrated, this culture has amazing similarities whether it is looked at in North America, in Latin America or even in other parts of the Western world. This is what Lewis says about it:

> Some of the social and psychological characteristics include living in crowded quarters, a lack of privacy, gregariousness, a high incidence of alcoholism, frequent resorts to violence in the settlement of quarrels, frequent use of physical violence in the training of children, wife beating, early initiation into sex, free union or consensual marriages, a relatively high incidence in the abandonment of mothers and children, a trend toward mother-centered families and a much greater knowledge of maternal relatives, the predominance of the nuclear family, a strong predisposition to authoritarianism, and a great emphasis on family solidarity—an ideal only rarely achieved.[9]

While Lewis speaks with great sympathy about this type of family (which he has studied in great detail in Puerto Rico and in Mexico), one still gets the impression from the above description that he is thinking of it in primarily negative terms, the negative evaluation

[7] Seeley, *op. cit.*, p. 176.

[8] See E. Digby Baltzell, *Philadelphia Gentlemen* (New York, Free Press, 1958).

[9] Oscar Lewis, *The Children of Sanchez* (New York, Random House, 1961), p. 26.

no doubt coming from a comparison with North American middle-class norms. In recent years, especially as a result of the reassertion of black culture by black intellectuals in the United States, the negative evaluation of some of the characteristics of this type of family has been seriously questioned. A good many of Lewis's above characteristics do apply to the black family in the United States. Sociologists and other commentators, white or black, have habitually decried these characteristics and emphasized, in a negative way, the instability and ineffectiveness of the black family. This may well have been a distortive point of view. If one speaks of an institution as "ineffective," one must always ask, "Ineffective for what?" Very probably this type of family is not effective in terms of promoting the individual's movement into the middle class. It may be very effective, however, in promoting the norms that exist within his own community, and quite possibly also in providing emotional satisfactions to the individuals in it. To mention but one aspect of this in terms of the black family: it is far from clear that the frequent absence or transitory character of father figures in this type of family has produced the nefarious psychological results that have often been attributed to this.[10]

CRISIS AND NEW COMMUNITIES: CLANS AND COMMUNES

The modern family is today in a state of crisis. Increasingly, its virtues as well as its practicability are being questioned within Western society—most strongly, as one would suspect, among the young. The paradox of this crisis is that at the same time as the institution is being vigorously questioned in its societies of origin (and in some instances proclaimed there to be obsolete), the same institution is

[10] See Franklin Frazier, *The Negro Family in the United States* (Chicago, University of Chicago Press, 1939). The recent works of Jesse Bernard are useful in balancing Frazier's materials. A violent, and instructive, debate over the meaning of changes in the black family erupted in the wake of the so-called "Moynihan Report." For the latter's text and a good overview of the debate, see Lee Rainwater and William Yancey (eds.), *The Moynihan Report and the Politics of Controversy* (Cambridge, Mass., M. I. T. Press, 1967).

continuing its more or less triumphant invasion of societies outside the West in which it previously did not exist. The family, incidentally, is not the only institution to which this is happening in our contemporary situation. Be this as it may, the crisis has affected almost every aspect of both the value set and the social form of the family.

While the family, and especially the marriage arrangement within it, continues to be looked upon as a place of personal fulfillment, there is increasing frustration with its capacity to meet this expectation. The modern family unit seems to many to be too small and too fragile to accomplish such a purpose. As a result, there have been many experiments in recent years which have tried to enlarge and to change the character of this basic unit of private life. A more extreme form of this has been the commune movement which has rapidly developed in America (to some extent also in Western Europe). Here the attempt is made to break through the alleged egotism of the conjugal nuclear family in the West and to provide something like a new version of the traditional clan or extended-kinship unit. A number of adults will live together and jointly operate a household; all of them will regard themselves as being married to each other; and the children either emerging from this group or having initially been brought into it are regarded as being the children of all of them. The economic arrangements are typically communitarian, and there is a general aversion to the very idea of private property. In more moderate forms of the same phenomenon, numbers of married couples have settled together or near each other in order to promote economic cooperation, joint ventures in child rearing and general social contacts. Here the attempt is made to combine the virtues of the old extended family with the individualism and privacy of the later nuclear family.

Many of these experiments are very recent, and not much has yet been done to study them systematically. One predecessor of the contemporary commune movement, however, has been studied in some detail. This is the kibbutz movement in modern Israel.[11] The kibbutz is a communal agricultural settlement. It goes back to the

[11] See Bruno Bettelheim, *The Children of the Dream* (Toronto, Collier-Macmillan, 1969).

early days of Jewish settlement in Palestine, and represents the attempt by a highly idealistic and socialist group to experiment with a new and more perfect form of society. There are now quite a number of different types of kibbutz in various parts of Israel, but there still exists the socialist type that tries to realize the old communal ideals of the founding generation. No attempt was made here to abolish marriage as such, but strong emphasis was placed on the collective rearing of all children. This has meant in practice that while husband and wife lived together in separate housing units, their children did not live with them but were housed in a "children's house" with all other children of the kibbutz. It is very difficult to say whether the kibbutz has lived up to the expectations with which it was founded. Undoubtedly, it was strongly affected by the fact that it was only an enclave or, rather, a set of enclaves within the larger society; the Jewish community in Palestine and later the independent state of Israel never became socialist societies as a whole. The domestic arrangements of the kibbutz, therefore, remained a minority phenomenon. It is fairly clear, though, that the child-rearing practices of the kibbutz have had an effect on its products. Very broadly speaking, kibbutz children when they grow up seem to be both less neurotic and less individualistic than children raised in conventional families. Whether one will welcome or deplore this change will evidently depend on how one values different things in the development of personality.

READINGS

The following four studies of contemporary family life have been briefly discussed in the text. Any one may be used to help the reader get a more detailed impression of what is involved in the sociology of the family (the books are also available in paperback).

Bettelheim, Bruno, *The Children of the Dream* (Toronto, Collier-Macmillan, 1969).

Gans, Herbert, *The Urban Villagers* (New York, Free Press, 1962).

Lewis, Oscar, *The Children of Sanchez* (New York, Random House, 1961).

Seeley, J. R., R. A. Sim and E. W. Loosley, *Crestwood Heights* (New York, Basic Books, 1956).

Chapter **6**

THE
COMMUNITY

WE GROW UP in landscapes. Although there is not much evidence for this, it is quite likely that the physical, natural landscape of our childhood greatly influences our future life. Thus it seems quite plausible that a person whose childhood was spent alongside the sea would develop differently in some fashion from someone who spent the same years atop high mountains. Perhaps poets know more about this than sociologists. There can be no question, however, but that the *human* landscape in which the individual grows up decisively determines his character and a good part of his further career in life. When sociologists speak about the community, one may usually substitute the term human landscape to make what they are saying more graphic.

EXPLORING: WHAT KIND OF COMMUNITY IS OUT THERE?

By and large, the term "community" is not used in a particularly technical sense. It simply means the immediate social context of the individual's life. Or, if one wants to put it this way, the context of which the outermost limits are what may be *personally* experienced or encountered by the individual in his everyday life. In this sense, the community is the natural area into which the child moves as he leaves the immediate circle of his family. As soon as the child leaves his family, he encounters the specific structures of the community in which he lives. Needless to say, there are vast variations in these structures—say, between a child growing up on a farm and a child growing up in an urban neighborhood. In each case, however, the child learns to move about in structures that greatly transcend the context of his own home. Learning to do this the child learns to participate in a larger society.

RURAL AND URBAN COMMUNITIES: SIZE, DENSITY AND COMPOSITION OF THE POPULATION

There is one fundamental difference between communities that has fascinated sociologists, especially in America. This is the difference between rural and urban communities. At the time when sociology began to develop in America, this was still a country in which most of the population lived in the countryside and in small, basically rural towns; but it was rapidly changing. Thus the contrast between rural and urban life was at the same time a contrast between the old and the new. Whether this contrast was experienced with a feeling of nostalgia or with eager anticipation of the urban future, it deeply impressed itself on the minds of all observers. The city was one of the first subjects, and in some ways continues, to fascinate American sociologists.

As we have remarked in a previous chapter, urban sociology in America flourished particularly in Chicago during the 1920's and 1930's. Quite apart from the influence of intellectual history, the locale is not incidental. Chicago was the most tumultuous, the most rapidly growing and, in some ways, perhaps the most American metropolis in the country. Its growth was phenomenal. In 1860 its population was slightly over 100,000. By 1900 it had grown to a little over 1.5 million. In 1930 its population was over 3.3 million. During the decade that urban sociology developed there first (that is, during the 1920's), to have lived in Chicago must have been like living at the center of an enormous explosion. One can well understand the excitement and fascination that this particular city engendered in the sociologists of the Chicago School.[1]

Urban and rural sociology developed hand in hand in America.[2]

[1] For an authoritative statement of the approach of the Chicago urban sociologists, see Robert Park, Ernest Burgess and Roderick McKenzie, *The City* (Chicago, University of Chicago Press, 1925). A good discussion may be found in Maurice Stein, *The Eclipse of Community* (Princeton, N.J., Princeton University Press, 1960), pp. 13ff.

[2] For an overview of rural sociology, see Charles Loomis and Allan Beegle, *Rural Social Systems* (London, Bailey & Swinfen, 1955).

But it was in urban sociology that most of the exciting ideas were developed, that new methods were constantly being tried, that—in a word—the action was to be found. In some ways it might be said that rural sociology mainly developed as a foil to urban sociology; that is, the rural community was very largely analyzed to bring out the peculiarity of the urban one, rather than the other way round. (Incidentally, rural sociologists have suffered from a sort of status discrimination within the profession as a result of all this—a thoroughly unjust situation, which may perhaps be rectified now when many people in America have become disillusioned with the mystique of urbanism.)

At the beginning there is a problem of definition. What do the words "urban" and "rural" signify? Of course it is possible to evoke very clear imagery to refer to these two terms, and everybody has some sort of an idea of what is meant by it. But the question of definition becomes clear when we ask where the one type begins and the other ends. The census, of course, makes arbitrary mathematical distinctions. Clearly that does not make much sense for the sociologist, who is not interested in drawing an arbitrary dividing line between these two types of community but, rather, who must ask what their fundamental characteristics are. This, indeed, was the primary interest of the Chicago urban sociologists. One of their most prominent representatives, Louis Wirth, defined the city as being determined by three fundamental characteristics: large size, high density and heterogeneity of population.[3] The three characteristics *together* define what the city is—each one could exist alone without producing an urban form of community. Cities are places in which a large number of people live together (Wirth, not being employed by the census, was not interested in drawing precise limits to size); also, cities are places where people live together very closely; finally, cities are places where very different kinds of people live together and engage in very different kinds of activities.

[3] Louis Wirth's major work is *The Ghetto* (Chicago, University of Chicago Press, 1928). For a good anthology, see Albert Reiss (ed.), *Louis Wirth on Cities and Social Life* (Chicago, University of Chicago Press, 1964).

CONSEQUENCES OF LIVING IN THE CITY

There are some general sociological consequences to these three characteristics. Because of the size and diversity of the city, and despite the density of its settlement, it is difficult to maintain in the city the kind of direct and all-embracing solidarity that is characteristic of rural communities. Put differently: the city is not a social context in which traditional ways of thinking and acting have a good chance of maintaining themselves. As traditional solidarity and traditional controls weaken in the city, more formal associations between people and more formal controls take their place. Organizations and associations of every kind multiply in the city. Some of them are designed to draw different groups closer to each other, others are designed to facilitate contact and cooperation between groups.

Life in the city is largely a life with and among strangers. As a result, relationships between people become, in the main, quite superficial and very functional (that is, limited to highly specific and circumscribed functions). At the same time that there is an increase in strangeness in the city, there is also an increase in closeness—that, of course, is the result of the high density of settlement. Inevitably, this is the cause of much anxiety and tension. It is this area of urban life which the Chicago sociologists (not very happily) termed "social disorganization." By and large what they meant by this was all the expressions of conflict that the city brought about, both conflict within individuals and conflict between individuals. It was under this rubric that they studied crime, juvenile delinquency, mental illness, suicide and a variety of other phenomena which, at least from the point of view of law and order, could be called "social problems."

But it was the element of heterogeneity—that is, the tremendous diversity of people and social milieus in the city—that largely fascinated the Chicago sociologists. It was the paradox of incredibly discrepant worlds existing side by side with each other in the city, sometimes completely isolated from each other all the same. Most of the sociologists engaged in these studies came themselves from small-town backgrounds, the kind of background that today one would refer to as "middle-American." Chicago attracted and repelled them at the same time. In either case, the overwhelming contrast with the world of their own childhood and early youth proved to be very fertile for their sociological imagination. There is another interesting aspect to this. Chicago hit the sociologists very much as it hit the rest of America, or, more precisely, as *the city* hit the rest of America. Their own wide-eyed fascination with the city thus represented a much wider cultural attitude. No wonder that their studies became very influential.

THE CHICAGO SCHOOL: "PARTICIPANT OBSERVATION"

This point can be made by reference to a classic study of the Chicago School, Harvey Zorbaugh's *The Gold Coast and the Slum,* which was first published in 1929.[4] Zorbaugh carefully studied a rather small section of the North Side of Chicago. He showed in great detail how entirely different social worlds coexisted side by side in this small territory. Within a few blocks of each other Zorbaugh found a slum, an upper-class residential area, an area of rooming houses, a Greenwich Village type of bohemian settlement and, finally, a skid row inhabited by hoboes and other derelicts of society. Each one of these worlds is described in what one cannot but call loving detail. Zorbaugh's work is also a classical illustration of the method of so-called "participant observation" for which the Chicago School has become famous—that is, a method of research in which the researcher participates as much as possible in what he is observing.

Perhaps the most impressive account in this book is Zorbaugh's description of the sad and harassed world of the rooming-house inhabitant. This chapter is, as it were, the climax of the vision of urban life by the Chicago sociologists. It is a vision of individual

4 Harvey Zorbaugh, *The Gold Coast and the Slum* (Chicago, University of Chicago Press, 1929).

isolation, loneliness and, at the same time, freedom. However, Zor-baugh did not make the mistake of thinking that this atomism of individuals in the urban situation meant an absence of institutions. On the contrary, the inhabitants of the world of rooming houses re-lated to a large number of institutions, including those institutions which particularly catered to their peculiar needs—such as the taxi dance hall and the all-night restaurant (both of which, incidentally, were studied in great detail by other Chicago sociologists). The point about city life is not that it is bereft of institutions; indeed, it has a much more intense and complex network of institutions than the rural community. The point is the manner in which people re-late to these institutions. Again, these relations are very largely in a mode of strangeness or estrangement.

COMMUNITY STUDIES: THE URBANIZATION OF "MIDDLETOWN"

A counterpoint to these delvings of the sociological mind into the labyrinthine depths of the city has been a number of studies of smaller communities. The unques-tioned classic in this series of Amer-ican community studies is the work by Robert and Helen Lynd on the community which they called "Middletown," and which, in fact, was Muncie, Indiana.[5] The Lynds studied Middletown twice: once before and once after the coming of the Great Depression. These two studies were published in 1929 (*Middletown*) and in 1937 (*Middletown in Transition*). Again using the method of participant observation, the Lynds moved into Middletown like two ethnolo-gists moving into the inner recesses of a native village. They tried to observe everything, describe everything, taking everything down without letting their own value judgments intrude. The result is what is probably one of the most comprehensive pictures of an American community ever drawn.

For their description, the Lynds used the guidelines developed by

[5] Robert and Helen Lynd, *Middletown* (New York, Harcourt Brace, 1929), and *Middletown in Transition* (New York, Harcourt Brace, 1937).

a cultural anthropologist, W. H. R. Rivers. These were: getting a living, making a home, training the young, using leisure, engaging in religious practices and engaging in community activities. The Lynds assumed that these various areas of community life would be related to each other. They further assumed that the first area—that of getting a living—would be the decisive one. And, accordingly, they paid special attention to the effects of industry and business upon community life. They were interested not only in what Middletown was like at that particular moment of their investigation but in its history as well. And this historical perspective made clear that the fundamental thing that had happened to the community had been the introduction of modern factories. Middletown thus represents small-town America under the impact of industrialization.

The most steady and pervasive change was the one that made it increasingly impossible for people in Middletown to understand their lives primarily in terms of that community. Increasingly, forces and people from the outside shaped their lives. This change is particularly noticeable between the two studies of the Lynds, that is, as having taken place during the time of the Great Depression and the early New Deal. But as people in communities such as Middletown are drawn into a wider interplay of social forces in the society, the nature of the community and its social ties changes. Indeed, keeping in mind the previous description of Wirth's characterization of urban life, it could be said that even if the size and density of a community such as Middletown would remain the same, these outside forces would, in effect, *urbanize* its style of life. As local traditions and local loyalties wane, people turn to larger organizations and identifications for material as well as psychic security. Labor unions are a case in point.

THE AMERICAN IDEOLOGY OF THE SMALL TOWN

The vision of the small community has had a very deep hold on the American mind. There has been a great reluctance to give up not only the values of the small community but even its self-image in times of great change. People in such communities have continued to maintain their sense of independence, even if the facts of the situation have made it very clear that such independence no longer exists. Similarly, people in such communities have consistently refused to face the facts of class and class conflict and of deep tensions within the community. Tenaciously they have clung to a vision of themselves in terms of an earlier and supposedly happier America. This ideology of the small town has been effectively documented in a recent community study, this one of a small town in the northern part of New York State, by Arthur Vidich and Joseph Bensman, *Small Town in Mass Society*.[6] The study showed how the people in this town, which in its basic structures was determined by forces of the larger society, kept holding on (against the evidence of the facts) to the view that the town was essentially what it had always been.

SEEKING A NICE PLACE TO RAISE CHILDREN: THE MOVEMENT TO SUBURBIA

However, in recent decades, it has been above all in suburban community that a serious attempt has been made to revive the vision of the small-town community.[7] The great expansion of suburbs in America following World War II was only in part a negative phenomenon in the sense that it was a flight *from* the city and its problems. Its positive side is really more interesting, namely, its aspect as a move-

[6] Arthur Vidich and Joseph Bensman, *Small Town in Mass Society* (Princeton, N.J., Princeton University Press, 1958).

[7] William Dobriner (ed.), *The Suburban Community* (New York, Putnam's, 1958)—a good overview.

ment *to* a certain vision of the good life. That vision can rather accurately be described as a refurbishing of an earlier American small-town ideology. Physically, it has been a vision of small, one-family houses, of trees and grass, of quiet streets and good air. Socially, it has been a vision of life lived with neighbors whom one knows and with whom one shares certain basic values—all in an atmosphere of friendliness and cooperation. Indeed, the new suburban way of life has been closely related in its motivations to the new family ethos that we described in the previous chapter. In a very large number of cases, the move to the suburbs was motivated by concern for children more than for adults; it was the children, above all, who were supposed to enjoy the trees, the quiet streets and the good air, and it was for the sake of the same children that a "desirable" social environment was sought.

In recent political controversies the charge has often been made that the basic motive involved in all of this has been "racism," that is, the desire to get away from black and other minority groups within the city. Undoubtedly this has been a motive among many, but it would be a grave distortion of the situation if this were regarded as the *principal* motive. The migration to the suburbs has indeed been a flight, but not primarily a flight from other races; rather it has been a flight from the tensions, the conflict and the anonymity of urban life. And it has (at least in part) been motivated by what is generally regarded as a most praiseworthy motive indeed, namely, concern for one's own children.

THE SUBURBAN SEARCH FOR BELONGING: "THE NEW PEASANTRY"

There exists a fairly large number of studies by now that have delineated this new suburban type of community. *Crestwood Heights* has already been mentioned, a book which has attained the rank of a classic of this genre. Another work, not usually regarded as being primarily a community study, is William Whyte's *The Organization Man,* published in 1957.[8] Whyte was above all interested in analyz-

[8] William Whyte, *The Organization Man* (Garden City, N.Y., Doubleday-Anchor, 1957).

ing (and also criticizing) the social world of the rising executive in large corporations. However, in the process of doing this, he also went to great lengths to describe the physical habitat of this social group. He did this by analyzing a suburban community near Chicago, which he called Park Forest, and that part of his study is a model analysis of its kind.

Whyte's study, as others of its type, has shown, among other things, how deceptive the suburban vision turns out to be for most of its followers. To be sure, the physical expectations are generally met—although even they may be soured after a while by the tax cost attached to all of this and by various urban problems (such as air pollution, traffic congestion, crime and overcrowded schools) which have had a way of late of moving into the suburbs. But it is the social aspect of the vision which is most apt to be frustrated. The search for belonging and social roots is frustrated, if by nothing else, by the very great transience of suburban populations. In Park Forest, for example, about 35 percent of the population changed every year. The new suburbanites—most of them middle class or upper middle class in status—are highly mobile, both socially and geographically. Under such circumstances, the manifestations of small-town solidarity are apt to be quite artificial.

The serenity of social life that is sought in the vision is marred by the constant intrusion of occupational and status anxieties into the suburban context. And the flight from the anonymity of the city may be frustrating in precisely the degree to which it is achieved. Suburbanites find themselves surrounded by neighbors who are most curious about every aspect of their personal life; and, what is worse, many of those neighbors are also relevant in terms of business and occupational relations. Thus suburban community, while it may indeed be a deliverance from urban anonymity, often enough turns out to be an entrapment in the social tyranny of a strange new kind of peasant society. The major consequence of this is a cloying conformity which has made the suburban vision turn sour for many, and especially for the young. A main escape from this conformism has been the automobile, and the suburban community has developed, above all, as a culture of the automobile. Family life tends to revolve around the car or cars which the family possesses. This has imposed a new, and often bizarre, structure on the carrying-on of everyday activities. The individual most affected by this has undoubtedly been the housewife-mother, who finds herself spending a good part of the day chauffeuring her children around from one activity to another.

URBANIZATION AND SUBURBANIZATION

The general process of transformation from a predominantly rural to a predominantly urban society is called *urbanization*. The fundamental causes of this process are two—industrialization and population growth. An industrial economy both requires and makes possible the concentration of large populations. A vast labor force is assembled in strategic locations. The so-called "infrastructure" of an industrial economy—its highly organized networks of transportation, communications and administrative agencies—allows these human agglomerations to exist. The demographic revolution (which is closely linked to the nutrition and medical care made possible by modern technological know-how) has meant a steady increase in the sheer size of this population. The urban centers became the places of opportunity, and thus a magnet attracting masses of migrants from the still "backward" areas. It is today not only an American but a worldwide phenomenon.[9] As far as America is concerned, however, it is important to keep the suburban phenomenon in mind in this connection. By census criteria it is quite true that there has been a constant shift of population from rural to urban areas. At the same time, however, there has been a shift from urban areas of great concentration of population to urbanized or suburban areas of smaller concentration. The census statistics bring this out very clearly.

The population living in rural areas has decreased from 54.3 percent in 1910 to 30.1 percent in 1960, while conversely, the population living in urban areas has increased from 45.7 percent to

[9] See Gerald Breese, *Urbanization in Newly Developing Countries* (Englewood Cliffs, N.J., Prentice-Hall, 1966) and Kingsley Davis and Hilda Hertz, *The Pattern of World Urbanization* (Englewood Cliffs, N.J., Prentice-Hall, 1954).

69.9 percent in the same period. But in the period from 1910 to 1930, the population living in urban areas of one million inhabitants or more increased from 9.2 percent to 12.3 percent. Between 1930 and 1960, however, the same proportion decreased once more to 9.8 percent. In 1960, 18.9 percent of the urban population in the United States lived in areas populated by 200,000 to one million inhabitants as compared to 12.9 percent in 1910, while 25.8 percent of the population lived in urban concentrations of 25,000 to 100,000 people as compared to 14.9 percent in 1910. Similarly, 19.5 percent of the American population in 1960 lived in urban areas comprising between 5,000 and 25,000 people, while the same proportion in 1910 was 14.7 percent. At least as far as the United States is concerned, it is thus important to keep in mind that urbanization does not mean that places like the inner cities of Chicago or New York are getting bigger and bigger. On the contrary, the latest census figures indicate that the population of such urban centers has a tendency now either to remain stationary or even to decline slightly. It is the suburban-exurban or semi-rural areas in process of urbanization that are seeing the greatest increase in population.

It would be a mistake, however, to see the process of urbanization as primarily a geographical or demographic one. It is, above all, the spread of a culture, of a way of life, with quite peculiar attitudes and habits. It is this urban way of life that has triumphantly swept across the country in recent decades, to the point where very few, if any, areas are left in which an unambiguously rural or small-town society is still surviving. Probably one of the most important factors in this has been the spread of the mass media of communications, especially of television. It is urban images, urban attitudes, urban values that are carried by these media. Rural and small-town culture in America has simply not had the resources to resist this onslaught of urbanity. Interestingly enough, it is within the city itself—within its urban culture—that the resistance has now emerged, especially among young people. The city is seen now more as threat than as promise. Not only is there a widening sensitivity to its physical discomforts (pollution, crowding and the like) but suspicion of its "sophisticated" culture. There is much nostalgia for simpler, allegedly "healthier" ways of life, such as is associated with smaller communities. The ecology movement has brought all this into sharp focus.

The fundamental characteristics of this urban ethos have already been analyzed by the classic sociologists, notably by Georg Simmel and Max Weber.[10] Simmel was particularly interested in bringing out what he called the "mental life" of the city. He emphasized that urban life produces a peculiar kind of consciousness, brought about inevitably by the conditions under which people live. This consciousness is marked by a strong intellectual bent, a matter-of-fact rationality, anonymity and "sophistication." Weber was particularly interested in the innovative role of the city in human history. The city, with its large concentration of heterogeneous people, has always been the place where traditions have weakened and where new forms of social life have emerged. Already in antiquity, cities were the places where things happened, where the "action" was to be found. This is still true today.

Many of the characteristics of the modern world—including, most importantly, its rapid rate of change—are directly related to the importance of cities in it and to the overall process of urbanization. For better or for worse, our social landscape today is primarily and increasingly an urban landscape. Very few children today, as they move beyond the circle of their immediate families, move into the world of non-urban structures. Rather, they move from one sector to another of the gigantic city which is modern society.

[10] See Simmel's essay on the metropolis in Kurt Wolff (ed.), *The Sociology of Georg Simmel* (New York, Free Press, 1950). Also, see Max Weber, *The City* (New York, Free Press, 1958). For overall historical studies of the city, see Gideon Sjoberg, *The Preindustrial City* (New York, Free Press, 1960) and Lewis Mumford, *The City in History* (New York, Harcourt Brace, 1961).

READINGS

The reader may read one of the following American community studies; asterisk indicates paperback edition:

David, Allison, Burleigh Gardner and May Gardner, *Deep South* (Chicago, University of Chicago Press, 1941).

* Lynd, Robert and Helen, *Middletown* (New York, Harcourt Brace, 1929).

* ————, *Middletown in Transition* (New York, Harcourt Brace, 1937).

* Seeley, John, R. A. Sim and E. W. Loosley, *Crestwood Heights* (New York, Basic Books, 1956).

* Vidich, Arthur, and Joseph Bensman, *Small Town in Mass Society* (Princeton, N.J., Princeton University Press, 1958).

Warner, Lloyd, and Paul Lunt, *The Social Life of a Modern Community* (New Haven, Conn., Yale University Press, 1941).

West, James, *Plainville, U.S.A.* (New York, Columbia University Press, 1945).

* Whyte, William Foote, *Street Corner Society* (Chicago, University of Chicago Press, 1955).

* Whyte, William H., *The Organization Man* (Garden City, N.Y., Doubleday-Anchor, 1957).

* Wirth, Louis, *The Ghetto* (Chicago, University of Chicago Press, 1928).

Zorbaugh, Harvey, *The Gold Coast and the Slum* (Chicago, University of Chicago Press, 1929).

Chapter 7

THE
STRATIFIED
COMMUNITY

MEETING DIFFERENT TYPES OF PEOPLE: SOCIAL DIFFERENTIATION

To grow up in society is to learn more and more about how very different people are from each other. Little boys are different from little girls; all children have something in common against adults; there are old people and young people; there are Protestants and Catholics; there are people who speak with an accent; there are doctors, teachers, babysitters, mailmen, policemen and handymen. All these people are not just different as individuals, but they are different as social types. That is exactly the point: differences are made in society between people not only because of their individual characteristics but because of the larger groups to which they belong.

Broadly speaking, it is this experience which underlies what sociologists commonly call *social differentiation*. A very basic question for the sociological analysis of any society is the manner in which it is differentiated, that is, the social typology which is operative in that society for the classification of its members. Learning this typology is one of the basic tasks of socialization. However, hand in hand with the experience of social differentiation goes another experience. People are not only different from each other in terms of their assignment to a certain typology but they are *ranked* differently in accordance with these assignments. The doctor is not only different from the handyman but he is deemed to occupy a higher position in society. This, of course, is not so with all cases of social differentiation. The doctor is generally deemed to be on the same level as the lawyer. *Some* differences, then, have a kind of altimeter attached to them—as soon as we know which social type an individual belongs to, we are in a position to say how high up he is in the ranking scale of society. This phenomenon of ranking is what sociologists call *social stratification,* and the various ranks are called *strata.*

Little Johnny is the son of a doctor. Little Jimmy is the son of a handyman. Their meetings (say, in a public school or public playground) are occasions of mutual wonder and, quite possibly, terror. Not only is it very clear that little Johnny has more money invested

in him than little Jimmy, and not only does this particular difference have all sorts of obvious consequences—from the size of the
family residence to the quality of Johnny's dental care—but there
are many other differences not so readily translated into money
terms. Johnny has been taught a whole set of "good manners"
which, to Jimmy, just look plain sissy. Jimmy, on the other hand,
appears to Johnny as frighteningly prone to violence. In situations
of conflict in which Johnny has recourse to verbal argument,
Jimmy is ready to fight with his fists. But if Johnny is frightened by
Jimmy's physical aggressiveness, he is also fascinated by Jimmy's
independence. At an age when Jimmy is free to roam not only the
playground but the whole neighborhood, Johnny is still accompanied everywhere he goes by mother, mother's helper, babysitter or
other irritating adults. The language of the two boys differs, too.
Jimmy probably has a more colorful repertoire of obscenities, but
Johnny is much more free to use whatever obscenities he knows,
even at home. Music that Johnny has learned to appreciate as
beautiful is just dull noise to Jimmy—and quite possibly, vice
versa. Moral judgments differ as well. Thus little Jimmy may find it
perfectly natural for a black child to be chased from the playground, while Johnny may develop acute guilt feelings about this
act of persecution.

In all of this, for both boys there takes place a process by which
the essentials of stratification are learned. Needless to say, the full
implications of what is learned become clear only much later. This
learning process not only conveys information about the world but
provides measurements to place others on a ranking scale. Much
more basically, because of the fundamental dynamics of socialization that we have discussed earlier, the same learning process leads
to a definition of self. The child learns to identify *himself* within a
ranking scale. And normally, the social patterns, manners, tastes
and values that go with his particular rank become important in-
gredients of his identity. To be sure, he may later rebel against
these, but they will nevertheless have played a very important part
in the shaping of his biography in society.

THE SHARPNESS OF THE EXPERIENCE: GEOGRAPHIC DIFFERENCES

Such a learning process will take place regardless of the type of community a child happens to be born in. But clearly there are differences in the experience of stratification between types of community. Thus there would be considerable differences in the relationship between little Johnny and little Jimmy depending upon whether they are growing up in a large city, a small town or a suburb. Very probably, it is in the small town that the experiences of stratification are sharpest and most clearly perceived. In the large city, to be sure, there are many more different types of people and a much more complex order of stratification, but also different groups of people are more segregated from each other so that the movements of confrontation are fewer. The suburban situation is generally characterized by considerable homogeneity of strata. Thus, in many suburbs in which people like Johnny's parents live, it is quite possible that he would go right through childhood without ever meeting anyone like Jimmy in a situation of close contact.

CLASS, RACE AND ETHNICITY

The phenomena of stratification that we have just alluded to are those which are commonly called (not only by sociologists but in ordinary usage) phenomena of *class*. Just what this term may mean we will discuss presently; for the moment, suffice it to say that all the differences between Johnny and Jimmy that we have just talked about are those deriving from the different class positions of their respective families. In American society, however, the experience of stratification is further complicated by two other factors, namely, those of *race* and *ethnicity*. The latter is a term coined by American sociologists and peculiarly applicable to American society only. It refers to those cultural traits retained by immigrant groups to this country from their original home culture. If, for example, Johnny's parents are the grand-children of Yiddish-speaking Jewish immigrants from Eastern Europe, while Jimmy's father was born in Greece, there is likely to be a strong ethnic component to their mutual bewilderment that will be added to the experience of class differences. It is quite clear that if Jimmy's father should be black rather than of Greek origin, the sharpness of the experience of difference will be very much increased. Both race and ethnicity are intertwined with class in America, making for an extremely complex and often hard-to-analyze stratification system.

SOCIOLOGICAL EXCAVATION: WHAT CRITERIA?

As we shall see, sociologists differ considerably in the manner in which they understand and study stratification. What practically all sociologists agree upon, though, is the universality of the phenomenon. All known societies have *some* system of ranking their members in terms of higher and lower positions. The term stratification quite deliberately arouses geological imagery. It suggests a mountain in which one can locate different strata of rock and soil, one located on top of another. This is precisely the image which the sociological term wishes to suggest. There is an additional suggestion, which is that one has to break open the surface in order to discover the precise organization of strata. Mountains are very rarely cut open in such a way that one can, in one glance, discover what their geological stratification is. The same is true of societies. Any sociological inquiry into stratification, therefore, commonly requires a good deal of digging and of eliminating surface materials that hide from view what is really going on underneath. What is more, sociologists, like geologists, frequently do not have confidence in each other's excavation projects.

All human societies are stratified. But they differ greatly from each other in the *criteria* of stratification. Thus members of a society may be ranked in accordance with age, with physical prowess, with learning and so on. There are many human societies in which old age, even taken as a factor by itself, is a quality that bestows high rank upon the individual possessing it. Traditional China is a classic example. In many primitive societies, in which people live close to the subsistence line and must constantly struggle for survival both against nature and against other men, physical prowess is very frequently an index of rank. The same, curiously enough, is the case with many groups of children and young people in our own society. Thus it is quite possible that little Jimmy's high rank on the playground derives exclusively from his ability to beat up anyone in sight. Possessions have very commonly been an important element of rank, but learning has been the same in many societies. In some, learning has been more important than possessions. For example, in the traditional Jewish world of Eastern Europe (from which we assumed Johnny's family to derive), it was very common for a well-to-do merchant looking for a suitable husband for his daughter to give preference to a completely impoverished rabbinical student whose only claim to fame was his Talmudic erudition. Some of this, incidentally, may very well have rubbed off on our little Johnny, who might look upon the acquisition of a Ph.D. as something much more significant than the acquisition of an impressive portfolio of stocks.

CRITERIA FOR RANKING: OBJECTIVE, SUBJECTIVE OR MAJORITY VOTE

A conceptual problem suggests itself as soon as we talk about ranking. It can be expressed in the form of a one-word question—*whose?* Are we talking about the ranking being undertaken by an outside observer such as the sociologist? Are we talking about the rank that the individual being ranked gives to himself? Or are we talking about the ranking engaged in by others in the individual's situation? These three possibilities already suggest three quite distinct approaches to the study of stratification. First, stratification can be analyzed in terms of objective criteria set by the sociologist. Take the matter of possessions and learning. Even a cursory study of stratification in American society will reveal that both income and education are important factors by which people's rank is determined. Thus middle-class individuals have more income and more education than working-class individuals. The sociologist, based on whatever reasoning of his own, might now draw dividing lines between the middle class and the working class on the basis of these two factors. Thus anyone having more than x amount of income would be defined as middle class, while anyone having less than y amount of education would be assigned to the working class; more precisely, a scale would be worked out in which the factors of income and education taken together would decide where an individual is placed in terms of the class system. Needless to say, other criteria could be used in the construction of such a scale.

Second, stratification could be analyzed in terms of the subjective consciousness of the people in question. Most simply, individuals can be asked how they view themselves in terms of class. In America, incidentally, it has been found that when asked this question the great majority of people reply that they consider themselves to be middle class (which, taken at face value, would create utter havoc with the neat differentiating scheme concocted by our first sociologist above). And third, stratification can be studied in terms of the way in which people see each other. Thus, if one wants to locate a particular individual in terms of stratification, one can ask a variety of people where *they* would locate him, and then make his assignment on the basis of some kind of majority vote. The same method, obviously in a more complicated way, can be used to stratify an entire community.

Now, quite clearly there can, and will be, considerable discrepancies between the results achieved by these three methods. The sociologist using objective criteria may place individual A in the working class. Individual A, informed of this assignment through some mismanagement of research, will fly into a rage and denounce the research project as a Communist plot. A, of course, has always thought of himself as middle class. But there may be equal disagreement between his self-ranking and the way in which others (not counting the sociologist) rank him. Nor is there any assurance that a careful matching of all the others' rankings will, in the end, have much relationship to objective criteria worked out by the sociologist. One should not draw hasty conclusions from these discrepancies. It is, of course, possible that the sociologist is an armchair philosopher who thinks up criteria that have nothing to do with the social reality he is investigating. It is also quite possible, however, that people living in a particular situation are quite ignorant of the real forces that determine their lives. Indeed, it is quite possible that the very rage with which our individual *A* responds to his classification by the sociologist derives from his own lingering suspicion that he may be living in a great illusion as to his own position in the world. Put simply: sociologists can be very wrong about the reality of other people's lives, but people can also be quite wrong about the reality of their own lives. Being in a situation is no guarantee whatever that one understands it. (If this were not so, sociology would be a waste of time.)

WHICH CRITERIA ARE CAUSES AND WHICH ARE CONSEQUENCES?

A further conceptual problem that arises from the beginning is this: Which criteria are to be taken as basic causal factors for stratification, and which are only to be seen as consequences? In other words, what is it that basically determines stratification? Again, the relationship of income and education in our own society illustrates the point. Increasingly, it is clear that education is an extremely important factor in the position which an individual can hold or acquire in American society. Quite logically, therefore, a number of sociologists have given education and income equal weight in determining an individual's class position. A moment's reflection, however, will lead to the thought that, after all, education can be *bought*. An individual who greatly increases his income over a period of years can buy education as a purchasable commodity on the market, if not for himself then, most certainly, for his children. Thus other sociologists, with equally plausible logic, have argued that education is really only a consequence of income, and that it is income rather than education which is the basic factor determining the position of an individual in the American stratification scheme.

So far in this book we have tried to transmit a broad consensus existing among sociologists on the various topics that we have discussed. Unfortunately, we cannot do this in connection with the topic of stratification. There are far-reaching differences of approach between different sociologists and sociological schools in this area, and we cannot proceed without paying attention to these differences. The purpose of this book is a general introduction to sociology and not a propagation of our own position on controversial subjects in the field. Therefore, it cannot be our purpose here to distribute merit or demerit badges among the different approaches to the study of stratification. In other words, it cannot be our purpose to arbitrate these disputes. What we must do, however, is to indicate where the disagreements lie and (equally important) what difference it makes in terms of the understanding of the phenomenon if one decides on this or that approach.

KARL MARX: THE CONCEPT OF CLASS

The most influential approach to the study of stratification has been that of Marxism.[1] This is so not only in terms of direct influence but also in terms of having been the provocation for alternative approaches to the phenomenon. Conventionally, Karl Marx (1818–1883) has not been regarded as a sociologist (of course he himself did not call himself that), but his own work and that of the Marxist tradition that has emerged from it have been regarded as an alternative method for the study of social phenomena—which, in the course of its history, has had quite varied relationships with the tradition of sociology that is conventionally regarded as beginning with Auguste Comte (1789–1857). In our discussion of the history of the discipline, we have followed this convention. This, however, does not change the fact that it is Marx who brought about a fundamental transformation in the way in which scholars of various disciplines have looked upon human affairs, a transformation that has left a fundamental impact on every

---

[1] References to class are scattered throughout Marx's work. For the beginnings and the basic conceptions of the Marxian theory of class, see Karl Marx, *Early Writings* (New York, McGraw-Hill, 1964).

scientific discipline dealing with man. (A comparable influence was exerted later by Sigmund Freud, 1856–1939, and the various psychological approaches emanating from his works.) Nowhere is this more evident than in the area of stratification. It was Marx who made the concept of class a central one for the sciences of man. Everyone who followed him (be it historian, economist or social scientist) had to confront Marx's ideas about class. Indeed, the greater part of studies on stratification taking place within the sociological tradition proper has been a result of this confrontation with the Marxist approach.

THE KEEPERS AND THE TAKERS: THE STRUGGLE OVER SCARCE RESOURCES

For Marx, class is determined by the relationship of a group to the means of production. He understood this relationship rather narrowly in terms of the ownership of the means of production. Thus classes are defined by how much or how little their members own not only of the wealth of a society but of the means by which this wealth is produced. Some later Marxist scholars have modified this definition by placing less emphasis on the legal matter of ownership, instead stressing the element of control over the means of production. They have insisted that the really important determinant of class position is not so much what an individual can legally call his own but over what resources he has effective command. Be this as it may, the Marxist approach to stratification, and its concept of class itself, is basically an *economic* one. This is very much related to the basic Marxist conception of society as such. What society is essentially all about is a struggle over the scarce resources that human beings want or need. Different groups of people, for various historical reasons, have differential access to these resources. History is the story of the struggle between groups over this control. In other words, history is the story of the struggle between classes. In the Marxist approach, therefore, class is not only an important but the central category for any analysis of society.

In different historical situations, the class struggle can be quite complex and involve a number of groups with different characteristics. Fundamentally, however, the Marxist approach sees the struggle as between two fairly clearly defined groups, the haves and the have-nots. In terms of the society of his day (that is, early nineteenth-century capitalist society in Europe), Marx saw the fundamental struggle as taking place between the bourgeoisie and the proletariat. By Marx's time, the old upper class—the aristocracy —had pretty much been eliminated as an important social group in most European societies. It was the old middle class—the bourgeoisie—which had taken effective control, at least since the French Revolution. This bourgeoisie was the capitalist class which both owned and controlled the economic machinery of these societies. The proletariat, on the other hand, is defined in terms of its lack of ownership and control. The relationship between bourgeoisie and proletariat is seen as a relationship of exploitation and oppression. Political disputes (such as the revolutionary turmoils of nineteenth-century France and Germany that Marx wrote about) are only the surface manifestations of the underlying conflict between classes. For reasons that we cannot go into here, Marx thought that the inevitable outcome of this struggle would be a victorious proletarian revolution. While Marx's economic approach stresses the objective factors that determine stratification, he was also very much aware of the subjective dimension, which he called that of *class consciousness*. Very often, he insisted, there is a discrepancy between the objective circumstances of class and the subjective awareness that people have of their position in the class system. Quite often, people may delude themselves about their real position in society, in which case Marx speaks of *false consciousness*. One of the important preconditions of successful revolution by an exploited class is precisely the growth of class consciousness, that is, of the awareness of people that they are indeed an oppressed group that has a common destiny.

A Marxist approach to stratification has been, and still is today, of obvious attractiveness to those who would like to radically transform society. Marx himself, of course, deliberately constructed his theory with that purpose in mind. There is also, however, an intellectual attraction to the Marxist approach that is quite independent of its political uses. However complex the Marxist analysis of a particular situation might become, its fundamental intellectual thrust is toward simplification. When all is said and done, every social situation resolves itself into a struggle between those who want to hold onto their prerogatives and those who want to take these away. This approach thus has a way of seeming to cut through irrelevant details to the essentials of any situation.

CLASS, STATUS, POWER: WEBER'S THREE-FOLD APPROACH

Next to the Marxist approach, the most influential approach to the topic of stratification has been that initiated by Max Weber.[2] As we have previously pointed out, Weber's entire approach to sociology was, in many ways, a long-lasting confrontation with Marx. This was very much the case with his approach to stratification. Weber felt that Marx's approach to these matters was far too simple and was, for this reason, likely to lead to a distorted view of stratification phenomena. To counteract this alleged simplicity of Marxism, Weber proposed a three-fold conceptual scheme. More precisely, he suggested that there were three quite different types of stratification.

First, there were the phenomena which, like Marx, he called *class*. Although Weber placed less emphasis on ownership of property than Marx did, he agreed with Marx that in this type of stratification the fundamental dynamic was economic. A class is understood by Weber as a group of people with similar *life chances*. This means that, because of a certain commonality of access to scarce resources, there exists the strong probability that people within one class will have similar biographies in terms of what they will actually achieve in this particular society.

Second, there is a quite different type of stratification based on *status*. Status simply refers to the degree of social esteem that is bestowed on an individual or a group. Needless to say, there is very

[2] Max Weber, *The Theory of Social and Economic Organization* (New York, Free Press, 1957); Hans Gerth and C. Wright Mills (eds.), *From Max Weber* (New York, Oxford University Press, 1946).

frequently a close relationship between class and status. But this is not a necessary or universal relationship. Thus there are cases in which people occupy a high position in the class system but do not attain comparable status. A simple example of this would be a wealthy parvenu trying to crash an aristocratic society. Conversely, there may be people, or groups, with high status that occupy relatively low positions in the class system. An example of this is the military in many societies. Closely related to the concept of status is Weber's concept of the *estate* as a stratum. An estate (the word here is, of course, used not in the sense of real estate but as, for example, when people spoke of the bourgeoisie as the third estate at the time of the French Revolution) is understood by Weber as a social group into which an individual is born and in which he remains by virtue of adherence to what Weber calls a code of honor. It follows that moving up in an estate system is considerably more difficult than moving upward in a class system. In the latter, the main mechanism of mobility is the acquisition of economic means. That, of course, is not enough in an estate system; one can buy any number of things, but one cannot buy the accident of one's birth —no matter how much money one has, one remains stuck with that. Actually, in a perfect estate system, it would not be possible for anyone to move up, although, because of breaches of the code of honor, it might be possible for some people to move down. In actual fact, there are possibilities of movement in an estate system, one of the most important ones being marriage. By marrying the right person, one can, as it were, correct the accident of birth.

And third, according to Weber, there is stratification based on *power*. Again, this may or may not be related to either class or status. Power is defined by Weber, rather simply, as the capacity to carry through one's intentions in society even against resistance. In discussing stratification based on power, Weber also uses such terms as political class or party. Other sociologists have preferred to use the term elite. Whatever term is used, it is quite clear that societies are stratified not only in terms of people's access to scarce resources, and to status, but also to power. Some groups are more powerful than others. The third type of stratification, then, is political.

The Weberian approach to stratification has been very influential in non-Marxist sociology, both in Europe and in this country. Its attraction lies in the fact that it provides a much more complex and calibrated conceptual scheme than the Marxist one. No attempt is made here to reduce the varieties of stratification phenomena to some one underlying force (though Weber would agree with Marx to the extent that he also regards modern society as primarily a class society and thus as primarily determined by economic forces). Weber, like Marx, was very much aware of the possible discrepancies between objective and subjective location in the stratification order. However, unlike Marx, Weber did not reduce this dimension to the question of class consciousness. Class, status and power here serve as a system of coordinates within which just about any question of stratification can be investigated.

THE STRUCTURAL-FUNCTIONALISTS: MOTIVATING INDIVIDUALS TO KEEP THE SYSTEM FUNCTIONING

The structural-functionalist school in American sociology has produced its own approach to stratification.[3] This was very influential for a while, though it is probably fair to say that it has been in decline in recent years. Whatever criteria may be used to determine location in the stratification system (and some sociologists of this school have been influenced more by Weber), the emphasis here is on stratification as maintaining the functioning of society by providing motivation and rewards for the members of society. It is necessary that certain tasks in society be

[3] The debate was initiated among structural-functionalists by Kingsley Davis and Wilbert Moore, "Some Principles of Stratfication," *American Sociological Review,* 10 (1945): 242ff. For modifications of the structural-functionalist approach to stratification, see Melvin Tumin, *Social Stratification* (Englewood Cliffs, N.J., Prentice-Hall, 1967), especially pp. 106ff., and Talcott Parsons, "A Revised Analytical Approach to the Theory of Social Stratification," in Reinhard Bendix and Seymour Lipset (eds.), *Class, Status and Power* (New York, Free Press, 1953), pp. 92ff. For a criticism of the entire approach, see Dennis Wrong, "The Functional Theory of Stratification," *American Sociological Review,* 24 (1959): 772ff.

carried on, and it is further necessary that people expend effort in performing these tasks. In order for people to do this, they must be motivated, and the best motivation comes from rewards being attached to successful performance of these tasks. In other words, stratification functions as a carrot-and-stick system. It is as if society were saying to people: "Do what you are expected to do and you will attain or maintain a rank that has certain privileges. Refuse to do what you are expected to do and you will either never get such rank or, if you now hold it, you will be thrown out of it." Unlike the Marxist emphasis on struggle, the emphasis here is on the integration and stability of society. In terms of Weber's trilogy, status is emphasized much more strongly than either class or power.

CRITIQUES OF THE DAVIS-MOORE HYPOTHESIS

In its sharpest way, as formulated above, the structural-functionalist approach to stratification has been associated with two American sociologists, Kingsley Davis and Wilbert Moore, and has consequently come to be known as the "Davis-Moore Hypothesis." This has not only been criticized by sociologists of different orientations but within the camp of structural-functionalists themselves. Melvin Tumin has pointed out that attainment of the "rewards" of the stratification system is dependent on the previous development of the attitudes and habits conducive to such attainment, and that these are available only to a limited number of people. In other words, Tumin has tried to show that the Davis-Moore view exaggerates the "openness" of the class system (presumably following general American ideology in this respect). Talcott Parsons has also modified the structural-functionalist approach to stratification, having started out with a position very close to the Davis-Moore Hypothesis and subsequently moving further away from it. Parsons particularly emphasized the necessity of understanding values and norms as they operate in stratification. It is not enough to understand the concrete, material "rewards" of the system, but the subtle network of normative judgments that people make both about the "rewards" and the means to attain them. What all structural-functionalist positions have in common is their perspective on stratification as part of a functioning social system, though they differ in how they look upon the complexity and the specific character of these functions. Indeed, values and norms (such as those motivating people to achieve) can themselves be viewed as "functional" for the maintenance of the social system.

The structural-functionalist approach has been attractive to many American sociologists because, in accordance with widely held American values, it emphasizes achievement and its rewards as against the much nastier imagery that both the Marxist and the Weberian approaches suggest. The major assumption of this approach is that the de facto system of stratification actually does function so as to maintain the integration and stability of society as a whole. This, many critics have argued, is quite an assumption and one that has very little support from the empirical evidence. Marxist critics, indeed, would maintain that the structural-functionalist approach to stratification is nothing but the theoretical elaboration of a widely prevalent form of false consciousness in American society. The major ingredient of this false consciousness is the illusion that people can make it to the top if only they will do what is expected of them. Structural-functionalists might reply to such critics that even illusion may be functional in maintaining the integration and the stability of a society. To say that a society is functioning is not necessarily to say that its order is an expression of either truth or justice.

THE CASTE SYSTEM AND AMERICAN RACIAL STRATA

Despite these overall differences in approach, there is general concurrence in American sociology on the usage of the two terms, class and status. Whatever the differences in general approach, almost everyone agrees that the former term refers to economically based and the latter to non-economically based forms of ranking. Because of the peculiar racial situation in America, the additional concept of *caste* has been added to the general terminology regarding stratification.[4] The term originally derives from India, but it has been given a much more general significance by American sociologists. By caste is meant a stratum into which one is born, within which one must marry and out of which (at least theoretically) there is no exit. In a continuum of rigidity, one might thus place the concept of class at one end, this concept of caste at the other, and Weber's concept of estate in the middle.

The concept can, of course, be applied quite successfully to racial stratification in America, and, indeed, it was specifically coined for such application. Needless to say, the addition of this concept makes the analysis of stratification even more complex. This is especially so because everyone familiar with the situation realizes that caste and class are very much related in the American situation. Thus, while it is true that, generally speaking, it is impossible for a black person to move into the white stratum (except by "passing," that is, by pretending not to be black), there are very wide class differences within the black group and these class differences have a lot to do with the way in which the racial situation is experienced. What is more, if one applies objective class criteria, a great part of the black group would fall below the middle class in American society. Some Marxist analysts of the American situation have used this latter fact to arrive at the conclusion that the conflict between the races in America is simply another manifestation of class struggle. Rather few non-Marxist sociologists would go along with this position, but it is quite clear that the American stratification system cannot be understood unless both caste and class are taken into consideration.

[4] On the general concept of caste, see the article by Gerald Berreman under "Caste" in the *International Encyclopedia of the Social Sciences,* Vol. 2 (New York, Macmillan, 1968), pp. 333ff.

LIFE-STYLE: DIFFERENCES BETWEEN CLASSES

Another key concept in American studies of stratification is that of *life-style*. This concept, originally coined by Weber, refers to the overall culture or way of life of different groups in the society. The differences we have pointed out at the beginning of this chapter between the worlds of little Johnny and little Jimmy are expressions of different classes' life-style. Some American sociologists have emphasized life-style in lieu of economic factors, and have thought thereby to provide an unambiguously non-Marxist way of studying stratification. This has been particularly true of the studies of stratification in America stimulated by the work of Lloyd Warner.[5] This approach began with an intensive study of the community of Newburyport, Massachusetts, by Warner and his associates (following the usual convention of anonymity in the field, Warner called the community "Yankee City"). Warner's work has stimulated many further investigations into the phenomena of class in America, especially in terms of the differential life-styles of different classes. Critics of this approach, however, have maintained that life-style is a *result* of class position and not, in itself, a determining factor of the latter. Everyone, though, will agree on the reality of the phenomenon of life-style and the fact that there are, indeed, significant differences between the life-styles of different classes. In other words, different strata live in different worlds.

[5] Lloyd Warner and Paul Lunt, *The Social Life of a Modern Community* (New Haven, Conn., Yale University Press, 1941).

ELMTOWN'S YOUTH,
"THE ELITE,"
"THE GOOD KIDS"
AND "THE
GRUBBY GANG"

Some of the foregoing considerations might have struck some readers as excessively abstract, as theories having nothing to do with the real lives of people outside of whatever sanctuaries sociologists sit in. Such an impression would be quite erroneous. Ordinary people living in ordinary American communities ex-

perience the reality of stratification every day of their lives. What is more, this experience begins very early. A very influential study of the impact of class on adolescents in a Midwestern town was August Hollingshead's *Elmtown's Youth,* published in 1949. Hollingshead's book had a considerable impact beyond sociology proper because it so radically challenged what many Americans then (and some still today) like to believe so strongly, namely, that in some fashion American society is classless, is a society in which no fundamental differences are made between people, and also that the primary locale for training individuals in this kind of democracy is the public school. All these assumptions were blown sky high by Hollingshead's data.[6]

Hollingshead divided the population of Elmtown into five classes (the details of his criteria need not concern us here), ranging from an upper class 1 to a quite depressed lower class 5. He then was able to show in great detail how class position determined just about every aspect of the adolescent's life in this community. Success or failure in school was directly related to class level. For example, in the Elmtown high school, 2.9 percent of children from class 1 failed to pass from one grade to another; the corresponding figure for class 5 was 23.1 percent. To some extent, no doubt, these differences are to be explained in terms of teachers' prejudices. But much more important, the underlying factor is a difference in lifestyle between classes and the simple fact that the school itself is

[6] August Hollingshead, *Elmtown's Youth* (New York, Wiley, 1949).

geared to the life-style of the higher classes and not to that of the lower ones. The private lives of the adolescents, however, are equally dominated by class. For example, Hollingshead found that 61 percent of dates in the Elmtown high school take place between people of the same class, 35 percent between people in adjacent classes and only 4 percent between people whose class position is farther apart than that. One hundred percent of the adolescents in classes 1 and 2 participated in some extracurricular activity of the school; 73 percent of those in class 5 did not participate in anything. The facts of class, while of course not expressed in sociological jargon, were well known to the children and expressed by them in their own terms. Thus Hollingshead found that the adolescents in this high school stratified themselves in three overall categories: "the elite," "the good kids" and "the grubby gang." To a large extent these, as it were, inner stratification categories were related to the class system in the larger community.

THE QUIET LIFE, TRYING HARD AND IMMEDIATE ENJOYMENT: CLASSES IN NEW ENGLAND

We have already mentioned the work of Lloyd Warner and his collaborators which was published at about the same time as Hollingshead's book. Warner divided the community he was studying into six classes, ranging from an upper-upper class descended from old New England families) to a lower-lower class (a kind of sub-proletariat). He tried to show how each one of these classes had a distinctive life-style that went far beyond the obvious differences in economic resources available. For example, he distinguished between the aforementioned upper-upper class and the lower-upper class, which consisted of much more recent arrivals on that social level. In some instances, lower-upper-class individuals had far more money than upper-upper-class people, yet they tried to emulate as far as they could the life-style of the latter. The best adjective with which to describe that life-style would be "quiet." This is quite different from the life-style of the upper-middle class from which most of the lower-upper individuals had recently come. In the upper-middle class, with whatever measure of taste, the fruits of one's economic endeavor are displayed openly and sometimes with a measure of aggressiveness. By contrast, the upper-class style dictates that wealth be hidden as much as possible. Corresponding to this, there is also a difference in ethos. Put very simply: the overall middle-class ethos is a pushing one. The same values which, in the middle class, are looked upon as showing healthy ambition are regarded as pushiness and vulgarity in the upper class.

Similar differences in ethos exist further down in the social scale. Thus Warner showed that the dividing line between what he called the upper-lower and the lower-lower classes is primarily one of morality. The upper-lower class (what most other sociologists would now call the working class) is poor, in some instances perhaps as poor as members of the stratum below it, but it is animated by an ethos of hard work, discipline and ambition. By contrast, the lower-lower class has no such virtues at all. The prevailing ethos there is one of immediate enjoyment, and there is mainly disdain for the rewards which people in the other strata strive for. In one respect there is actually a curious similarity between the uppermost and the lowest strata in Warner's scheme, and that is in the contempt for the middle-class ethos of driving ambition. That ethos dominates the greatest part of the class system as analyzed by Warner (thus, in a very real way, verifying at least the symbolic significance of the American belief that this is a middle-class society). Going from top to bottom, the middle-class ethos extends from the lower-upper class through the upper-lower. In these strata, everyone is trying hard. All this frenetic activity is viewed with sardonic detachment by people on the two extreme poles of the system, from the very top and from the very bottom.

THE KINSEY REPORTS: "SOCIAL LEVEL" AND SEX LIFE

During the same period, namely, in 1948, the first results of Alfred Kinsey's studies of sexual behavior in America were published.[7] Some of Kinsey's material showed, in the most graphic way possible, how far even the most intimate aspects of personal life were influenced by class. Kinsey, of course, was no sociologist, and, indeed, his works show a remarkable absence of sociological perspective. However, he did introduce indicators of what he called "social level" into the analysis of his data. The results were very striking indeed. For example, he found that the higher up one goes in the class system, the later do men begin to have sexual intercourse. Instead, he found a great variety of sexual practices (generally subsumed under the category of petting) which provided the satisfaction which, on the lower levels, is provided by actual intercourse. Generally speaking, the higher levels have a much more variegated and imaginative sex life, many aspects of which are regarded as perverse on the lower levels. Kinsey's later findings on American women followed the same pattern. There have probably been considerable changes in American sexual practices since Kinsey's first results were published. These details, however, need not concern us here. Now, as then, there are considerable differences between classes in this area of life as well.

It is thus possible to go through literature of quite different kinds and produce what could be called an ethnography of class in American society. Classes, far from simply being economic brackets, constitute cultural universes which, to a very large extent, dominate the lives of their members. As society changes (for example, in its sexual practices), the contents of each of these worlds changes, and sometimes the dividing lines between classes on specific matters are blurred or shifted. What continues through this change, however, is the underlying fact of class differentiation. The

[7] Alfred Kinsey, Wardell Pomeroy and Clyde Martin, *Sexual Behavior in the Human Male* (Philadelphia, Saunders, 1948).

practical result of this can be put very simply in terms of prediction: if we know the class location of an individual, we can predict a large variety of the details in his life. Of course, we cannot be absolutely sure in each instance. Prediction is a statement of probability; there are always exceptions. All the same, if, for example, we are able to assign an individual to the upper middle class, we can (knowing nothing else about this particular individual, and possibly never having seen him) predict with considerable assurance the distribution of several items in his family budget, the number of his children, the geographical location of his home and the manner in which he spends his vacation. But that is not all. We can also predict his political position on a variety of issues, his religious affiliation and the number and type of books he is reading. We can even predict whether he has intercourse with his wife with the light on or off (if we are talking about an upper-middle-class individual, chances are that the light will be on).

CASTE AND CLASS: STATUS COMPENSATION

As we move from stratification by class to stratification by caste (that is, in American terms, as we cross the race line between white and black), we shall continue to encounter this basic phenomenon of differentiated life-styles. However, the phenomenon becomes more complex. The black community itself is divided along class lines. Here too we find distinctive class-bound life-styles, some of which are quite similar to the differences existing between classes in the white community, while others are distinctive to the culture of the black community as such. We also find, however, sharp dividing lines between the two racial communities as a whole—as a result of which there are overall life-styles that are distinctively black, irrespective of class divisions.

An early and very influential study of the relationship of class and caste in an American community was John Dollard's *Caste and Class in a Southern Town*, originally published in 1937.[8] Dol-

    [8] John Dollard, *Caste and Class in a Southern Town* (New York, Harper, 1937).

lard showed very clearly how the dynamics of caste and class are combined in the everyday life of people in this Southern community. For example, he was particularly interested in the oft-noted fact that lower-class whites show much more intense hostility toward blacks than upper-class whites. One element in this is undoubtedly that there is sharper economic competition at those levels of the social system. There is, however, another very important dimension, which has to do with status as distinct from economic level. In the traditional Southern stratification system, the black community as a whole was ranked below the white community as a whole. Within the white community, however, there were quite sharp class antagonisms and resentments. Caste served as a status compensation mechanism for the lower-class white. Put quite simply: whatever the lowliness of his class position, the lower-class white is irrevocably ranked above the black within the caste system. What is more, the etiquette of relations between the races in the traditional South makes this fact unambiguously clear every time a white and a black meet.

BEING BLACK

This was an intricate system of regulating every single encounter between white and black in everyday life. Its basic rule was very simple: the black partner in the interaction was to constantly express, by word and gesture, that the status of the white partner was superior to his own. In other words, the racial etiquette was a systematic self-demeaning by the black who was, at the same time, of course, demeaned by the white partner in the interaction. For example, the proper mode of address of the white by the black was by the white's last name prefixed by a "Mr.," or by such honorific titles as "sir" or "boss." Conversely, the black was commonly addressed by his first name or by such non-honorific titles as "boy." This etiquette was consistently performed by whites of all classes, although upper-class whites generally put a more benign attitude into it than lower-class whites.

That this placed a very strong emotional burden upon the black and that its overall effect was one of depersonalization hardly need any emphasis. It also produced, however, another consequence of considerable importance, namely, the social existence of the black took on a strange double quality. There was, as it were, the official façade of his life which had to be constantly exhibited in relations with whites. This façade, for example, included the qualities of childlike and irresponsible cheerfulness that whites liked to ascribe to blacks. Behind this façade, however, an entirely different life-style could exist. This, of course, was the life-style engaged in by blacks when they were among themselves. Here, the masks could be dropped and quite different roles could be performed. This doubleness of black existence in the traditional South shows up the ironic quality of a very common notion of white Southerners, that they "knew Negroes very well." What, in fact, they did know was the public façade of Negro life. They were abysmally ignorant of whatever took place behind that façade. The blacks themselves, on the other hand, had a much more accurate perception of the white world since whites had no motive to engage in this kind of dissimulation in their dealings with blacks. Since Dollard's work, of course, there have been far-reaching changes in the racial system, both in the South and in other parts of the country. Many features of this type of caste stratification still remain, however. What is perhaps even more important, the emotional consequences of this caste system continue to play an important part in the attitudes of both whites and blacks toward each other.

GETTING AHEAD MEANS BECOMING WHITE?

More recent studies of black communities in America, whatever other changes have taken place, show that one fundamental aspect of the situation has remained very similar, namely, that the higher up a black individual is located on the class scale, the closer he is to the white community in terms of his life-style.[9] Again, of course, there is an economic aspect to this. Middle-class blacks quite simply have the economic resources to participate in a much wider range of activities in the overall white-

[9] See, for example, Andrew Billingsley, *Black Families in White America* (Englewood Cliffs, N.J., Prentice-Hall, 1968).

dominated community than is the case with lower-class blacks. Beyond this obvious fact, however, there are much subtler dynamics of opinion, values, tastes and manners. A middle-class white will much more readily feel at ease with a middle-class black than either he or a working-class white would feel in encountering blacks of lower levels in terms of class. Putting the same observation in terms of the black community itself, it can be said that it has been the lower-class black who has retained a much more distinctively black life-style as against the middle-class black. It is quite possible that the recent upsurge of black nationalism, in its various manifestations, will change this in the direction of producing a much more distinctive black culture that will embrace all classes within the black community. At this time it would be hazardous to make sociological predictions about this.

DIFFERENT LIFE-STYLES: CUTTING THROUGH CLASS LINES?

The mention of black culture raises a considerably broader question, namely, whether in American society today there may be life-styles with different statuses that cut right across the class system. Thus it has been suggested that religious affiliation plays an important part in establishing status in a situation in which ethnicity has become of doubtful value in determining personal identity and in which there is very high movement between classes.[10] It is also possible, however, that quite different types of life-style may be significant. The most important of these on the contemporary American scene, to which we shall return in a later chapter, is the youth culture. To be sure, there are class differences in the way in which young people relate to this culture. Nevertheless, as a whole, it seems to cut considerably through major class lines. Similarly, there are other life-styles (usually associated with certain patterns of consumption and leisure-time activity) which have gained importance in recent years in the determination of an individual's status. For example, on different class and age levels, one might mention the life-style which

[10] Will Herberg, *Protestant—Catholic—Jew* (Garden City, N.Y., Doubleday, 1955).

has been so very successfully symbolized by *Playboy* magazine and the life-style revolving around the motorcycle as a symbol.

Tom Wolfe, a writer with a keen eye on the changing American scene (for which most sociologists might well be envious of him), has called this phenomenon by the apt name of *status spheres*.[11] If Wolfe is correct, then in the world of these status spheres the old criteria of class and class-bound life-style have lost importance to a great degree. What now provides status are objects and activities that are obtainable by a broad spectrum of people in the society. Thus the young people of quite different class backgrounds may adopt the activities, dress, language and group patterns of the motorcycle culture—and, what is most important, derive status from this fact. Again, it is too early to predict with any degree of assurance whether status spheres of this kind may eventually become more important than class in the stratification order of American society. If they do, many sociological statements in the area of stratification will have to be drastically revised.

[11] Tom Wolfe, *The Pump House Gang* (New York, Farrar, Straus & Giroux, 1968). Parsons has made the same point much earlier (using more complicated language, to be sure).

R E A D I N G S

The reader might at this point choose one of two tracks—further readings that will help clarify the basic concepts of stratification, or further readings that will bring out the everyday realities of stratification in American society. The following are suggested for the first track:

Bendix, Reinhard, and Seymour Lipset (eds.), *Class, Status and Power* (New York, Free Press, 1966).

Dahrendorf, Ralf, *Class and Class Conflict in Industrial Society* (Stanford, Calif., Stanford University Press, 1959), available in paperback.

Tumin, Melvin, *Social Stratification* (Englewood Cliffs, N.J., Prentice-Hall, 1967).

The reader wishing to pursue the second track may turn to the following:

Dollard, John, *Caste and Class in a Southern Town* (New York, Harper, 1937), available in paperback.

Hollingshead, August, *Elmtown's Youth* (New York, Wiley, 1949), available in paperback.

Mills, C. Wright, *White Collar* (New York, Oxford University Press, 1951), available in paperback.

Warner, Lloyd, and Paul Lunt, *The Social Life of a Modern Community* (New Haven, Conn., Yale University Press, 1941).

Chapter 8

THE
STRATIFIED
SOCIETY

MAN IS THE ANIMAL that makes plans. He undertakes projects. He dreams of the future, most likely of a future that will be better than the present. The child imagines what he will be like as an adult. The adult, too, projects himself in images of future fulfillment. Commonly, these projections are not only in time but in space. In terms of future fulfillments, man not only thinks of other times but of other places—faraway places or, at any rate, places that are more spacious than his present location. Especially in childhood and youth, the micro-world is experienced as an antechamber to the macro-world. The micro-world is the locale in which one waits and works for the future which, hopefully, will transcend its limits.

There is nothing new about this. Project-making appears to be an intrinsic element in man's constitution. As far back as we have any evidence, human beings have always projected into the future. What is peculiar about contemporary society is the belief of most people that their projects for improving their overall position in the world have a good chance of succeeding and that, therefore, it makes sense to work systematically for a better future. What is more, there is a moral ingredient to this belief. Thus there is not only the factual judgment that a better future is actually possible but the moral judgment that one has a right to a better future. These ideas have a long history in Western civilization that we cannot possibly go into here. Having gained a place of dominance in the world view of Western humanity, they have now been very effectively diffused through most of the world. Almost everywhere the expectations of the future have become more ambitious and more urgent, introducing an element of restless movement into most societies in the world today.

All of this entails a view both of the individual's biography and of society as a whole. The individual looks upon his own life as an achievement ladder. Each phase of life is supposed to be a rung in this ladder, an upward step. Society as a whole is then looked upon as a context that makes possible such achievement. There is either the belief that society, in fact, is such a context or, if it appears not to be, the pressing conviction that society ought to change in such a way as to live up to this expectation. It should be strongly emphasized that the wide prevalence and strength of these ideas in contemporary societies are quite new. For most of human history most people took it for granted that their dreams were likely to remain just that, that their general location in society was likely to remain the same throughout their own lifetimes (though, of course, some of their projects might make little improvements here and there) and that there was little point in rebelling against this—this being what the world had always been like and would always remain. Very commonly, this conviction as to the inevitability of one's social fate had a foundation in religious beliefs about the nature of the world and man's place in it.

STATUS ASCRIPTION AND ACHIEVEMENT

Sociologists make the distinction between *ascribed and achieved status*.[1] Ascribed status belongs to the individual by virtue of his birth or some other biographical fact that is not due to his own efforts. For example, both a prince and a leper have a specific status ascribed to them, and there is nothing which the former did to attain it or that the latter can do to get rid of it. Achieved status, on the other hand, is attained by the individual as a result of his deliberate efforts. Thus a person rising from office boy to office manager (assuming that he is not a relative of the boss) occupies the latter status on the basis of his own achievement. Again, for reasons that have a long history, contemporary society —and especially American society—is permeated with an achievement ethos. The individual is expected to want to achieve better things in life and the society is expected to provide him with the opportunity to do so. Indeed, some psychologists have maintained that socialization in our society instills a strong need for achievement. Most games played by American children are competitive. From early childhood, acts of achievement are applauded and rewarded, and the failure to achieve is presented to the child as a very serious thing indeed.

In terms of the stratification system, this achievement ethos is

[1] The terms were originally coined by Ralph Linton, a cultural anthropologist, but they have now become common sociological usage.

translated into a mobility ethos, that is, into an ambition by the individual to improve his position in the stratification system, to move upward. In America, this mobility ethos has been, just about from the beginning of American history, an intrinsic element of the national ideology. America is supposed to be the land of opportunity. Ideally, it is supposed to be a society in which *all* status is achieved, a society which discards all distinctions between men that are produced by ascription. This, indeed, was to be the major difference between the new world and the old. The same national ideology proposes that the major institutions of American society should be so arranged as to facilitate such movement by individuals. American free enterprise, American government and (very importantly) the American public school system are permeated with the notion of equality of opportunity—or, if such was deemed to be lacking, with the ideal of equalization of opportunity.

LIFE CHANCES: IS THERE EQUALITY OF OPPORTUNITY AT BIRTH?

The obvious question that suggests itself is how realistic these expectations and assumptions are. Is there really equality of opportunity in American society? If not, is there a tendency toward such equality? In terms of the individual looking at his own life, the same question becomes one concerning the degree of illusion in which the individual exists. Given the individual's position in the stratification system, what may he realistically expect of life? And what are his chances of improving his position?

We may here once more refer to Max Weber's concept of *life chances* which, as we have previously seen, is a crucial element of Weber's concept of class. Class position, according to Weber, determines the chances that an individual's life will follow certain patterns. We can then ask, in terms of the American stratification system, what life chances are entailed by the position which an individual occupies in it. To some extent, of course, this question is already involved in the differences in life-style between classes that we have discussed previously. But differences in life-style still have, if one may put it this way, a milder character than differences in life chances. When we talk about the latter, we are talking very starkly about what people hope for and what they fear when they look into the future. From the viewpoint of the American national ideology of equal opportunity, sociological data about class differences in life chances are quite shocking. At the very least they reveal a profound gap between the society's rhetoric and its realities.

One can begin with the most elementary meaning suggested by the term life chances, namely, with life expectancy.[2] This term, of course, means the likelihood that an individual will live to a certain age. In 1940, the total life expectancy of Americans (total in the sense of being undifferentiated by male/female, by race, income or any other differentiating category) was 62.9 years. Measured in terms of income, the lowest census category (male and female combined) had a life expectancy of 58.7 years, while the highest category had a life expectancy of 67.8 years. What this means is very simple: a person born at the top of the American stratification system could reasonably look forward to nine more years of life than a person born at the bottom. The racial differences are equally stark. In the same year, the lowest-income white group had a life expectancy of 60.2, and the highest-income white group a life expectancy of 67.8. By contrast, the life expectancy of the lowest-income non-white group was 49.9, and of the highest-income non-white group 55.9. Again, what this means is quite simple: even if, in terms of class achievement, a non-white individual was lucky enough to reach a high-income bracket, his life expectancy was still almost five years less than that of a white person in the lowest-income bracket, and more than eleven years less than a white in an income bracket comparable to his own. As to those at the bottom of the income scale, whites could reasonably look forward to about ten years of life more than non-whites in the same income category.[3] By 1967, the total life expectancy had risen to 70.5. Al-

[2] A psychologist, David McClelland, has built up an entire theory on the need for achievement and how it can be produced. See his *The Achieving Society* (Princeton, N.J., Van Nostrand, 1961). Many social scientists have been skeptical of McClelland's approach.

[3] Albert Mayer and Philip Hauser, "Class Differentials in Expectations of Life at Birth," in Reinhard Bendix and Seymour Lipset (eds.), *Class, Status and Power* (New York, Free Press, 1953), pp. 281ff.

though both class and race differences have narrowed, there still were differences in considerable degree. Thus the total life expectancy of whites was 71.3, of non-whites 64.6. The gap had indeed narrowed. In terms of total life expectancy (not differentiated by income groups), the difference between whites and non-whites in 1940 was 11.1 years, in 1967 only 6.7 years.[4] Indeed, since the turn of the century, the gain in life expectancy among non-whites has been twice that among whites. Nevertheless, it remains true even today that the accident of one's birth on different levels of the stratification system literally determines one's chances of living to a certain age.

INCOME, HEALTH, MENTAL HEALTH AND MIDDLE-CLASS ORIENTED INSTITUTIONS

The reasons for these differences are not hard to find. The higher strata in society enjoy much better nutrition, have patterns of living more conducive to health and (very importantly) have better medical care available to them. Take only one example of medical care to make this point, namely, the number of visits paid to the dentist per year per person. For 1966, this number was 0.8 times in families with an income under $2000 per year, 1.4 times in families with an income of $4000 to $7000, and 2.3 times in families with an income of $7000 or more.[5] People in the lower strata of the society are more frequently ill, have fewer resources to prevent or treat illness and are therefore more likely to die earlier. What is true about physical illness also seems to pertain to mental illness. A number of studies have shown a considerably higher rate of mental illness among lower-class than upper-class individuals, and among non-whites than whites.[6]

Sociological studies of the relationship of class to mental illness,

[4] U.S. Bureau of the Census, *Statistical Abstracts of the United States, 1969* (Washington, D.C., 1969).

[5] U.S. Bureau of the Census, *Statistical Abstracts of the United States, 1966* (Washington, D.C., 1966).

[6] The best-known study in this area is August Hollingshead and Fredrick Redlich, *Social Class and Mental Illness* (New York, Wiley, 1958).

however, have brought out another interesting point, namely, that lower-class patients are perceived, and therefore dealt with, in a manner different from higher-class patients. Thus it appears that quite similar clinical symptoms are diagnosed as psychotic in lower-class patients and as only neurotic in higher-class patients. It follows that the lower-class patient having recourse to medical help for mental symptoms is much more likely to end up in a mental hospital than a higher-class individual would be. This brings us to an important element related to the life chances within the stratification system: most institutional agencies with which an individual has to deal in his life are controlled and operated by higher-class individuals. Thus psychiatrists, social workers, welfare officials and lawyers (all people who would be involved in the commitment of a lower-class patient to a mental hospital) all occupy positions of middle-class status. It is not necessary to assume deliberate favoritism or even prejudice to explain the difference in treatment accorded by them to individuals of different class backgrounds. The middle-class professional, in such circumstances, has an immediate rapport and a much better understanding when he has to deal with another middle-class person. Such rapport and understanding are not readily given when he is dealing with lower-class people. This very elementary sociological fact has far-reaching consequences for the life chances of lower-class people in a society where they constantly have to deal with middle-class oriented institutions.

CLASSES OF PEOPLE, CLASSES OF CRIME, CLASSES OF JUSTICE?

This fact is highly relevant with regard to crime and punishment. Consistently, there are higher rates for crimes and for convictions for lower-class as against higher-class individuals, and for non-whites as against whites.[7] There are two explanations (which are not at all contradictory) for these differences. First, it is almost certainly true that more crimes (especially certain types of crime such as those in-

[7] See, for example, Richard Quinney, *The Social Reality of Crime* (Boston, Little, Brown & Co., 1970), pp. 129ff.

volving violence) are committed by lower-class and by non-white individuals. The social context in which people in these strata live is, for obvious reasons, more productive of crime than higher-strata contexts. But there is an additional reason for the differences, and that is the discrimination in treatment accorded to individuals by the law-enforcement and judicial systems.

Certain types of crime common among middle-class individuals (especially the type commonly referred to as "white-collar crime," such as misappropriation of funds and other illegal or semi-legal financial operations) are easier to conceal than crimes common among lower-class individuals. Thus there may already be class discrimination in the crime reports themselves. Police and other law-enforcement agents tend to be more tolerant of middle-class offenders. Thus there are almost certainly class differences in arrest rates that are not simply due to class differences in the commission of the offenses in question. The same discrimination, though perhaps in a subtler form, tends to continue when an offender is dealt with by the judicial system. The discrimination is obvious in the much greater ability of higher-class individuals to secure competent legal assistance. The discrimination is blatant in the ability to put up bail. More subtly, it may be manifested in the prejudices and attitudes of judges, juries and prosecuting agencies.

WHO'S HAPPY? SOME CLASS DISTINCTIONS

In the American national ideology, the pursuit of happiness has been elevated to one of the foremost principles to which the society is supposed to adhere. If there is to be equality of opportunity anywhere, surely it is to be here. The sociological data make depressingly clear that chances of success in this pursuit vary greatly from class to class. Divorce rates in the lowest-income group of the census are almost four times those to be found in the highest-income group. Perhaps the relation between divorce and unhappiness is debatable. The following data are less debatable. In one study, 30 percent of unskilled workers reported that they had no close friends. As against this, only 10 percent of professionals and upper-echelon business and government employees made a similar report.[8] Lower-class individuals live lives that are lonelier and more fragile in terms of abiding human ties. After all this, the following data should not be surprising. In one recent study people were asked to group themselves on a scale of happiness and unhappiness. At the top of the scale were the people who replied that they were, indeed, "very happy." Of those with an annual income of over $10,000, 38 percent replied that they were "very happy." The number fell to 26 percent among those with an income of between $5000 and $6000, and to 14 percent among those with an income under $3000.[9]

CLASS POSITION AND EDUCATIONAL ATTAINMENT

A crucial relationship pertains between class position and the chance to obtain a certain level of education. Thus in a recent study it was found that 44 percent of children from families with an annual income of $10,000 or more attended college; only 17 percent did from families with incomes of from $5000 to $7500; and that figure fell to 9 percent of the children from families with an income under $5000.[10] This difference could be understood in terms of differences in life-style and thus could involve something as, after all, rather innocuous as the relative chance of a higher-class and a lower-class individual to really appreciate Shakespeare or Milton at the age of twenty. Important though such differences may be in terms of a liberal-arts point of view, education, alas, has much more vulgar relations to an individual's life chances. Specifically, education is directly related to income. In figures for 1967, individuals with less than eight years of school had a mean annual income of $3606; those with eight years of school, of $5139; those with four years of high school, $7629; those with one to three years of college, $8843; and, finally, those with four years of college or more,

[8] Joseph Kahl, *The American Class Structure* (New York, Holt, Rinehart & Winston, 1957).

[9] Norman Bradburn and David Caplowitz, *Reports on Happiness* (Chicago, Aldine, 1965).

[10] Herman Miller, *Rich Man, Poor Man* (New York, Crowell, 1964).

$11,924.[11] Thus, to be sure, the individual who did not finish grade school undoubtedly had a lesser appreciation of Shakespeare than the college graduate (if, indeed, he has ever heard of Shakespeare). But what is perhaps more relevant to him, the college graduate makes more than three times as much money a year than he does.

The relation between class and education points up another very important fact about stratification, namely, the vicious-cycle effect of many locations in the stratification system—most glaringly, of those locations on its lower levels. The lower-class individual has fewer chances of acquiring education. As a result of his deficient education, he has a deficient capacity for income. The latter, in turn, inhibits his chances of improving his position in the class system and, what is worse, his chances of providing an adequate education for his children. Once more there is a double explanation for these relationships. First, there is a direct relationship here between life-style and life chances. The life-style of the middle class is highly conducive to educational achievement. A brief recollection of the differences in child-rearing patterns between middle-class and working-class families, which we discussed in a previous chapter, will make this quite clear. Almost everything that happens in the middle-class family is conducive to motivating the middle-class child to make successful use of the educational system. The lower-class background is far less conducive to such motivation.

Second, however, the same middle-class orientation that we have just discussed in connection with medicine and law also pertains here. Schools are taught and administered by middle-class professionals. What is more, the standards of achievement are set by these same middle-class professionals. Often, and quite unintentionally, they discriminate against the lower-class child simply because his language, thought patterns and imagery are geared to a different class context. The lower-class child, therefore, is at a disadvantage in the educational system from the beginning, even if everyone he comes in contact with is trying to be helpful, and even if he himself has the requisite intelligence and achievement orientation. The

---

[11] U.S. Bureau of the Census, *Statistical Abstracts, 1969.*

aforementioned study of high-school youth in Elmtown has made this point very clearly. In recent years, these linkages between class and education, and their mobility-inhibiting effects, have been studied with particular reference to black children.

WHERE AM I HEADED? TYPES OF SOCIAL MOBILITY

It is very clear, then, that the life chances of an individual are decisively affected by his starting position in terms of the stratification system. One should be very careful how one chooses one's parents. Again, an obvious question follows: To what extent can fortune be corrected? If one has been careless in the choice of parents, what are one's chances of making good this mistake? In sociological terms, this question concerns one's chances of *social mobility*.

Social mobility is defined as any movement within a stratification system. Very often in sociological literature, the term "mobility" is used by itself to designate the same phenomenon. A number of further conceptual clarifications are necessary, though. The distinction is made between *social and geographical mobility*. The latter simply refers to movements of people in physical space and in itself need have no particular relationship to social mobility. For example, nomadic Arabs are constantly moving about in space, but these movements do not normally entail any changes in position on a stratification scale. In our society, however, there is a relationship between these two kinds of mobility. Very often, social mobility requires a geographical movement as well. To take another example: opportunities for social mobility are typically smaller in rural than in urban communities. Consequently, migration of rural people into cities is commonly associated with social mobility, or at least with aspirations to such mobility. A further distinction is made between *upward and downward mobility*. Both concepts refer to social mobility. In terms of American values, it is only upward mobility that is in most people's minds when they speak about the subject. Individuals not only move up, however, but they do move down in the stratification scheme, and it is important to keep this in mind.

There is also *vertical and horizontal mobility*. Only the former refers to social mobility properly speaking, that is, to upward or downward movement within a stratification system. Horizontal mobility refers to changes in social position that remain within the same strata. For example, a schoolteacher who becomes a principal undergoes vertical mobility. But a teacher who changes his subject from mathematics to geography undergoes horizontal mobility that does not, in all probability, affect his rank in the stratification scheme of his profession. A further distinction is made between *career and generational mobility* (sometimes also referred to as *intra-generational and inter-generational mobility*). By career mobility (or intra-generational mobility) is meant such movement as occurs within the adult life of one individual—as, for instance, in the movement from teacher to principal. Generational (or inter-generational) mobility, on the other hand, refers to the respective ranks of two successive generations. For example, if the teacher's father was the school janitor, the son has undergone generational mobility, even if, having once become a teacher, he never moves beyond this position.

Finally, the difference is made between *individual and group mobility*. The aforementioned examples, of course, all refer to individual mobility, but it is also possible for entire groups within the stratification system to move. Thus it could happen—perhaps as a result of labor-union activity—that school janitors as a group triple their income, change their designation (say, to "building engineers") and require a college degree for admission to their ranks. In such cases, which are far from rare in our society, all individuals in the group undergo considerable social mobility by whatever criteria one might wish to measure it, despite the fact that then, as now, they are janitors.

MONEY, MARRIAGE, EDUCATION, POLITICS AND "IMPRESSION": FIVE MEANS TO MOBILITY

Within a stratification system such as ours, there are five major mechanisms of upward social mobility for individuals. These are related to each other, of course, but can nevertheless be seen as distinct for purposes of sociological analysis. The first, and probably the most obvious mechanism of mobility, is through economic activity. By hard work, by luck, by connections or by fraud the individual operates within the economic system to improve his position. In most cases this simply means that he increases his income and thus his purchasing capacity—not only for the material but also the non-material benefits of status.

The second mechanism, still much more important than many people would readily recognize, is marriage. That is, a person improves his or her position by "marrying up." Clearly, this mechanism is more readily available for women than for men in our society, but it is by no means limited exclusively to women. The third mechanism of mobility is education. As we have already pointed out, this is very much related to the first mechanism of economic activity and position, but it is nevertheless distinct from it. The efforts of the individual here are primarily exerted not at his place of work or business but in movement through an educational process.

A fourth mechanism of mobility is political. This takes place when improvements in the position of individuals or entire groups are achieved through political pressures, negotiations or guarantees. It is a particularly important mechanism in terms of group mobility. Thus American blacks and other non-white minorities are today using political means to pressure society to grant and guarantee a collective improvement in the position of their members in the stratification system.

Finally, there is a mechanism which is perhaps best described by the term coined for different purposes by the contemporary sociologist Erving Goffman—"impression management." This is mobility achieved through the manipulation of status symbols and personal attraction. It is most readily evident in such social contexts as that of "café society," in which all kinds of hangers-on, confidence men and alleged inside dopesters try to advance themselves by making an impression on those who have already made it in that particular sector of the stratification system. While in terms of the society as a whole this mechanism is probably of minor importance, it is almost certainly one element in the use made by many individuals of the first four mechanisms.

AREAS OF AGREEMENT: THE *SHAPE* OF SOCIAL MOBILITY

How much upward mobility is there in American society? It is very difficult to answer this question in a direct way. Data about social mobility are surprisingly scarce, and most of them are ambiguous in their implications. There are differences in interpretation caused not only by the ambiguity of the data but by differing theoretical presuppositions of the interpreters. The most accessible data are those concerning occupation and income (the basic data for this, of course, are provided by the United States census). As we have seen, however, class and stratification generally are much subtler phenomena than simply raw expressions of occupational and income standing. There is therefore a problem of relating data on occupation and income to the subtler phenomena of class-related life-style and class consciousness. A full discussion of this topic would completely break the framework of a book such as this, requiring very extensive and at times very complicated treatment. The best we can do here is to summarize a number of trends in social mobility about which there is fairly general agreement among sociologists, and to point out a number of important areas in which there is disagreement.[12]

[12] Bendix and Lipset, *op. cit.;* Harold Hodges, *Social Stratification* (Cambridge, Mass., Schenkman, 1964); Kahl, *op. cit.;* Gerhard Lenski, *Power and Privilege* (New York, McGraw-Hill, 1966); Seymour Lipset and Reinhard Bendix, *Social Mobility in Industrial Society* (Berkeley, Calif., University of California Press, 1959).

1. As measured by occupational mobility between generations (that is, between fathers and sons), there is considerable upward movement, though there are sharp differences in this between different occupational categories. Figures for 1950 indicate that 77 percent of professionals have moved upward to their present position from the position held by their fathers, but only 56 percent of skilled workers and foremen have gone through a similar movement.[13] In other words, a considerable number of individuals manage to improve their position vis-à-vis that of their fathers in terms of occupation, but middle-class individuals are in a more favored position to do this.

2. As measured by occupation, most mobility is between occupational categories that are adjacent or close in status (to which should be added that the relative status of different occupations has remained remarkably the same in recent decades). For example, it is much more likely that the son of an unskilled worker will become a garage mechanic than that he will become a lawyer. Similarly, it is more likely that a lawyer's son will become a law professor than the director of a large corporation. The most difficult line to cross remains that between manual and non-manual work. Individuals whose occupation is farming are least mobile.

3. As measured by occupation, mobility rates in America have remained very similar during the last half century. That is, roughly similar proportions of people have moved upward in the occupational structure. Moreover, these mobility rates are quite similar to those prevailing in other Western industrial societies. There is disagreement as to whether mobility into the highest strata of the system has become harder or easier or has remained the same. However, most sociologists who have looked into this aspect of the matter are of the opinion that the highest strata in America have become more closed to newcomers from below.

4. It is likely that most mobility has been the result of changes in the overall occupational structure. An important factor in this has been the increase in demand for clerical, technical and other skilled labor, and a concomitant decrease in the demand for unskilled labor. The same relationship between changes in the occu-

[13] Kahl, *op. cit.* These data are derived from a study by the National Opinion Research Center.

pational structure and mobility seems to prevail in other industrial societies (including the Soviet Union).

5. Education has become the most important mechanism for mobility. This makes particularly serious the vicious-cycle relation between class and education that we have referred to above. This also makes it easy to understand why the educational system has become the main target for political pressure on the part of blacks trying to improve their chances in the society.

6. For the foregoing reasons, mobility has become more difficult, and may actually have decreased, for the lowest strata. This trend has been particularly severe for blacks and other racial minorities. If one combines this fact with the aforementioned opinion of some sociologists that the highest stratum has become relatively closed, an interesting picture emerges with regard to mobility; namely, most mobility takes place in the broad sector *between* the highest and the lowest strata of society; both the top and the bottom of the system participate least in this mobility. Individuals in these two strata are most likely to remain where they are—though this, very obviously, has different connotations at the bottom than at the top. As measured by occupation, it is the middle sectors of the stratification system that have expanded the most. In other words, it is, broadly speaking, the middle class that has grown the most. To some sociologists, this has suggested the image of a diamond to represent the stratification system—as against the pyramid, which has been the apt image for stratification in most older societies.

8. There has been a steady decrease in self-employed individuals. Even professionals are increasingly on payrolls rather than in independent business for themselves.

9. There has been a steady increase in income of almost all strata over the last half century, so that, in absolute terms, almost all strata have experienced upward group mobility. To measure differences in income, economists have coined the term "real income," by which they mean that income figures for different periods are translated into standardized dollars to take cognizance of differences in purchasing power between these periods. Thus, between 1939 and 1950, real income, so defined, increased 176 percent among unskilled workers, 172 percent among skilled workers, 111

percent among clerical workers and 95 percent among proprietors and managers.[14] In terms of income, the entire national pudding has grown very much, and everyone has experienced a slice of this growth. Indeed, for the lower strata this growth in income has been relatively greater.

10. Nevertheless, the income differential between different strata has remained fairly similar over the same period. That is, there have been no dramatic shifts in the proportions of total national income accruing to different strata, though it is claimed by some that the gaps between the different strata have steadily diminished. It should be noted that although the census provides very reliable data on these matters, it is sometimes difficult to know just how to use them. For example, there are people with very small running incomes who, nevertheless, own their own homes. There are various sources of hidden income in all strata of the population—most spectacularly so in the higher strata. Thus there is also disagreement as to whether the share in the total national income of the highest strata has changed or not.

11. Again, the relations between income and mobility appear to be similar in Western industrial societies, though the increase in total national income has been highest in America. There is disagreement as to whether income differentials are higher or lower in the Soviet Union. There is general agreement that these differentials are everywhere higher in the less-developed societies than in the industrial ones.

DIFFERENCES IN INTERPRETATION: A "CLASS" OR "STATUS" EMPHASIS

Even if all these propositions are agreed to, quite different interpretations are possible. Specifically, there are strong differences between Marxist and other radical approaches in sociology as against more conventional sociological views. The former will emphasize the discrepancies between the mobility ethos, based as it is on an ideology of equal opportunity, and the facts about mobility

---

[14] Hodges, *op. cit.*

chances. They will also stress the decrease in occupational independence, that is, self-employment, coupled with an alleged closing up of the highest strata. The theoretical differences in the approach to stratification are very important in all of this. If one follows the traditional Marxist line of defining class in terms of the ownership or lack of ownership of the means of production—and in these terms only—then it makes some sense to say that what has been happening is really nothing new, that there continues to be a basic split between a small group of capitalists owning the society and a growing mass of proletarians—no less proletarians because they are now well fed and often engaged in white-collar occupations.[15] Similar views have been expressed with regard to blacks in American society, with the emphasis here on the decreasing ability of the lowest strata in the system to move out of their underprivileged position.[16] As against this, other sociologists less committed to a radical critique of American society have emphasized the upward movement of the entire system in terms of occupational opportunity, education and income, as well as the alleged decrease in the income gaps between different strata in the system.[17] Such a view of the situation becomes more plausible in theoretical perspectives that operate with a more elastic concept of class than the Marxist one, and especially in approaches that emphasize the subtler elements of status as against ranking based on starkly economic criteria only.

HOW DO PEOPLE *FEEL* ABOUT THEIR "CHANCES"?

What seems quite clear in all of this is that the consciousness of what is going on is a decisive factor in the way the situation is perceived. As we have just suggested, this is very much true of sociologists themselves. Different theoretical positions produce a different consciousness of the empirical reality. And, of course, those holding a partic-

[15] See, for example, Gabriel Kolko, *Wealth and Power in the United States* (New York, Praeger, 1963); T. B. Bottomore, *Classes in Modern Society* (New York, Pantheon, 1966).

[16] See Thomas Pettigrew, *A Profile of the Negro American* (Princeton, N.J., Van Nostrand, 1964).

[17] Hodges, *op. cit.*

ular consciousness are prone to believe that those who disagree with them are caught by what the Marxists call "false consciousness." But there is something much broader involved in this than the consciousness of sociologists.

Objective criteria, such as those referring to occupational mobility or income distribution, do not tell us anything about the way people feel about their condition in society. For example, as we have pointed out before, there is general agreement that mobility rates in American society have not greatly changed in recent times. They certainly have not decreased, if one looks at the broad central sectors of the stratification system. Nevertheless, there has taken place a great change in, let us say, "mood" regarding mobility. In the earlier part of this century there still continued, with unbroken vigor, the American ethos of open horizons, of limitless opportunity, including the great myth of the self-made man. A very different "mood" seems to prevail today. We are not in a position here to inquire into the historical causes for this change—except to point out that whatever evidence we have seems to indicate that the change is not to be explained in terms of the objective situation with regard to mobility. Yet the way people feel about society is an important causal factor in what happens afterward. The disillusionment and the lack of faith in the national ideology of movement are in themselves factors of considerable sociological importance that may have far-reaching consequences.

To take another example: we have pointed out that most sociologists agree that mobility rates in the major Western industrial countries have been very much the same. Yet the consciousness of mobility has varied very much. In Germany, for example, there has been a much greater feeling of movement than in France, despite the fact that the actual mobility rates are very similar. Again, we cannot go into the reasons for these differences here (which are cultural and political, rather than rooted in differences in the stratification systems in these two countries), but we would emphasize again that such differences in consciousness become causal factors in the situation in their own right and thus influence what takes place as far as stratification is concerned.

FEELING DEPRIVED: WITH REFERENCE TO WHOM?

Also involved in this dynamic is what sociologists call *relative deprivation:* people will feel deprived, depending upon whom they are comparing themselves with. Take lower-class immigrants from Europe coming to America. Despite the fact that these people may now be located at the bottom of the American class system, they are comparing themselves not with those above them in this society but with the people they have left behind in Europe. This comparison generally puts them in a rather favorable position; in other words, their relative deprivation will then be low. It may be a quite different situation with their children. They are no longer interested in their country of ethnic origin. They may, instead, compare themselves with other Americans who are much better off than they, and their relative deprivation may be very high. Thus there may be a completely different consciousness of the situation despite the fact that (let us assume) the objective conditions of these two generations have remained the same. When people say that they are underprivileged or deprived, it is a good sociological rule of thumb to ask immediately, "With reference to whom?" Sometimes the answer will be in terms of the past, sometimes in terms of strata in the same society, sometimes with other societies and, not infrequently, with utopian conditions that do not exist anywhere in empirical reality. Whatever his theoretical position, the sociologist studying stratification will have to take these elements into account very seriously, or he will arrive at a distorted picture of what is going on.

DISAGREEMENTS AND A CHANGING LANDSCAPE

One final word of caution here: the reader of this and the preceding chapter has undoubtedly noted how much disagreement there is on important questions within the field of sociology. This will be depressing or challenging depending upon one's point of view. (We would suggest that, at the very least, it is in-

164 SOCIOLOGY

teresting.) The reader should also note, however, that one particular difficulty of the sociologist—as of other social scientists—is that he is studying a situation that is changing very rapidly. This, of course, is true of most areas of sociological inquiry, but it is true in a particularly acute way when it comes to stratification. For example, works written on American blacks even five years ago now have about them a certain quality of obsolescence if not incredibility. A number of things happening in American society today (such as the movement within the black community toward separate subsocieties, the widespread "dropping out" of upper-middle-class youth from previously established career patterns and a new ethnic and political self-consciousness in the white working class) may have far-reaching influences on the American stratification system in the not too distant future. One very important virtue that should be cultivated by anyone who engages in sociological thinking is the virtue of having theoretical perspectives that are sufficiently flexible to take cognizance of new developments.

READINGS

Again, we would suggest two tracks for additional reading—one, following up on overall views of stratification in America; and the other, following up on social mobility in America and elsewhere. For the first, two general books on class in America that give an excellent idea of the basic data and problems are Joseph Kahl, *The American Class Structure* (New York, Holt, Rinehart & Winston, 1957) and Harold Hodges, *Social Stratification* (Cambridge, Mass., Schenkman, 1964). Good summaries of materials on the relation of American blacks to the stratification system may be found in Thomas Pettigrew, *A Profile of the Negro American* (Princeton, N.J., Van Nostrand, 1964), also available in paperback, and on the poor in general in Herman Miller, *Rich Man, Poor Man* (New York, Crowell, 1964). A radical view of class in America may be found in Gabriel Kolko, *Wealth and Power in the United States* (New York, Praeger, 1963), also in paperback.

For the second track, a standard work is Seymour Lipset and Reinhard Bendix, *Social Mobility in Industrial Society* (Berkeley, Calif., University of California Press, 1959), also in paperback. A standard reader is Reinhard Bendix and Seymour Lipset (eds.), *Class, Status and Power* (New York, Free Press, 1953). An excellent summary of different approaches to class and mobility in contemporary societies is Ralf Dahrendorf, *Class and Class Conflict in Industrial Society* (Stanford, Calif., Stanford University Press, 1959), also in paperback. For a more left-leaning view, compare T. B. Bottomore, *Classes in Modern Society* (New York, Pantheon, 1966).

Chapter 9

WHAT IS SOCIAL CONTROL? THE CASE OF EDUCATION

SUDDENLY THE DAY HAS COME—the first day of school. Perhaps it has been eagerly anticipated, or perhaps there have been feelings of anxiety connected with it. In either case, for most children this day is experienced as a most significant one, as the crossing of an important threshold. Good-byes are said to members of one's family, at the door of one's house or at the school. And then one is alone, in a new place, with other children, facing a new authority in the figure of the teacher. A new kind of life begins.

BEING "HANDED OVER" TO SCHOOL

For most children in our society, the educational system represents their first experience of being subjected to what sociologists call a *formal organization*. By that is meant, quite simply, an institution whose rules are explicitly laid down and are administered by special personnel. By crossing the threshold from family to school, the child passes not only under a new jurisdiction but under a new kind of jurisdiction. He is, as it were, "handed over" by the family to a quite different kind of agency. Different rules apply, and they apply not only to him but to all others in the same situation. What is more, however benevolent the school may be, the child is now treated as one of many (if you will, "as a number"). And he can no longer count on the unique status he occupies within his own home. In this new situation, for better or for worse, he "must make his own way." By entering school, the child takes his first step into a larger world, which the school both represents and mediates.

BEING HANDLED BY SCHOOL

It should be emphasized that this is a peculiar feature of education in modern society. It is possible to define education very broadly as all forms of socialization that occur after primary socialization has been completed (if one prefers, all forms of secondary socialization). In that case, of course, education is a well-nigh universal phenomenon. What is peculiar about education in our society, however, is that it is in fact administered by formal organizations that have no other purpose except education. Education, in other words, is separately institutionalized, and by the same token is segregated from other spheres of social life. Specifically, education is segregated from the family which, in earlier times, carried out many of the activities that now fall under the jurisdiction of the formal educational system. Thus the crossing of a threshold that we have just described is not a universal human experience but one that is peculiar to modern society. In the latter, however, it is a crucially important experience. For many years, ranging from childhood through youth into early adulthood, the educational system is the most important large institution with which the individual must deal. But even after he is formally released from its jurisdiction (at whatever stage of the educational ladder he finally attains), this does not mean that he is finished with education as such. In one way or another, educational organization and educational activities will pursue him into adult life.

Indeed, education is one of the most pervasive institutions in contemporary society. In many occupations advancement and success are dependent upon continuing education (even more, the higher the individual climbs on the occupational ladder), and frequently upon recurring periods of time in schools of one sort or another. But even the formal educational system has a strong tendency to expand in terms of duration. In modern society, people go to school for longer and longer periods. Ever longer periods of educational preparation are required for every variety of job in the society. What is more, particularly in recent years, the formal educational system has reached earlier and earlier into the individual's biography through kindergarten, nursery schools, play groups, head-start programs and the like. Educational activities of all sorts now constitute a major sector of the occupational system and consume a very large portion of the gross national product, to the extent that one prominent economist has aptly spoken of the "knowledge industry." [1]

In view of the prominence of education in our society, it is not

[1] Fritz Machlup, *The Production and Distribution of Knowledge in the United States* (Princeton, N.J., Princeton University Press, 1962).

surprising that an increasing number of sociologists have concerned themselves with it. Indeed, there now has developed a special field known as the sociology of education. A broad range of problems have been investigated under this rubric, problems ranging from the classroom as a social situation to the broad questions of the relationship of education to society at large (notably, to the mechanics of social mobility as discussed in the previous chapter).

GOING TO SCHOOL: THE EDUCATOR'S VIEWPOINT

How is passage through the educational system experienced by the individual? There is an ideology of education, with deep roots in the history of Western civilization, that says what this experience *should* be. Education is supposed to transmit skills and bodies of knowledge which the individual will need to be successful in the world. It is also (and, in the classical tradition of Western education, more importantly) supposed to shape character and expand the mind, quite apart from the criteria of success in a particular society. While there are clear tensions between the utilitarian ("education for life") and non-utilitarian ("education for its own sake") elements of educational ideology, both have at least been paid considerable lip service in the American educational system. Undoubtedly, these ideological purposes are frequently realized, and many individuals actually experience at least segments of their passage through the educational system in these terms. It is also clear that the years spent in school contain a variety of experiences, sometimes associated with but not directly programmed by the educational system as such, that are "educational" for the individual in one or both of the above-mentioned senses—experiences of learning through social relations with others (teachers as well as peers), through books, art or sports. It is important to keep all this in mind, especially since the sociological analysis of education has mainly emphasized quite different aspects of this experience.

THE STUDENT'S
VIEWPOINT:
BEING PRESSURED

Yet, a central aspect of the experience is that the individual undergoes *pressure,* and not only pressure but *systematic* pressure. To some extent, this is already implied as soon as

one speaks of education as an institution, which is how sociologists have viewed it as soon as they began to be interested in it.[2] To say, however, that education is an institution is not enough. One must ask further what kind of institution it is and how it relates to other institutions in the society.

One important thing to see is that education is today a *universal* institution—whatever may be its unique importance or characteristics in American society, it has become an institution of paramount importance all over the world.[3] One sharp critic of contemporary education, Ivan Illich (whose main concern has been the relation of education and "development" in Latin America), has even called the school the new "universal church." [4] North American suburbanites and Mexican *campesinos,* capitalist corporation executives and socialist revolutionaries, people of just about every imaginable ideological hue, all seem to share a common faith in education as one of the greatest goods and in the school as its organizational vehicle. Churches represent a religion, and Illich has made a good argument for saying that the school represents much more today than the process of education by itself. Rather, it represents some very deep aspirations of modern man for a better life. If the school can be seen as a kind of church, then its religion is that of progress— for each individual, for entire societies and (in its most universal expression) for mankind as a whole.

[2] On the sociology of education generally, see Ronald Corwin, *A Sociology of Education* (New York, Appleton-Century-Crofts, 1965); Robert Havighurst and Bernice Neugarten, *Society and Education* (Boston, Allyn & Bacon, 1967); Donald Hansen and Joel Gerstl (eds.), *On Education—Sociological Perspectives* (New York, Wiley, 1967).

[3] See Robert Havighurst (ed.), *Comparative Perspectives on Education* (Boston, Little, Brown, 1968).

[4] Ivan Illich's papers on education have recently been published, *The Schooling Society* (New York, Harper & Row, 1971).

None of this negates what was just said about the experience of pressure. Churches, indeed, have been magnificent producers of pressure throughout human history, and religions of universal benevolence have often been experienced by people as intolerable oppression in actual social life. Contemporary education and contemporary schools prove to be no exception to this.

THE STUDENT'S VIEWPOINT: RESPONDING TO PRESSURE

Different individuals respond differently to this pressure. Some of these differences can probably be accounted for in terms of the psychological and perhaps even physiological makeup of individuals. Others must be explained sociologically. As we have seen earlier, the location of an individual in the stratification scheme of the society is a crucial sociological factor with regard to his relation to the educational system. More than any other single factor, this location influences whether the individual starts out with favorable or unfavorable prospects on his journey through the system.

If we look at the white middle-class child in America, we can see clearly that he will begin his educational career under very favorable auspices. Chances are that the attitudes and habits he has learned before ever entering school are conducive to success in school. Chances are that he will receive all manner of support (financial as well as psychological) from his family at every stage of his passage through the educational system. It is also likely that his teachers will respond to him with sympathy and understanding, even when he does not measure up to the highest expectations. Last but certainly not least, the sector of the educational system that he will traverse is likely to be relatively well financed, well equipped and well staffed. Even if we focus on this favored population, however, we perceive a network of pressures that falls very hard on many, eliminates quite a few from the higher reaches of the educational ladder, and strongly influences everyone.

AM I *BAD* IF I FLUNK?

First of all, there is the pressure of the ideology of the "universal church" as such. "Progress" is not just something that all are supposed to believe in; they are all supposed to *contribute* to it. In other words, the "religion" is not one of passive contemplation but of very active effort. What this means in practice is that the individual is supposed to achieve, *to want to achieve*. Inevitably, this means achievement *in the terms set by the educational system*. Conversely, failure to achieve is interpreted as a moral deficiency. Assuming that the individual has been "properly" socialized, such failure will induce *guilt*. This ideological constellation contains an interesting contradiction: supposedly, success in the educational system is based, at least to a large extent, on intelligence. Failure is then, simultaneously, attributed to lack of intelligence (for which, one might assume, the individual can hardly be held responsible) *and* given a stamp of moral disapproval. Faiths, alas, are rarely exercises in logic. Since the educational system contains an endless series of hurdles, it is impossible that all should succeed in it; it is predetermined that some (indeed, many) should fail to reach the top. The individual who fails is thus simultaneously beset with the notion that he is stupid *and* with guilt for the consequences of his alleged stupidity. Added to this, of course, is the knowledge of the realistic consequences of such failure in terms of diminished life chances in all areas ranging from income to the choice of a marriage partner. The fundamental pressure exerted by the educational system upon the individual is precisely the fear of this failure, along with the multiple anxieties that reflect this underlying fear in the day-to-day experience of education.

Faith in progress has played an important part in American society generally; faith in education has been an essential ingredient of this larger faith. The virtues enjoined by the latter have been, among others, individual ambition and competitiveness. The American educational system is based on these virtues and in turn fosters them, beginning with nursery school and going on through college. The games that American children play are very largely competitive, indeed are training devices for competition. Essential to this is the win/lose formula. In every game, in the end, somebody wins and somebody loses; the aim, of course, is to be a winner. It is only very young children who sometimes wish, wistfully, that "everyone should win"; they soon learn that this is "impossible"—in American society, that is, for there are other societies in which children actually play games in which "everyone wins."

The educational system not only fosters competition but (except in some sports) *individual* competition. Each individual competes with all the others. The academic sin of "cheating" brings this feature out very clearly. To give help to a weaker peer in an examination is defined and morally reproved as "cheating" in American education; in another society (and, indeed, sometimes in the sub-society of the peer group even in America) the same act may be defined as an expression of "friendship," and morally approved or even required as such. A further refinement of this particular definition of the situation is the so-called "honor system," still operating in many schools and colleges. Here, the individual is not only not supposed to "cheat" but to keep an eye on all the others to make sure that *they* don't—and to report them to the proper authorities in case they do. All of this expresses a morality both competitive and individualistic, and by the same token discouraging of such solidarity between individuals that would impede successful achievement in the system by each one of them.

PACKAGED
KNOWLEDGE ON
MY RECORD

The educational ideology does not just exist as moral rhetoric. It is tightly organized in bureaucratic processes to which the individual is subjected.[5] The entire educational career of the individual is structured in these terms: knowledge is "packaged" in courses, each a unit (numbered, to boot) added to other units, the sum total of which represents the specific educational goal (graduation from this or that curriculum, attainment of

[5] See the chapter aptly entitled "Bureaucratization of the Talent Hunt," in Corwin, *op. cit.*, pp. 191ff.

this or that degree) that the individual is supposed to achieve. The credit system represents this quantitative and cumulative conception of learning. Thus a sociology course is supposed to "cover" a certain quantity of knowledge; course #202 follows course #201, and taking both presumably means that one is learning "more" sociology; and if one has taken, say, ten courses at three credits each, one is officially defined as having absorbed enough of the stuff to graduate as a sociology major. If, that is, one has achieved the right grades. Grades and grade averages measure the pilgrim's progress through the educational system. They are the recording angel's verdict as to salvation or damnation—only *this* recording angel is a bureaucrat with a full-time job and the day of judgment comes, at the least, at the conclusion of every academic term. What is more, a judgment once made is hard to eradicate. It is entered on all the forms, cross-indexed and maybe even computerized, sent out in transcripts and handed over to heaven knows what data banks, and it follows the individual from educational stage to educational stage like an ancient malediction. Not so invisibly carrying this ever-thickening "record" on his back, the child becomes an adult as, over long years, he progresses through the labyrinth of examinations, certifications and diplomas.

WHO ARE THE WINNERS?

The avowed purpose of all this is to ensure competent performance of various socially necessary tasks, and conversely to bar those who are deemed incompetent from these tasks. Even if one is very critical of the educational system, one will have to admit that, in a rough way, it does some of this. Its criteria of "competence" and "incompetence," however, are debatable. It is fairly certain that, by its very nature, the system weeds out many who, under different circumstances, could become "competent." An important reason for this has to do with personality. The system rewards a certain personality type, one that is introvert, conformist and compulsive—in short, a bureaucratic type. Conversely, it comes down hard on a different type that resists or finds it hard to adapt to its processes—the extrovert, non-conformist, non-compulsive and bureaucratically inconvenient type.[6] This bias often correlates with, but is not at all identical with, the previously mentioned class bias.

WHAT IF I NEED "HELP"?

The educational system is humanitarian in its ideology. Its pressures are benign. Consequently, the system has all sorts of provisions for the individual who falters and needs "help." American education, at all stages, is covered with a network of counseling and therapeutic agencies. There can be no doubt that these very often "help" the individual—optimally, by getting him to succeed in the system after all; minimally, by softening the shock of failure. But this network is itself part and parcel of the educational pressure machinery. Its ideology, most of the time, is identical with that of the whole system. Its battery of "objective" tests and measuring devices furnishes an additional mechanism for "placing," channeling and weeding out individuals.[7]

AM I EFFICIENT? ARE WE EFFICIENT? WHY?

The educational system exists within a society that is highly technological and has corresponding personnel needs. American society, originally because of the capitalist creed of competitive ambition and then, added to this, because of the necessities of modern technology, is strongly imbued with an ethos of "efficiency." This ethos has had an immense impact on the educational system.[8] The system is to be maximally efficient in the production of efficient people, and this is supposed to guarantee the efficiency of the society as a whole. In 1956, when the Russians

[6] For data on this, see R. Lynn, "Two Personality Characteristics Related to Academic Achievement," *British Journal of Educational Psychology* (1959) : 29.

[7] See Aaron Cicourel and John Kitsuse, *The Educational Decision Makers* (New York, Bobbs-Merrill, 1963).

[8] See Raymond Callahan, *Education and the Cult of Efficiency* (Chicago, University of Chicago Press, 1962). On the relation of this to the requirements of contemporary business organizations, see William Whyte, *The Organization Man* (New York, Simon & Schuster, 1956), especially Chapter 8.

launched their first earth satellite, the faith in the efficiency of American education suffered a severe shock. Critics of the schools shot out of the ground like mushrooms after a big rain, and the call for "quality education" became a national outcry.[9] One result of this was a vast infusion of public funds into education, something that had begun to happen earlier but that reached huge proportions in the 1950's. Among other consequences, this led to very large salary increases for teachers at all levels. At the level of colleges and universities it led to an academic entrepreneurship that Robert Nisbet, in a recent sociological study of academia, has called "the higher capitalism." [10] The 1960's saw a widespread revolt against all this, first among some intellectual critics (such as Paul Goodman, who said that the educational system condemned youth to an existence of absurdity), then in the student movement that exploded onto the academic scene with the Berkeley revolt of 1964.[11] We shall return to this once more in the chapter on youth.

The same overall educational system faces the non-white, non-middle-class child, but with much more devastating effects. This confrontation has been most fully documented for the experience of black children in the inner city.[12]

For reasons already touched upon in our discussion of racial stratification in America, the black child begins his educational career with an unfavorable starting position. By and large, the educational system not only fails to make up for this but adds to his handicap through the external conditions in which it deals with

[9] See the book by Admiral H. G. Rickover, *Education and Freedom* (New York, Dutton, 1960), significantly described on the cover of its paperback edition as "a vigorous demand for higher standards in American education, *the foundation of our national security*" (italics ours).

[10] Robert Nisbet, *The Degradation of the Academic Dogma* (New York, Basic Books, 1971), pp. 71ff.

[11] Paul Goodman, *Growing Up Absurd* (New York, Random House, 1960). For a good overview of various critiques of contemporary American education, see Ronald and Beatrice Gross (eds.), *Radical School Reform* (New York, Simon & Schuster, 1969).

[12] For a general discussion of the problems of urban schools, see Harry Miller and Roger Woock, *Social Foundations of Urban Education* (Hinsdale, Ill., Dryden, 1970). For an influential and radical critique of schooling for black children in the inner city, see Jonathan Kozol, *Death at an Early Age* (Boston, Houghton Mifflin, 1967).

him. Among these are dilapidated buildings, inferior equipment, poorly prepared and frequently resentful teachers. "Success" in the terms set by the educational system thus not only is hard to achieve by the black child but frequently fails to impress him as a desirable goal to strive for. What is more, he early develops an awareness of the realities of racial discrimination in the society, and is then led to doubt whether educational "success" will necessarily lead to the "success" in the larger society that the educational ideology promises. As a result of all this, large numbers of black children and young adults experience education not only as a system of pressures but as an alien force in their lives—as meaningless, or even as a cruel oppression. The demands for "community control" over schools educating black children in the inner city are, at least in part, a reaction to this situation.[13]

THE STUDENT'S VIEWPOINT: BEING CONTROLLED

The preceding pages will have given some idea of the problems dealt with by the sociology of education (though we have overemphasized the aspects that are critical of the educational status quo.) Here, we are interested in staying close to the experience of the child with which we opened this chapter and in asking what this experience means in broader sociological terms. The experience is, above all, one of *social control*. And it is as a basic agency of social control that we would look at education. In this, our interest in education is not so much as a formal organization in its own right but as the most important case of social control first encountered in the individual's life and as a pervasive system of social control extending through a great part of his lifetime.

What is social control? The term was coined by an early American sociologist, Edward Ross, in a book of that title.[14] The term

[13] See, for examples, the articles by Kenneth Clark and Preston Wilcox in Gross and Gross, *op. cit.*, pp. 116ff.

[14] Edward Ross, *Social Control* (Cleveland, Press of Case Western Reserve University, 1969). The book was originally published in 1901.

has now become part of general sociological usage, quite independent of Ross's original use. By social control is meant any social mechanism by which individuals are compelled to abide by the rules of society or of a particular segment of society. In other words, social control is the means by which society keeps people "in line." If the reader will recall our earlier discussion of institutions, he will recognize that social control is an intrinsic element of *any* institution. Thus even language can be said to exercise social control. The term, however, is usually restricted to those institutional processes that have explicit and specific sanctions connected with them. That is, we speak of processes or agencies of social control when the individual faces specific penalties for specific offenses. In this sense, a further distinction is made between *external and internal controls*. External controls threaten the individual with punishments in his social life. Such punishments may range, in the extreme case, from the threat of death or physical mutilation, through milder penalties such as economic sanctions, to the subtle controls of social disapproval, gossip or ostracism. Internal controls are those in which the individual is not threatened from without but from within his own consciousness. Internal controls are, of course, dependent upon successful socialization. If the latter pertains, then the individual—if he commits certain transgressions against the rules of society—will be sanctioned by his own conscience which is, in effect, the internalization of social controls. Both of these aspects of social control are highly relevant to education.

THE STUDENT'S VIEWPOINT: LEARNING DISCIPLINE
Of the great classical sociologists, only Émile Durkheim devoted a substantial part of his work to education. In one of his major works on the subject (appropriately entitled *Moral Education*), one of the first chapters is headed "The First Element of Morality: The Spirit of Discipline." [15] This must be understood in terms of Durkheim's

---

[15] Émile Durkheim, *L'Education morale* (Paris, Presses Universitaires de France, 1963). To date, this work is not available in English.

overall view of society as a moral order. The fundamental function of education, then, for Durkheim was the transmission of morality —but this could only be done by infusing children with the kind of discipline that would inwardly predispose them toward morality even if no external sanctions were imposed. In other words, education fosters morality by instilling a conscience in the individual which, in turn, will discipline him in accordance with the moral rules of society. Durkheim, it must be added, thought that this was a fine thing. One may or may not agree with this evaluation, but Durkheim was certainly correct in seeing society as being, at its very root, a moral order, and education as the internalization of moral discipline in every new generation.

At this point it will be useful to introduce two other concepts which were developed by the American sociologist, Robert Merton. These are the concepts of *manifest and latent functions*.[16] A function here is understood as any social process that keeps society together. Manifest functions are those that are deliberate and intended; latent functions, those that are unconscious and unintended. Thus, for example, the manifest function of a student coming to a sociology class is to learn sociology; the latent function of the same activity may be to get closer to a certain girl who is also attending this class.

THE MANIFEST FUNCTIONS

The manifest functions of education can be enumerated quite readily. Education, in the view of some, is concerned with the transmission of knowledge for its own sake. In the view of others, it is concerned with the transmission of knowledge that will have practical use for life. In either case, the functions of education are viewed as relating to individuals by themselves and their individual careers in life. Furthermore, education is supposed to transmit values or, as many parents put it when asked what they expect of the schools which their children attend, to teach children the difference between right and wrong. Finally, ed-

[16] Robert Merton, *Social Theory and Social Structure* (New York, Free Press, 1957), pp. 19ff.

ucation is supposed to form character, to develop certain socially desirable types of human beings.

Already when looking at these manifest functions of education, the control aspects of this institution become fairly obvious. For example, human knowledge is, in principle, nearly infinite, yet it is *particular* knowledge that is actually transmitted by the educational system—which means that other types of knowledge are *not* transmitted. A guidance counselor, let us say, when talking to a high school student about his future, will inform him of any number of educational possibilities but will hardly mention bank robber or prostitute as possibilities. In an only slightly subtler way, the teaching of the nation's history, for example, will accentuate those elements of the past that are conducive to upholding nationally recognized values and ideals. Similarly, the values and personality traits fostered by the educational system are those that are established as legitimate by a society, and, by the same token, values and traits that are not so established will be either ignored or explicitly condemned. Whatever else these manifest functions of education may be, most of them can quite easily be subsumed under the category "the spirit of discipline" in Durkheim's sense. However, the social-control aspects of education become even clearer when we look beneath the surface, namely, when we look at the latent functions of education.

THE LATENT FUNCTIONS: BEING "PLACED"

Most broadly, the function of education is *placement* (a term used extensively, and quite appropriately, by educators themselves). This has a double meaning. It means, as a manifest function, to place a child "correctly," that is, to evaluate his status in terms of some recognized criteria, and thus to put him in a career program that seems appropriate to this evaluation. Secondly, it also means—subtly and as a latent function—to teach a child what "his place" is, that is, to make him accept the criteria of evaluation as just and therefore to legitimate the career that follows logically from this evaluation. Thus, for example, the educational system will evaluate a particular child as being "slow." It will place him accordingly within its several "streams"—in a vocational rather than an academic high school perhaps. Needless to say, this placement will have far-reaching consequences for the child's future. At the same time, however, precisely by inculcating its own morality in the child, the educational system will seek to have the child accept this placement as just and to motivate him to operate within the channels which the system has provided for him. What we have here is a very effective combination of external and internal controls.

IS THERE EQUALITY OF OPPORTUNITY?

We have previously referred to the fact that in America the educational system is supposed to provide equality of education for all children. It is very important to understand that the control function of education will be present regardless of whether the educational system lives up or does not live up to these egalitarian ideals. Most of the sociological criticisms of education have dealt with situations in which the egalitarian ideals are violated. We have already referred in the preceding chapter to the findings on the relationship of education to social mobility. The basic question in this area has been aptly summed up in the title of an influential book on the sociology of education published in the 1940's—*Who Shall Be Educated?* [17] As we have seen, the data show quite conclusively that the schools systematically discriminate against children from the lower strata of the class system, and particularly so if these children come from non-white minority groups. Manifestly, then, education serves as a vehicle of mobility, but latently it also serves as an agency that controls mobility. Critics of the educational system have been particularly concerned with this discrimination and have urged that the educational system live up to its professed egalitarian creed. Very vocal in this in recent years have been spokesmen for the black community, as well as white

[17] Lloyd Warner, Robert Havighurst and Martin Loeb, *Who Shall Be Educated?* (New York, Harper, 1944).

radical critics. They have, of course, been quite right in pointing to the great lapses from the egalitarian goals that the educational system in America is supposed to serve. The relationship of education and social control is more complex, however, and (alas) more intrinsic than even a complete vindication of these critics would allow.

Hans Gerth and C. Wright Mills, in their book on social psychology, have emphasized that social institutions both select and form persons.[18] *Person selection* refers to the process by which individuals are chosen from the available manpower supply for specific tasks that the society requires. *Person formation* refers to the process by which society insures that the manpower for these needed tasks will remain in supply. These processes, in one way or another, take place in all human societies. In our society, though, it is primarily the educational system which administers them. If this is understood, it should be clear that the control aspects of education will remain important even if (and perhaps especially if) its egalitarian ideals are more fully realized.

It is possible here to engage in a rather chilling exercise of the imagination. One may then imagine a situation in which there is total equality of educational opportunity. In other words, by whatever means, a situation has been brought about in which there is no discrimination whatever on the ground of factors in the child's social background such as class, racial, ethnic or what have you. In that case, the placement of the child will be guided by no other criteria than the child's capacities as measured by the staff of the educational institutions. This will enable placement to proceed much more smoothly in both of the aspects mentioned before. Every child will be put in "his place" by the most scientific—and therefore most just—criteria imaginable. What is more, though, the child will be *taught* "his place" in a much more conclusive manner, because it would then become much more difficult to complain of injustices. Put more simply: there will be no more excuses. If we pursue this fantasy to its logical conclusion, we arrive at a totalitarian world in which every individual gets exactly what he deserves and

[18] Hans Gerth and C. Wright Mills, *Character and Social Structure* (New York, Harcourt Brace, 1953), pp. 165ff.

is even deprived of the subjective comfort that he really deserves more than what he got. This is not the place to speculate on possibilities of educational reform that would preserve us from *both* the present discriminations *and* such future vistas of totalitarian nightmare. We only wanted to make the point that the removal of inequalities of educational opportunity would not, in and of themselves, end the relationship of education and social control.

THE STUDENT'S VIEWPOINT: *WHAT CAN I DO?*

With his entry into school, then, the individual starts out on a lifelong relation to formal control networks. Indeed, one of the most important things an individual learns in school is how to cope with this fact. (One could say that a latent function of schooling is to teach the individual a kind of rudimentary and practical sociology.) Given the network of social controls, what can the individual do about this? There are four broad reactions that are possible: straight conformity, tongue-in-cheek conformity, withdrawal and rebellion.[19]

The straight conformist is the individual who has learned his place, has accepted it and acts accordingly. In terms of the latent functions of the educational system, this individual is, of course, a very successful type—or, rather, the educational system has brilliantly succeeded with him. Outwardly, he may be undistinguishable from the tongue-in-cheek conformist. The latter has also learned his place, but he only pretends to accept it and to act according to the rules of the game. He is engaged in what Erving Goffman has called "working the system." Another possibility is to withdraw from the entire "rat race." This may be involuntary withdrawal, as in the case of many rejects of the educational system who, quite simply, give up. On the other hand, it may be a deliberate withdrawal, usually coupled with a commitment to values and life goals that are at variance with those propagated by the educational system. Finally, there is the possibility of rebellion, that is, of

[19] These are a slight modification of a typology developed by Robert Merton. See *op. cit.*, pp. 140ff.

the deliberate attempt to basically change the system in accordance with allegedly better values. These possible reactions, of course, refer to society and its controls in general and are by no means limited to the way in which individuals react to the educational institutions. We can see them, though, quite clearly at work within the educational system itself. Indeed, for many individuals in our society, these basic reaction patterns are formed quite early in their school careers and often persist from that point on throughout their adult life.

Thus the threshold experience of the first day in school is anything but an illusion. It is—if we may put it this way—a quite valid sociological insight. If this has not happened to him before, the child will from now on be obliged "to take society seriously." His life, in increasing measure, becomes "serious." He must learn to cope with this. Chances are that the means of coping he develops while in school will greatly influence, if not determine, his later career in society and his relation to other institutions and systems of social control.

READINGS

The reader who wants to penetrate further into the specialized field of the sociology of education might start with the books mentioned in footnote 2 on page 170. Or the occasion might be used to read one of the most poisonous pieces of writing in the history of American sociology—Thorstein Veblen's *The Higher Learning in America*. Originally published in 1918, it is available in a paperback edition published in 1957 by the Sagamore Press. Though it is very much dated, in addition to being distorted by Veblen's passionate revulsion against educational administrators, it makes the key point of this chapter in a particularly devastating manner.

Chapter 10

BUREAUCRACY

THE EXPERIENCE OF *BEING* *PROCESSED*

As we pointed out in the preceding chapter, for most individuals in our society the experience with bureaucracy begins as they come into contact with the educational system. It certainly does not end there. As the individual grows into adulthood, he is compelled to have contact with an ever-widening circle of bureaucratic institutions—government, private economic enterprises and even cultural organizations. The underlying experience which is common to all these different types of bureaucracy can be described as the experience of *being processed*. It should be emphasized that this does not necessarily mean an experience of being subjected to malign forces that oppress one. It does mean, however, that the individual is dealt with by largely anonymous functionaries in terms of highly regulated and impersonal procedures. For better or for worse, it means that the individual is "treated as a number."

Indeed, the ever-widening relation to bureaucratic organizations can be measured by the different numbers that an individual is assigned. In terms of government, for example, this means the assignment of a Social Security number and a Selective Service registration number (to mention two that usually are experienced as respectively benign and malignant). As the individual grows older, there is likely to be added to this number a variety of licenses, diplomas and authorizations of various kinds, ranging from the number of his driver's license to the sometimes astronomical reference numbers which government agencies will ask him to refer to in answer to their communications. The individual's relation to the economic institutions of society will again enmesh him in a tangle of bureaucratic agencies that assign him numbers of all kinds, from his utilities bills to whatever credit cards or bank accounts he may hold. But even his church, or the bird-watching society to which he belongs, may assign him a number and refuse to have any dealings with him unless he identifies himself in terms of this number. In all these cases it is increasingly probable that the communications that go back and forth between the individual and the various bureaucratic headquarters are handled by computerized procedures.

Computerized or not, every one of these bureaucratic organizations will be perceived by the individual as some sort of gigantic office in which there are masses of files. In the midst of all these files, somewhere and somehow, there is one that deals with his own "case." In all likelihood he will never meet the individuals who handle his case, but will either deal with their remote representatives or be limited to written communication with them. It is important to stress that the same principle of anonymity applies to all these various types of bureaucracy, to the church no less than the government and the utility company. We would maintain that this perception of anonymity on the part of the individual being processed is sociologically correct, and it points to an important sociological insight, namely, that there is a fundamental similarity to bureaucratic processes regardless of the institutional context in which they operate. To put the same thing in slightly different words: bureaucracy establishes its fundamental dynamic on whatever social context it operates in. Essentially similar procedures are employed, similar relations obtain between the persons involved, a similar ethos pervades the different bureaucratic structures.

The term "formal organization," which we employed in the preceding chapter, is not synonymous with bureaucracy. There may be formal organizations, as previously defined, that are not bureaucratic in character. The army of Genghis Khan, say, had a distinctive staff organization and probably more or less fixed rules of procedure, thus qualifying for the designation formal organization but certainly not for that of bureaucracy. When one is talking about contemporary society (and that, incidentally, definitely includes contemporary armies), the two terms are, in fact, overlapping. The reason for this is simple: most formal organizations in modern society are bureaucratic in character. This observation by itself would be enough to indicate the very great importance of the phenomenon of bureaucracy today.

BASIC CHARAC-
TERISTICS: A
STAFF

Bureaucracy is a phenomenon that is very difficult to contain in a brief definition. Rather than attempt such a definition, most sociologists have instead tried to describe the various elements that seem to be intrinsic parts of the phenomenon of bureaucracy. The classical description of bureaucracy is that undertaken by Max Weber, and most subsequent sociologists have (sometimes with some reservations) accepted his description as supplying the basic social characteristics that will have to be taken into account.[1]

First of all, bureaucracy is characterized by a separate organization with a full-time staff (in this basic characteristic it may be said to be similar to other forms of formal organization). What is more, this separate organization is segregated from the private life and activities of its staff members. We may take here a rather venerable illustration for this characteristic. A recurring figure in the New Testament is the "publican." This term refers to the people who collected taxes for the Roman government in Palestine in the days of Jesus. In addition to their tax-collecting activity, they usually carried on any number of other occupations, such as being tavern-keepers, small shopowners or craftsmen. Typically, they carried on all these activities in one place, which was also the place in which they lived with their families. The United States Internal Revenue Service furnishes a convenient contrast. Here, the organization is distinct from every other type of activity and is concerned with nothing else but tax collecting. Its employees are occupied in this activity in full-time jobs and, needless to say, they neither carry on this activity in their homes nor do they bring their children to play in the office. To what extent this bureaucratic structure prevents the corrupt practices that made the "publicans" so odious in the eyes of their fellow countrymen in first-century Palestine need not concern us here. Whatever his opportunities for graft and extortion,

---

[1] Hans Gerth and C. Wright Mills (eds.), *From Max Weber* (New York, Oxford University Press, 1958), pp. 196ff.

the modern bureaucratic tax collector operates in a vastly different milieu from that of his ancient cousin.

BASIC CHARAC-TERISTICS: FIXED AREAS OF JURISDICTION

Bureaucracies arrange their work into fixed areas of jurisdiction which are ordered by specific regulations. Thus, for example, both the Internal Revenue Service and the Department of Immigration are bureaucracies of the Federal Government. Yet they deal with quite distinct sets of problems. It would be futile to go to the Internal Revenue Service in order to obtain a visa for a foreign relative, just as the Department of Immigration would refuse to accept one's income tax declaration. In either case, the bureaucrat to whom one would address such a misbegotten request would reply, with varying degrees of courtesy, that he is "not competent" for this particular problem. This is a sociologically far-reaching statement. The notion of "competence" is one of the fundamental characteristics of any bureaucracy. It means that each bureaucratic agency and each bureaucrat within it works on a particular area and no other. The advantage of this kind of setup is essentially the same as that of an assembly line. It insures, at least in principle, orderliness and speed in the work process. What is more, each unit in the process, and the relationship between each unit, is governed by explicit and highly specific procedures. This means that any bureaucrat challenged as to his precise competence (or, for that matter, incompetence) can normally appeal to one of these regulations (say, I.R.S. directive No. 5423–W–5b of July 12, 1970) which, supposedly, will then legitimate his action or inaction on the matter at hand.

BASIC CHARAC-
TERISTICS: A
HIERARCHY

Bureaucracy, in order to accomplish this kind of operation, is organized in orderly and stable hierarchies— say, from a national headquarters through various regional headquarters to a local office, which, again, has its own mini-hierarchy covering each member of the staff. Connected with the principle of hierarchy is a supervision system. Each bureaucrat, from top to bottom, is responsible to a specific other bureaucrat who supervises his work with more or less diligence. Again, the relations between these various hierarchical agencies, as well as the obligations and rights of all the staff members, are governed by highly specific regulations. Ideally, each bureaucrat knows exactly what is required of him and what, in turn, he may expect from the organization by way of rewards. Built into such a bureaucratic hierarchy are the notions of accountability and appeal. Each bureaucrat is accountable to another bureaucrat (occasionally to an outside agency) in case anyone complains about his performance. Conversely, the bureaucracy's clients can usually have recourse to some specified appeals procedure if *they* have any complaints. In principle, the regulations governing the conduct of the bureaucracy cover all conceivable problems that might arise in this way. If it is found that they do not do this, then they will have to be expanded accordingly in order to do so. In other words, there is a built-in principle of expansion in any body of bureaucratic regulations.

The means of communication between different offices and individuals in a bureaucracy are fundamentally impersonal and do not take place in face-to-face situations. Traditionally, bureaucracies have depended upon written communication. This has been somewhat modified in recent times with the advent of the telephone and electronic methods of communication. The impersonality and indirectness of the communication process, however, have not thereby changed. The mass of communications that flow from one office to another must somehow be stored. The file, for this reason, is one of the fundamental elements of bureaucratic equipment (and the perforated I.B.M. card is simply a technological improvement of the same tool).

BASIC CHARAC-TERISTICS: A RATIONAL SYSTEM OF EXPERTISE

A bureaucracy assumes that each staff member is trained in a rational manner for his particular position in the scheme. In other words, bureaucracy presupposes a rational system of expertise. Consequently, careers in a bureaucracy are supposed to depend upon expert training of this sort and a rational system by which individuals are evaluated as to their expertise. Civil Service examinations in this country are a typical case in point. Ideally, advancement within the bureaucracy depends on nothing except the successful ascent on such a career ladder—although, obviously, this principle is often sinned against. Different types of expertise will, of course, be required in different types of bureaucracy. In all bureaucracies, however, an essential element of expertise is the knowledge of the office procedures that are used. In other words, whatever areas of social life a bureaucracy may administer, it also produces its own body of knowledge, which is only indirectly connected with problems of social life outside the bureaucracy. For example, a staff member of the Department of Agriculture, depending upon his position, may have to have expert knowledge about various kinds of crops. But equally important is his knowledge of office procedures between the particular place he occupies in this bureaucracy and, say, the Washington headquarters. Each bureaucracy thus develops what Weber called "secrets of the office." Usually, these secrets have nothing or little to do with the outside world and thus are impenetrable to the outside observer, such as the client or an elected politician trying to penetrate the inner workings of the agency. Because of this, bureaucracies have a high degree of durability and a capacity to resist outside pressures. Governmental bureaucracies, for example, have an amazing capacity to frustrate the policies of democratically elected politicians who, supposedly, are in charge of such bureaucracies. A new party is voted into office and one of its politicians takes over, say, Agriculture on the Cabinet level. He may want to push a particular agricultural policy that his party is committed to. In theory, of course, his bureaucratic subordinates are supposed to assist him in this. In practice, if they really want to oppose the policy, they can sabotage him at each stage by entangling his program in a maze of bureaucratic procedures. *They* know all the procedures; he knows only his policy goals. At the very least, they can make life difficult for him.

BASIC CHARACTERISTICS: AN ETHOS OF "OBJECTIVITY"

Finally, a bureaucracy cultivates a particular kind of ethos. It is an ethos of "objectivity." Ideally, for better or for worse, each "case" that comes before a bureaucrat is supposed to be handled according to the applicable procedures regardless of the bureaucrat's personal feelings or relation to the matter. Again, of course, this is a principle that is often sinned against. Yet, compared to non-bureaucratic forms of organization, it is realized to a very high degree. Cases of "personal influence" are, in greater or smaller measure, exceptions in modern bureaucratic administration, while they are the rule in most pre-modern forms of non-bureaucratic administration. The main fruit of this is what Weber called "calculability." This means that the workings of the bureaucracy are, as far as possible, protected against the personal emotions and whims of those who administer its policies. As a result, the performance of a bureaucracy is highly predictable. Once one knows the regulations and procedures that apply in a particular matter, it is possible to calculate, in a reasonable way, how the bureaucracy is going to deal with the matter and, therefore, what one's own chances are as to the outcome. Bureaucracy thus introduces an important element of stability into society. It is very difficult to see how a complex technological society could survive without this. By the same token, it is very difficult to conceive of such a society without bureaucratic forms of administration—at least of its principal political and economic institutions. It may be added that this remains true regardless of whether a modern economy is capitalist or socialist, and regardless of whether a modern state is based on democratic or non-democratic political processes.

WEBER'S THEORY OF RATIONALIZA-TION

In this way, the sociological notion of bureaucracy has led to a general conception of *bureaucratization*. This term simply signifies that in modern societies bureaucratic forms of administration proliferate in every major institutional area. Weber himself related this to his overall theory of *rationalization*, by which is meant the proliferation of rational procedures in society (by rational, in turn, is meant a logical connection between means and ends of social action, both in the minds of the actor and of the scientific observer). Bureaucracy, whatever its faults and imperfections, is the most rational form of social organization. Such rationality becomes a necessary requirement for societies that operate on a modern technology. While historically it was the state which gave birth to modern bureaucracy, today it is the requirements of a technological economy which make its continuation inevitable. Today, bureaucracy is not only the dominant form of administration in the political and economic institutions of industrially advanced societies (be they capitalist or socialist in character), but bureaucratization has become a seemingly intrinsic component of modernization in the societies of the so-called Third World.[2] The experience of bureaucracy with which we began this chapter is becoming universal.

DIFFERENCES AND DISCREPANCIES

While the aforementioned features are to be found in all bureaucracies, there are significant differences between bureaucracies administering different aspects of social life. While the bureaucracy of the Episcopal Church has basic features that are similar to the bureaucracy which administers the Bell Telephone

[2] Edward Shils, *Political Development in the New States* (The Hague, Mouton, 1962); Myron Weiner (ed.), *Modernization* (New York, Basic Books, 1966).

Company, there are significant differences between the two bureaucracies that are dictated by their respective enterprises. Historically,
modern bureaucracy originated in the absolute state as it developed in the seventeenth century in Europe, first in France and then
elsewhere. From actual administrative organs of the state, it spread
to every group participating in one way or another in the political
process. Two such groups were political parties and labor unions.
The domination of such groups by small bureaucratic elites is, of
course, in a state of tension with the democratic ideology that such
groups have in Western countries. Sociological analysts have, nevertheless, commonly taken the position that this domination is just
about inevitable. Roberto Michels, an Italian sociologist of the generation that immediately followed Weber, gave this phenomenon the
name of "the iron law of oligarchy." [3] In its most general reference,
this term refers to the fact that it is always the few who rule over
the many. Applied to modern societies, the term refers to those few
who are in control of a bureaucratic apparatus.

A very interesting area of bureaucratization in American society
over the last half century has been the economy. Here, the startling
discrepancy is not between a democratic ideology and the rather
non-democratic facts, but between the ethos and imagery of free
enterprise and the facts of gigantic bureaucracies in charge of all
important economic operations. James Burnham aptly described
this transformation as "the managerial revolution." [4] Burnham's
ideas on the consequences of this transformation were probably a
little exaggerated. Yet there can be no doubt that any economic enterprise using methods of modern technological production and distribution must be administered along bureaucratic lines. This has
been shown over and over again in comparative studies, and it becomes especially interesting when what is compared are economic
enterprises in capitalist and socialist countries.[5] Whatever other differences there may be between the automobile industry in the
United States and in the Soviet Union, the way in which a large car
factory is actually managed must, of necessity, be very similar in

[3] Roberto Michels, *First Lectures in Political Sociology* (Minneapolis, University of Minnesota Press, 1949).

[4] James Burnham, *The Managerial Revolution* (New York, John Day, 1941).

[5] Reinhard Bendix, *Work and Authority in Industry* (New York, Wiley, 1956).

both cases—and, in fact, it is. Some sociologists and other social scientists have actually deduced from the latter fact a "theory of convergence," suggesting that the basic institutions of American and Soviet society are becoming increasingly similar. Again, this has probably been an exaggeration based on an overly great emphasis on some factors in social life as against others. There is, however, an important element of truth contained in this very term, namely, the fact that the bureaucratization of societies all over the world has made them more similar in some respects and, by the same token, has made it easier for them to communicate with each other in a large number of areas.

ORGANIZED RELIGIONS AND EDUCATIONAL BUREAUCRACIES

We have previously referred to bureaucratization extending even into areas of social life that are quite distinct from either the state or the economy. One of these areas is organized religion. A very dramatic illustration of this is provided by a study made some years ago by Paul Harrison of the organization of Baptists in this country.[6] This case is dramatic because of the very strong tradition of opposition to central authority in the Baptist denomination. This opposition goes so far that when Baptists hold a national convention they call their delegates "messengers" to underline that they are accountable only to the individual congregations that sent them and not to some national authority. The historical roots of this tradition are in the strong emphasis on the autonomy of the local congregation, to which Baptists have always adhered. Despite this, Harrison was able to show that, in fact, a national bureaucracy is operating within this denomination, and his book contains the usually beautiful tables of organization of which bureaucrats are so fond. In other words, bureaucratization is a fact among American Baptists, despite the fact that their theology and their rhetoric summarily deny it.

[6] Paul Harrison, *Authority and Power in the Free Church Tradition* (Princeton, N.J., Princeton University Press, 1959).

We have already referred to the bureaucratization of education, a process of particularly far-reaching consequences. Especially in America there has emerged a large population of educational bureaucrats, whose modes of operation (and probably modes of thinking) are very similar to those prevailing among bureaucrats in political and economic bureaucracies. The traditional notion that education has two parties, the teachers and the taught, has become obsolete in all stages of the educational career, from kindergarten to graduate school. In every one of these stages a third party has obtruded its increasingly massive presence—namely, administration. What is more, it is the administrators who are generally in control of what goes on.[7]

DYSFUNCTIONS, DISPLACEMENT OF GOALS AND DEPERSONALIZATION

Robert Merton has drawn attention to what he calls "the dysfunctions of bureaucracy"—that is, the unintended and often disruptive consequences of bureaucratization.[8] An important element here is the "displacement of goals," a shift of emphasis from ends to means. Bureaucracies and bureaucrats have a tendency to forget what it was they were originally supposed to do. A bureaucracy is set up to administer a certain area of social life and to accomplish certain tasks in that area. For example, the assigned mission of a city board of education is to run the schools and to carry out certain educational objectives. Over and over again, the social dynamics of bureaucracy bring about a situation in which the attention of the bureaucrats shifts from those official goals to the means that they themselves have developed within the bureaucratic apparatus. The

[7] For a study of bureaucracy on the high-school level, see Neal Gross, Ward Mason and Alexander McEachern, *Explorations in Role Analysis* (New York, Wiley, 1958). For a study of bureaucracy in higher education, see Nicholas Demerath, Richard Stephens and Robb Taylor, *Power, Presidents and Professors* (New York, Basic Books, 1967).

[8] Robert Merton, *Social Theory and Social Structure* (New York, Free Press, 1957), pp. 195ff.

bureaucrats become fascinated by their own procedures and by the intricacies of life within the bureaucratic hierarchy. Thus it is possible to visit some boards of education and to listen to the conversation of bureaucrats who work there and to begin to doubt that the schools supposedly being administered from this place exist at all. Their concern is now focused on the smooth operation of the bureaucratic machine as such, and its original goals become subordinated to that purpose. A paper grid is superimposed on social reality, and the bureaucrat finds himself incapable of perceiving the latter underneath the former. Success and failure are now defined in new terms. In the extreme case, this bureaucratic formulation follows the old adage, "The patient died but the operation was a success." This also means that the vested interests of bureaucrats may increasingly diverge from the interests of their clientele, and in some cases may be diametrically opposed. Thus, in a certainly unintended and often unperceived way, the dynamics of bureaucracy engender social conflict.

Also, as we have previously pointed out, bureaucracy brings about a transformation in the quality of social relations. The shift is from what sociologists call *primary relations* to *secondary relations,* that is, from relations between people that are face-to-face, personal and endowed with rich, diverse meanings, to relations that are remote, anonymous and limited to rigorously limited topics. Bureaucratization thus brings about an overall depersonalization of everyday life. It therefore significantly increases the risk of what Émile Durkheim called *anomie,* that is, a condition in which people feel that they have no significant social ties with anyone and that they exist in a world that they cannot understand, let alone control. Almost certainly, this feature of bureaucratization is closely related to what nowadays is commonly called "alienation."

THE BUREAUCRAT'S PERSONALITY: CAUSES AND CONSEQUENCES

Bureaucracy also leads to the emergence of a particular personality type. We may refer here once more to the concepts of *person selection* and *person formation*. It is personalities of a certain type that are successful in bureaucratic careers. But what is more, bureaucracy engenders socialization processes that actually form this type of personality. Karl Mannheim, another European sociologist of the generation following Weber, has described bureaucratic psychology as being primarily concerned with security.[9] In other words, the bureaucrat develops an overall attitude in which his main concern is not to upset any apple carts, and, more specifically, to keep his own cart intact.

This is the result of a combination of factors. One important factor is the aforementioned calculability of the bureaucratic process. The intended function of this is, as we have seen, to insure the predictability of social processes. In an unintended way, however, the psychology that this produces stands the original intention on its head, so to speak. The bureaucrat now finds himself psychologically incapable of dealing with anything that is *not* calculable. When this becomes an organizing principle of life, all human phenomena of spontaneity and surprise are experienced as severely disturbing. Another factor in the development of this psychology is the bureaucrat's position of dependence and ongoing accountability in the office hierarchy. Except for people at the very top of any bureaucratic apparatus, each person is continuously subjected to someone else's supervision. Occupational survival and career chances are continuously dependent on one's relations with people in the hierarchy. Bureaucrats have effectively limited this insecurity of their occupation by the invention of the tenure system which, of course, makes things much more calculable and therefore secure. Nevertheless, bureaucracies are, just about inevitably, locales for intrigues

[9] Karl Mannheim, *Essays on the Sociology of Knowledge* (New York, Oxford University Press, 1952), pp. 266ff.

and manipulations of one kind of another. To some extent, of course, this is true in any activity in which people make careers. But in other occupations, the aforementioned "displacement of goals" is less likely to take place or to dominate what goes on. For example, a team of engineers building a bridge will also probably contain people with considerable anxieties as to how their performance will be evaluated by their superiors on the job. The very activity of building a bridge, however, is so concrete and time-consuming that it is likely to detract attention from these career preoccupations. Bureaucratic work, on the other hand, is highly abstract and takes place totally within the segregated world of the office; bridges, if any, are reduced to circulating files. Bureaucratic expertise, as it were, is always turned inward, to the bureaucratic reality itself, rather than to outside events and actions. It is the anxieties produced by this characteristic which lead to the overriding concern with security that Mannheim indicated.

In addition, as both Weber and Mannheim pointed out, bureaucracy necessarily entails a sharp separation between public and private life. Again, in this it is similar to other occupations in modern society—for example, to all occupations that have to do with industrial production. But because of the closedness, and even secretiveness, of the bureaucratic world, this separation is particularly sharp in the life of the bureaucrat. As Mannheim put it: "He lives in two worlds, and he must therefore, so to speak, have two souls." [10] This has important psychological consequences. It leads to a dichotomy both of values and emotions. An individual believes and feels one thing in the office and quite another thing at home. An individual can be sensitive and considerate with his family and absolutely ruthless in the office—or, for that matter, the precise reverse. This separation of life into public and private sectors has the further consequence that one can compensate in one sector for the frustrations existing in the other. Again, this can cut both ways. The person who is humiliated or frustrated in his bureaucratic career can go home and play the role of big fish in a small pond. But conversely, the office can serve as an escape from the bickering and

[10] *Ibid.*, p. 269.

irritations of family life. We shall have occasion later on to return to this particular dichotomy, which is generally true of modern societies although it takes on a particular character in the case of bureaucracy.[11]

SOCIOLOGICAL VIEWPOINTS: FROM THE SYSTEM AND FROM THE "CLIENT"

Two quite different approaches have been taken in the sociological analysis of bureaucracy. The first is one that essentially deals with the phenomenon from the viewpoint of the bureaucratic system itself. The other does so from the viewpoint of individuals "caught" in it. In recent American sociology, the former has been by far the most successful, though it has recently been subjected to sharp criticism.

The first approach is characteristic of structural-functionalism and to what is now known as systems theory which, in its basic sociological presuppositions, is quite close to structural-functionalism. A key category in this approach is *system maintenance*. This concept has two implications: first, that a bureaucracy functions as a more or less closed mechanism with processes that unfold according to a logic of their own; and, second, that one of the, as it were, basic "instincts" of such a system is to safeguard its own survival in society. Philip Selznick, one of the foremost analysts of bureaucracy in recent American sociology, has helped to clarify this approach through a number of what he calls "imperatives"—by which he means principles that will, of necessity, govern the operation of bureaucratic systems.[12]

[11] On this dichotomy, also see C. Wright Mills, *White Collar* (New York, Oxford University Press, 1951), and William Whyte, *The Organization Man* (Garden City, N.Y., Doubleday-Anchor, 1957).

[12] Philip Selznick, "Foundations of the Theory of Organization," in Amitai Etzioni (ed.), *A Sociological Reader on Complex Organizations* (New York, Holt, Rinehart & Winston, 1969), pp. 26ff.

SELZNICK'S "IMPERATIVES OF THE SYSTEM"

These imperatives refer both to the internal workings of the system and to its relations with the larger society in which it operates. The very first imperative, therefore, is the security of the organization within the larger social environment. While this is an imperative for all bureaucratic systems, clearly its implications will be different from case to case. Thus a bureaucracy of the Federal Government has a quite different relationship to its larger social environment than the bureaucracy of the Baptist denomination. Both, however, will have to be concerned with their security against forces that might challenge their policies or even endanger their social survival. Another imperative is the stability of the lines of authority and communication within the organization. Again, the term "security" might be applied to this imperative. It is essential that each agency and staff member within the organization know precisely who is responsible for what, and who is accountable to whom. Furthermore, in a communication process as complex as that of a modern bureaucracy, it is essential that individuals and individual agencies have reasonable certainty that their messages get to where they are supposed to get. This is especially important for communications that originate at the top of the hierarchy—otherwise the control of the bureaucratic apparatus becomes endangered.

A very interesting imperative mentioned by Selznick is the stability of informal relations within the organization. This refers to a whole area of bureaucratic life that has been particularly emphasized by American sociologists, taking up where Weber left off. There is the general notion that every bureaucracy also has an *informal structure* that exists, as it were, beneath its formal tables of organization. Individuals in a bureaucracy not only relate to each other through the formal channels established for this purpose by office procedure but also in a great variety of unofficial, and sometimes even illicit, relations. This informal structure is not necessarily antagonistic to the formal structure of the system. On the contrary, it might serve to maintain the system by smoothing difficult situations, filling in gaps left open by the formal procedures and generally giving staff members feelings of belonging and personal satisfaction. These informal relations, however, must not get out of hand. Whatever the degree to which they may be officially recognized within the organization, it is necessary that they be "kept in their place" and not allowed to interfere with the formal workings of the system. Another imperative is the continuity of policy within the organization. Drastic shifts and transformations of policy endanger the entire rationale by which a bureaucracy works. This does not mean that bureaucracies cannot adapt to change, but they do so more readily when the change is gradual. Finally, there is the imperative of homogeneity of outlook on the organization and its mission among its staff members. Again, this need not necessarily mean a rigid conformity, but it does mean that it is necessary that there be a general consensus as to what the organization is and what it is about.

SYSTEMS IN EQUILIBRIUM; "OPEN" AND "CLOSED" SYSTEMS

In this approach, a view of bureaucracy emerges that emphasizes stability or even equilibrium. This view, however, does not imply a static situation; it does not say that bureaucracies always *are* stable, let alone in equilibrium. Rather, it suggests that bureaucratic organizations will *tend toward* such a condition. All institutions undergo continuous change, and bureaucratic institutions are no exception. What is peculiar to them is a particular genius for adaptation. A well-functioning bureaucratic system has the capacity to modify or expand its procedures to deal with new situations. Minimally, the classification scheme by which files are ordered will have to be revised. Maximally, there will be a new table of organization. Different bureaucracies, however, will vary in their degree of "openness," in terms of their interaction with other systems or social forces. Relatively "open" bureaucracies will be in an ongoing process of adaptation to the social forces of their larger environment, while relatively "closed" bureaucracies will function as far as possible

without responding to this environment. This difference will obviously be basically determined by the degree of power which the
bureaucracy's clientele has or can threaten to mobilize against the
bureaucratic staff. Thus a bureaucracy dependent in greater or
lesser measure on the interplay of democratic processes will tend to
be more "open" than a bureaucracy which does not have to worry
about such things. The latter can afford to follow the old adage,
"Never apologize, never explain"; the former will have to engage in
all sorts of public relations activities in order to keep its clientele
reasonably happy.

THE ADVANTAGES AND DISADVANTAGES OF THE VIEWPOINT FROM THE SYSTEM

An important assumption of this approach is the autonomy of functions
in such a system. It is assumed that
many of these functions are (in Merton's sense) *latent* in terms of the
awareness or intentions of the people who participate in these social
situations. This approach suggests
that "processes are unfolding"
rather than that "here are people
doing things." In a very curious way, the sociological analysis itself
reflects the bureaucratic ethos of objectivity and impersonality.
Conversely, the subjective meanings that are operative in the situation are de-emphasized, and the actions of individuals tend to appear only as imperfections or disruptions in the functioning of the
system. There are distinct advantages to this approach. It provides
a comprehensive and comprehensible view of organizations in motion; it permits the sociologist to view them as wholes and to understand what is going on in terms of an integral logic that seems to
originate in the system as a whole rather than its individual participants. Such a view, of course, is characteristic of structural-functionalism in general, no matter what the institutional area it investi-
gates, and it is suggested the very moment that one uses the concept
of system. It is especially plausible when applied to bureaucracy
because the latter is indeed dominated by a highly rational orientation. In other words, more than most other social institutions, bu-

reaucracies actually function like systems and, therefore, can quite adequately be viewed in these terms.

There is, however, also a distinct disadvantage to this approach —namely, it has a tendency to view everything from a "management" point of view and to absolutize this perspective. This can be seen most easily when what is being analyzed are "problems" in a bureaucracy. Take a case in which a group of parents, dissatisfied, for one reason or another, with the education their children are getting in school, band together to oppose a program of a city board of education. If the parents' actions are successful to any degree, they will, of course, disrupt or at least interfere with the smooth operation of the system as designed by its bureaucracy. Seen from the viewpoint of the educational bureaucrat, it is the parents and their activities which constitute the "problem." Similarly, to a sociologist analyzing the situation in terms of the educational organization as a functioning system, the "problem" will again be the disturbance in that system produced by the parents. Needless to say, from the parents' point of view a quite different perspective prevails. *Their* "problem" is the allegedly bad education which their children receive—and the educational organization itself becomes a part of this "problem" to the degree that it does not help to remedy this condition. In other words, the structural-functionalist or systemic approach to bureaucracy is always in danger of overlooking important elements in the situation that are not part of the "official" or "management" view of what is going on.

THE ALTERNATIVE VIEWPOINT: FROM THE INDIVIDUAL

An alternative approach to the sociological study of bureaucracy is one that takes the viewpoint of the actors in the situation—not only those actors who are officially designated as representatives of the organization but, more importantly, those actors who are its clients or even victims. A by now classical instance of this approach is Erving Goffman's study (of all things) of the mental hospital as a bureaucratic institution.[13] While Goffman's approach has been particularly influential in the rather limited field of medical sociology, it has broad applicability to the study of bureaucracies. The mental hospital—as, indeed, all bureaucratically administered institutions —has an ideology by which the actions of "management" are legitimated in terms of "what is good for" the people being managed. Goffman magisterially brushes aside all these legitimations, including the psychiatric definitions of what is going on. Instead, he simply looks at the situation as one in which one group of people controls another group. And what particularly interests him is the way in which the latter look upon and react to this situation. What specifically interests him is what he calls "ways of making out," that is, the multiplicity of stratagems by which the clients of the bureaucratic organization manage to evade or circumvent the formal controls and to protect conduct which is often inimical to the professed goals of the organization.

Goffman distinguishes between what he calls *primary and secondary adjustments* to any organization. By primary adjustment he means the adaptation of the individual to what is the formal structure of the organization. The individual who does this, and does nothing else beyond this, he calls the "programmed member" of the organization. By secondary adjustment, on the other hand, Goffman means various unauthorized ways of coping with the organization. Some of these, through various informal and unofficial definitions of the situation, can be "contained" within the formal structure; others are more dangerously disruptive. Consequently, there will be different degrees of acceptance of secondary adjustment by "management." Sometimes, if only to preserve superficial harmony, there may be semi-official definitions of the situation that go very far in recognizing the various unauthorized things that are going on. The network of procedures and compromises with authority that are the consequence of secondary adjustment Goffman rather happily calls the "underlife" of organizations.

For example, every bureaucratic organization (and a mental hospital is no exception to this) has a communications system. The

[13] Erving Goffman, *Asylums* (Garden City, N.Y., Doubleday-Anchor, 1961).

purpose of this communications system, of course, is to channel directives and information from one bureaucratic position to another, both upward and downward in the bureaucratic hierarchy. The same communications system, however, can also be used for highly unauthorized communications. It can be used to place bets. Such use (as long as it is employed with some discretion) does not interfere with the formal purpose of the communications system and therefore can be "contained." The same channel of communication, though, can also be used for much more disruptive purposes. It can be used to forewarn various individuals of intended actions by the upper echelons of the bureaucracy, with the express intention of sabotaging these actions. In this case, "containment" will fail and the bureaucracy will have to take steps to regain control over that sector of its "underlife."

David Silverman, a British sociologist, has recently suggested that this kind of approach can be developed into a full theory of formal organizations which will be able to cope with its manifold phenomena more adequately than either a structural-functionalist or a systems approach.[14] In this approach, bureaucracy (or any other kind of formal organization) will be viewed as the meeting place of varying definitions of the situation. No privileged status will be given to the definitions of any party in the situation, be it "management" or anyone else. Rather, the attempt will be made to understand all the definitions that are operative in the situation and to see how they come together to produce the overall social reality of the bureaucracy in question. Such an approach will place emphasis on quite different factors. It will find it very difficult to operate with the concept of system or even of function. Instead, it will focus on the different groups that are in interaction in such a situation—on their intentions, perspectives and strategies. It will tend to see bureaucratic organizations as arenas of conflict or, in a lower key, of negotiation and compromise. It may be added here that these two approaches, whatever their differences, are not really contradictory. They simply focus on different aspects of the same overall phenomenon.

[14] David Silverman, *The Theory of Organisations* (New York, Basic Books, 1971).

WHAT IF I'M FRUSTRATED?

Let us return once more to the basic experience of bureaucracy with which we began this chapter. It is, as Weber pointed out, an experience of pervasive rationality and rationalization. And it is that not only for the personnel of bureaucracies but for all those who come in intimate contact with it—and, in modern societies, this is nearly everyone. But this means that the ethos of bureaucracy affects not only the bureaucrats themselves but vastly larger numbers of people. Specifically, the dichotomy of which we spoke before is something experienced by the clients as well as the staffs of modern bureaucracies.

For almost everyone in contemporary society, vast areas of his own life are, in effect, bureaucratized, and the individual can only operate in these areas by subjecting himself to the rationale of bureaucratic conduct; in Goffman's term, he must be "programmed." This has its own frustrations. Even if the individual does not come to feel downright oppression or alienation, he is very likely to be frustrated in various areas of his life by this programming. Most importantly, he is likely to be frustrated in his emotionality. In order to cope effectively with a bureaucratized world, the individual must continuously keep in control various emotions, such as affection, hatred, impatience, enthusiasm or anxiety. In other words, a bureaucratized world expects him to be "reasonable" at all times. This very expectation can produce a powerful desire to be "unreasonable"—to pound on the table, to fold or perforate the form that is supposed to be kept unfolded or unperforated, to talk back to the recorded announcement—in sum, to tell the bureaucracy to go to hell. Emotions and experiences, banned from expression in a bureaucratized world, seek outlets in one way or another. Sometimes (as we have recently had plentiful occasion to observe) these frustrations of bureaucracy may lead to directly disruptive outbursts against bureaucratic organizations. More generally, however, individuals will seek to compensate for bureaucracy and its discontents in other areas of life—in the private sphere or in such institutional areas as political or religious movements. In other words, the rationalization of life brought about by bureaucracy creates its own antagonistic force of irrationality. Weber himself foresaw this development. Depending upon one's point of view, one may see this as a great human hope or as a threat to orderly social existence. In either case, one will have to recognize that bureaucracy and its rationales must reckon with definite limits to their sway. What we know today as the "youth culture" is a prime example of resistance to the bureaucratization of life.

READINGS

A useful compendium of articles on the topic of this chapter is Amitai Etzioni (ed.), *A Sociological Reader on Complex Organizations* (New York, Holt, Rinehart & Winston, 1969). The major theoretical positions are well described in David Silverman, *The Theory of Organisations* (New York, Basic Books, 1971). The following are well-known case studies of bureaucracies at work:

Blau, Peter, *The Dynamics of Bureaucracy* (Chicago, University of Chicago Press, 1955).

Crozier, Michel, *The Bureaucratic Phenomenon* (Chicago, University of Chicago Press, 1964).

Selznick, Philip, *TVA and the Grass Roots* (Berkeley, Calif., University of California Press, 1949).

Chapter 11

YOUTH

SOCIETY'S AMBIGUOUS DEMANDS: "ACT YOUR AGE"?

It is not easy to be young: the comforts of childhood are in the process of disappearing, and the rewards of adulthood are slow in making themselves available. It is unclear when youth begins and when it ends. And it is far from clear what it means while it is apparently going on. No clear dividing lines separate the different stages of biography. Modern society has few, if any, of those "rites of passage" which, in many other human societies, mark the thresholds between clearly defined stages in the individual's progress through life. Young people in modern society are nevertheless frequently exhorted to "act their age," while, at the same time, society is very ambiguous as to what this actually means. The young individual in this society is subjected to a highly bureaucratic educational establishment and to fierce competitive pressures to succeed within it. And he is supposed to take all of this with great seriousness. At the same time, his capacity to participate in important decisions affecting his life is seriously doubted by adults. Young men are expected to serve in the military but (at least until very recently) they were not permitted to vote. Young women are subjected to completely contradictory expectations, one set of expectations in terms of a traditional value system that emphasizes the virtues of being "feminine," the other set vigorously affirming the equality of the sexes and both the right and the necessity for a woman to have an independent career. Young men and young women alike are presented with a bewildering choice not only of careers and occupations but of life-styles and belief systems. What is more, the adult world is not only fairly unhelpful in the face of the situation of youth but seems to react to it with hysterical inconsistency: one day youth is hailed as some sort of messianic hope for the society, the next day it is denounced as a sinister, subversive conspiracy.

HUDDLING TOGETHER AGAINST THE UPTIGHT

It is not surprising that people in this situation should band together. Thus there has developed a community of youth with very distinctive features of its own. In this community young people can huddle together and give each other solace in the face of the frustrations imposed by the world of adults. The identity of being young is loudly proclaimed in dress, language and aesthetic style. Within the confines of educational establishments, the community of the young presents itself as the antithesis, in just about every detail, of bureaucracy and the bureaucratic ethos. Where the latter seeks to impose order, the community of the young represents spontaneity sometimes approaching chaos. Where the bureaucracy promotes discipline, the community of the young glorifies pleasure. Youth's perspective on bureaucracy is very aptly caught in the term "uptight." Youth defines itself in precise antithesis to this "uptightness." It is loose, spontaneous, free. To be young in contemporary society is to look for refuges. The community of the young is experienced as a refuge.

BIOLOGY AND LAW: HAVING A MATURE BODY, BEING A JUVENILE

What is youth? Common sense would, first of all, suggest a biological answer. As in so many things, common sense would be rather misleading here. Obviously, there is a biological process of growth which sets in at birth (more precisely, at conception) and continues until the individual has reached maturity in terms of the species. After that point, alas, he begins to fall apart again, slowly, or fast, as his luck would have it. It is also possible that the time-span of biological maturation varies from period to period. Some anthropologists have suggested that over the last century or so sexual maturation has had a tendency to occur earlier and earlier. Be this as it may, it is clear that the biological growth process sets limits to what society can expect of the individual at a given moment. It would be futile for a society to expect a two-year-old to run the government or a seventy-year-old to excel in athletics. However, as we have seen much earlier in our discussion of socialization, these biological facts only set very broad parameters to socialization and to the social definitions of reality. In any case, the biological facts about human biography offer no definitive guidance as to either the duration or the cultural substance of youth. In strictly biological terms one might define youth as beginning on the day on which the individual has lost his last milk tooth and as ending on the day on which he sprouts his first white hair. There are no *biological* reasons why such a definition of youth might not be undertaken.

If common sense, on the other hand, is shaped by a bureaucratic imagination rather than a scientific one, it might look for guidance to law for an answer to the question about the character of youth. American legislation does, indeed, abound with a variety of statutes and legal institutions that are specifically aimed at youth. In fact, there is an entire jurisdiction, with its own court system, that deals with juvenile crime. The law then suggests, quite definitely, that there is such a thing as youth and that it must be distinguished from both the preceding and succeeding stages of biography. Beyond that, however, the law is not the best guide for grasping what the phenomenon is. One may get a driver's license at fourteen, stop worrying about statutory rape after sixteen, go to dirty movies and vote at eighteen. Even if one overlooks the fact that these ages vary considerably from state to state, which of these different thresholds is to be regarded as marking the boundaries of youth? The sociologist can only point out that law always reflects the society in which it has its being and that in this particular area the ambiguities of the law reflect the ambiguities of the society's conception of youth. We would again refer to the famous statement of the American sociologist, W. I. Thomas: "If people define a situation as real, it is real in its consequences." For a sociologist, at any rate, youth is neither a biological nor a legal fact. Rather, it is a matter of social definition. The biological facts merely set the parameters of this definition, while the legal facts are its consequences.

CHILDHOOD,
[YOUTH],
ADULTHOOD:
INSERTING A
NEW PHASE INTO
BIOGRAPHY

Different societies differ greatly in the manner in which they define the stages of biography, and they differ very greatly indeed in their definition of youth.[1] Every society is forced by the biological facts to differentiate at least between the earlier phases of childhood and what comes later in the individual's life.

Thus every human society has some definition of childhood. But many societies recognize no stage between that and the status of fully recognized adult. In other words, in many societies the individual steps directly from childhood into adulthood with no intervening stages.

The Israeli sociologist, S. N. Eisenstadt (one of the foremost sociological authorities on youth), has suggested that societies will develop a strong definition of youth to the degree that there exists a sharp cleavage in value orientations between the family and the larger institutions of society.[2] The period of youth is then required to help the individual in making the transition from the one world to the other. Be this as it may, the definition of youth in modern society has been greatly different from that existing in any other society that we know of. Not only is youth inserted between childhood and adulthood as a distinctive biographical phase, but that phase has been expanding in both directions and has increasingly created a social-cultural world of its own. The global tendency is for youth to begin earlier and earlier, and to last longer and longer. Life-styles and behavior patterns that only a few years ago were characteristic of college students have now penetrated the high schools and may yet reach even earlier age groups. At the other temporal border, anyone under thirty certainly thinks of himself as young today, and the symbols of youth may be exhibited at much

[1] See S. N. Eisenstadt, *From Generation to Generation* (New York, Free Press, 1956); Erik Erikson (ed.), *Youth: Change and Challenge* (New York, Basic Books, 1963); Muzafer Sherif and Carolyn Sherif (eds.), *Problems of Youth* (Chicago, Aldine, 1965); F. Musgrove, *Youth and the Social Order* (Bloomington, Ind., Indiana University Press, 1965).

[2] Eisenstadt, *op. cit., passim.*

later stages. Graduate degrees are frequently obtained today by individuals in their early thirties. As to politicians and executives, anyone in their early forties is commonly referred to as "young." These social facts are related to rising life expectancy, which, as we have seen in an earlier part of this book, has been one of the great changes in modern society. It obviously makes a difference whether an individual on his thirtieth birthday may reasonably look forward to another twenty or to another forty years of life. But the social definitions of youth cannot be fully explained in terms of demographic statistics. They are more subtle and complex and must be related to a variety of factors in modern society.

WHY DOES INDUSTRIALIZA- TION *CAUSE* "YOUTH"?

The basic causal factor for youth today is industrial society and its institutional dynamics. The phenomena that characterize youth in America are very similar to those that may be found in other industrial countries, while the situation of young people in the so-called underdeveloped world is quite different (and beyond our scope here). Why would industrial society produce the phenomenon of modern youth? We have previously mentioned the deepening of the division of labor, brought about by the industrial revolution. We have seen how this division of labor separated the family (and thus childhood) from the processes of modern production and administration. Modern youth is a further extension of the same process of institutional separation or differentiation. A British sociologist, F. Musgrove, has described this connection rather elegantly:

> The adolescent was invented at the same time as the steam engine. The principal architect of the latter was Watt in 1765, of the former Rousseau in 1762. Having invented the adolescent, society has been faced with two major problems: how and where to accommodate him in the social structure, and how to make his behavior accord with the specifications.[3]

The term "adolescent" is not quite adequate because the phenomenon of youth is broader than that of adolescence, but the general

---

[3] Musgrove, *op. cit.*, p. 33.

statement applies to youth as well. Put differently: the industrial revolution has produced an institutional structure which "allows room" for youth. Having first separated the family from the institutional areas of the economy and the state, the industrial revolution has created an, as it were, interstitial area in which "private life" could flourish in a variety of forms. Youth is one of many "luxuries" of this situation. It is similar to childhood in one fundamental characteristic, namely, its segregation from the "serious" activities of economic and political institutions.

SPECIALIZATION AND THE EDUCATIONAL ETHOS

Another effect of the industrial revolution in this area has to do with the occupational structure. The immense division of labor in modern society requires ever-increasing specialization. Whether this is always logical or not, this specialization has led to increasingly complex educational requirements for every conceivable type of job. Inevitably, this has meant a lengthening of the period the individual is expected to spend within the educational system. Also, there has been the general assumption that a fairly high level of general education is required for almost all jobs in this society.

The police is a case in point. Until very recently, the educational requirements for this occupation were minimal. Good physical condition, average intelligence and moral character (whatever that may mean) were the only prerequisites for entering this occupation. In most American cities today, a high-school diploma is an absolute necessity, and increasingly some urban police departments (for example, in New York City) deem it highly desirable that policemen attend college for several years as well. Once such an educational ethos is established in an occupational structure, it becomes difficult to say which educational requirements are really necessary for the adequate performance of a certain job and which are simply matters of status manipulation and one-upmanship. In other words, some occupations may force a candidate to spend three years in a certain kind of school because this period of time is necessary to impart the appropriate knowledge and skills. But another occupation may also impose a three-year schooling requirement because that will make it easier to demand legal and economic privileges from the larger society. In that case, if a curriculum extending over three years does not readily suggest itself, it will have to be invented by all necessary means.

TAKING THE YOUNG OUT OF THE FACTORY AND PUTTING THEM IN SCHOOL

Fortunately (though hardly fortuitously), these educational requirements of an industrial occupational structure have been linked to the educational ethos that was one of the major cultural products of the rising bourgeoisie.[4] This is not the place to speculate on which came first, the educational needs of industrial society or the educational ethos of the class most responsible for the formation of this society—or whether (as we would be inclined to think) these two phenomena fed on each other over a period of time. Whatever the historical chronology, as the (real or imagined) educational requirements of industrial society expanded, so did the faith in education and the educational system that institutionally embodied this faith. The law, with some inevitable delays, tried to keep pace with these developments. The separation of childhood and early youth from the processes of production was legalized by child labor laws. Logically enough, the institutional containment of childhood and early youth within the educational system was also legalized through compulsory schooling laws. In other words, the law followed the social definitions of reality; youth was assigned its proper place within the institutional order.

The participation of young people in the labor force has, accordingly, been steadily shrinking in industrial societies. In the United States, in 1900, 62.1 percent of males between the ages of 14 and 19 participated in the labor force. By 1930, that percentage had shrunk to 40.1 percent, and by 1963, to 36.5 percent.[5] Of course,

[4] See Philippe Ariès, *Centuries of Childhood* (New York, Knopf, 1962), pp. 137ff.

[5] Jacob Mincer, "Labor Force: Participation," in *International Encyclopedia of the Social Sciences*, Vol. 8 (New York, Macmillan, 1968), p. 474.

this shrinkage shows considerable class differences, being much more acute in the higher classes. Whether this relationship of youth to the labor force has a latent function economically or not is open to debate. If one assumes, as some economists have, that a modern industrial society could not absorb all of its available labor force, then keeping youth out of the labor market, for whatever reasons, is economically functional. If one were to question this economic position, then the same exclusion would be quite irrational. Whatever the economic logic of the matter may be, the term "youth" has increasingly referred to a population that is not engaged in gainful work.

Again, a demographic factor must be mentioned here, namely, the steep decline in child mortality that has been the consequence of modern medicine and nutrition. This has had a very simple consequence, in terms of the sheer numbers of young people in a modern society: there are more young people around. The institutions designed to deal with youth, notably the educational system, must therefore accommodate themselves to vast masses of young people. This mass character of modern youth has not only quantitative but also qualitative consequences.

SOCIAL-PSYCHOLOGICAL FACTORS: "ANTICIPATORY SOCIALIZATION" AND ESTRANGEMENT FROM PARENTS

Also, however, modern industrial society has produced more subtle social-psychological factors that bear upon the phenomenon of youth. It is probably an intrinsic element of the human condition that there be divisions between the generations. These divisions, however, have been greatly deepened in modern society. There are two reasons for this. One is the greater degree of social mobility of all types, which has led to the fact that very frequently people move into social milieus that are greatly different from those of their parents. Even if they do not do so, as a result of what Robert Merton has called "anticipatory socialization" they *aspire* to such different milieus and are already thereby estranged from the parent generation. The other reason is the sheer complexity of modern society, which has meant that different individuals live vastly different lives. These differences very frequently run right through individual families. Again, the separation of the family from the "important" processes of social life has been a factor in this. Seen from the perspective of the young, their elders seem to disappear into a strange world, reappearing from time to time within the limited context that they share with the young. Almost inevitably, the social-psychological effect of this is estrangement of one degree or another. As a result of the deepening separation between generations, there has been the powerful tendency for youth to become autonomous, that is, to establish norms and patterns of its own that are relatively independent of those prevailing in the adult world. Excluded from the "serious" concerns of the adult world and left to its own resources, youth has had to define itself anew with each generation in modern society. Not surprisingly, this definition—especially of late—has commonly been in deliberate opposition to the definitions of reality prevailing in the parent generation.

SOCIALIZATION INTO "OPEN-ENDEDNESS"

It is also possible that another causal factor is to be sought in the complex, and often ambivalent, processes of socialization that prevail in modern society.[6] While socialization in most pre-modern societies has been highly integrated and consistent, providing the individual with strong patterns to grow into, socialization in modern society has been characterized by high degrees of discontinuity and inconsistency. Such a situation is likely to produce personalities whose integration leaves something to be desired—in other words, individuals who are quite unsure of them-

[6] This point has been developed by Arnold Gehlen, a contemporary German sociologist whose work to date is unavailable in English. For works influenced by his approach, see Thomas Luckmann, *The Invisible Religion* (New York, Macmillan, 1967) and Anton Zijderveld, *The Abstract Society* (Garden City, N.Y., Doubleday, 1970).

selves. Primary socialization as well as the early stages of secondary socialization in modern society do not, as it were, complete the job. They leave the personality "open-ended." If that is so, it would follow that a period set aside for the individual to complete the process would be highly functional. Youth, as defined by modern society, meets this requirement. That is to say, the biographical stage of youth has the purpose of providing time for the individual to complete the process of socialization—in a word, to "find himself."

PATTERNS OF YOUTH: EMOTIONAL INTENSITY AND ROLE EXPERIMENTATION

Youth in modern society has had both formal and informal institutional consequences. The most important formal consequence has been the "containment" of youth in a gigantic educational establishment. We have already spoken of this. But there have been informal consequences as well, namely, there has been the development of autonomous social and cultural patterns for youth. Some of these have apparently emerged with a degree of spontaneity in the community of the young itself. Other patterns have developed in interaction between this community and the larger society. And some have undoubtedly been the result of direct and deliberate manipulation by the latter. In any case, youth in modern society is not just a vast mass of young people moving through the educational establishment. The phenomenon is much more complex and contains institutional forms that are different from, and in some instances directly opposed to, the educational establishment.

What are these autonomous patterns of modern youth? Probably most important of all, youth today is a period of emotional turmoil —or at least of considerable emotional intensity. To some extent this is probably due to simple biological facts. Just as the young organism is more vigorous, so it seems plausible to assume that the emotional makeup of the young is capable of sustaining more intense activity than that of their elders. This, however, is not enough to explain the degree of emotionality that the phenomenon exhibits, nor can it account for differences between modern youth and comparable biographical stages in other societies. Rather, we would contend that the emotional quality of contemporary youth is itself a consequence of its social definition. It reflects the ambiguity and the conflicts intrinsic to the modern definition of youth. An important element in this emotional structure is sex. Again, to be sure, there is a biological foundation for this. But youth as defined in modern society has a peculiarly intense sexual aspect. This is a period of sexual discoveries. Sexual means are employed to relieve the emotional tensions within the individual; on the other hand, youthful sexuality engenders its own emotional tensions and crises.

Much more broadly, however, youth is a period of role experimentation. Sexual roles are but one aspect of this. Another way of putting this is to say that within the limits of what is socially possible, the attempt is now made to realize the fantasies of anticipatory socialization. The individual now "tries out" different roles—with the other sex, in new and different social contexts, in different occupations (more usually in courses of study that are supposed to prepare for these occupations) and in connection with different aesthetic or ideological camps. Thus there is a playful and sometimes even theatrical aspect to youth, but this should not detract from the importance which this play-acting has for the individual. Sometimes, indeed, the performances are desperately serious. An essential element of the experience of youth in modern society is the instability of values (another way of putting this would be to say, their unreliability) and, indeed, of identity itself. "What is really worth doing?" "How should I spend my life?" "Who am I?" These are typical questions of youth. Again, while there is undoubtedly a universal human quality about these questions, they have received particular sharpness and urgency as a result of the modern definition of the situation of youth. Thus the period of youth is characterized very strongly by a search for "authentic" values and identity. Society expects that during this period the individual will "find himself," and to a very large extent this expectation is firmly internalized in the consciousness of young individuals. Society further recognizes that this process of self-discovery will involve experimentation of various sorts. In other words, the young individual is expected to "sow wild oats"—not only sexually but in every other significant area of social life.

YOUTH *CULTURE* OR *SUB-CULTURE*? We have suggested that these basic characteristics of youth today are derived from intrinsic structures of industrial society. These characteristics are not altogether new, and in some instances reach back at least to the late eighteenth and early nineteenth centuries. The notion of youth being engaged in some sort of noble struggle with the older generation is not new at all, finding its first powerful expression in the Romantic Movement about 150 years ago. For the aforementioned reasons, this conflict has been particularly sharp among the youth of the bourgeoisie, and especially that segment of it which attended institutions of higher learning. In a number of Western countries, student movements, under the banner of rebelling youth, have played an important cultural and political role since then.[7] Lately, however (in America, particularly during the last decade), all this has been greatly sharpened. The reasons for this are considerably in dispute, and this is not the place to suggest our own explanation. Suffice it to say that the conflict has erupted at several points where the community of the young confronts the bureaucratic structures of modern society—especially, of course, in the educational establishment. It should also be pointed out that this confrontation and the ensuing conflict have taken place in almost all advanced industrial societies, being in no way confined to America. However one may then wish to explain this phenomenon sociologically or social-psychologically, one would do well to bear in mind that no purely American developments are likely to serve as an adequate explanation.

It is indicative of this sharpening conflict that recent commentary on contemporary youth, both by social scientists and in the

[7] See Lewis Feuer, *The Conflict of Generations* (New York, Basic Books, 1969).

popular media, has come to accept the term *youth culture* as an adequate description of what is going on. The very word "culture" suggests, of course, that here is a separate entity with which the larger society must contend. This is a very recent development. About ten years ago the term was either not used at all or its validity was actively disputed or, at best, it was used rather loosely to refer to certain patterns of behavior in adolescents.[8] Today, it is broadly maintained not only that the youth culture is a social fact but that it stands in massive opposition to the social-cultural status quo, or even that it represents the future of the society.[9]

With regard to the youth culture, we are dealing with a very new phenomenon which as yet has not been fully studied by sociologists. Most comment on the phenomenon has been by journalists and popular writers, and the data are unsatisfactory at this point. Therefore we can only make quite tentative and cautious statements about the phenomenon here. All the same, we are speaking of a phenomenon of very great importance in contemporary society, and if nothing else we would like to convey the questions which this raises.

In strict sociological parlance, the term *sub-culture* would be more adequate to describe the phenomenon. As the word suggests, by sub-culture is meant a social-cultural formation that exists as a sort of island or enclave within the larger society. We have already touched upon sub-cultural phenomena in dealing with class, ethnicity and race in America. Thus the black community forms a sub-culture within American society. Whatever may be the eventual relationship of the youth culture to the larger society, at this point the former clearly exists as a sub-culture within the latter. As such, it has a number of characteristics which can be described, however tentatively.

[8] See James Coleman, *The Adolescent Society* (New York, Free Press, 1961); Ernest Smith, *American Youth Culture* (New York, Free Press, 1962).

[9] See Kenneth Keniston, *The Uncommitted* (New York, Harcourt Brace, 1965); Theodore Roszak, *The Making of a Counter Culture* (Garden City, N.Y., Doubleday, 1969); Charles Reich, *The Greening of America* (New York, Random House, 1970).

YOUTH AESTHETICS, COLLECTIVE PARTICIPATION AND MORALS

In properly cultural terms, we can distinguish two types of characteristics: aesthetic and moral. The aesthetic characteristics refer to a quite distinct style and taste existing within the youth culture. This can most readily be seen in the style of personal appearance, as expressed by clothes, ornamentation or hair styles. The youth culture has a marked artistic flair (related to its emphasis on spontaneity and creativity). Probably the most conspicuous expression of this is rock music which, much more than an art form, has become a kind of symbolic manifesto, not to say sacrament, for the sub-culture. In the visual arts, the taste has run in the direction of the highly colorful and turbulent forms generally called psychedelic (which bear a striking and interesting resemblance to what, a half century ago, was called *Jugendstil* in Germany). To the extent that the same taste has extended to the performing arts, such as dance and theater, it has also moved in the direction of unrestrained expression, turbulence and collective participation. This last element, indeed, is present in all the aesthetic expressions of the sub-culture. The emphasis is on community, on a sense of belonging, on collectively shared ecstasy—all values, it should be noted, which stand in the sharpest contrast to the ethos of bureaucratic society.

The theme of collective participation bridges the aesthetic and moral. Communalism appears as a moral value, again in sharp opposition to the individualism and competitiveness of middle-class society. Honesty, sincerity, "authenticity" are recurring themes, posited against the alleged "hypocrisy" of the adult world. There is a strong emphasis on liberation from all restraints and on a guiltless pursuit of pleasure. Here, the antithesis is to the Puritan heritage of American society, including the "Protestant ethic" which played, and still plays, such an important part in the ethos of capitalism. The widespread use of hallucinogenic drugs has been the most flamboyant expression of these themes. But it would be an error to identify these themes exclusively with the drug scene. A probably more important and more enduring expression of the same themes is in the area of sexuality, where their expression is closely linked to the so-called sexual revolution. Within the youth culture, sex has been firmly defined as one of the most important, if not the most important, area of life in which the individual is to experience himself and others with complete freedom and honesty. The current cult of nudity is a powerful expression of this aspiration toward "authenticity." The individual who exhibits himself nakedly supposedly puts away not only his clothes but the mask of insincerity under which he previously hid his true identity.

In all of this there is an intriguing combination of collectivism and individualism. On the one hand, the youth culture vigorously affirms community, and its major symbolic actions express an almost mystical fusion of many individuals in a common experience of ecstasy. Woodstock has become the most famous case in point, but every halfway successful rock concert replicates the experience on a less grandiose level. On the other hand, however, the youth culture has strongly affirmed the autonomy of each individual and his right "to do his own thing" to the limits of possibility. This is only a seeming contradiction. The underlying theme is the search for true identity. The community and its ecstasies are experienced as means to this end. We cannot be concerned here with whether these goals are ethically valid or empirically attainable. We can only describe this morality as it presents itself in the youth culture, and to try to understand how it makes sense in its own terms.

SUBSIDIZATION AND THE YOUTH MARKET

Every human culture or sub-culture has an economic foundation, and the youth culture is no exception. The economics of the youth culture is important for an understanding of its relationship to the larger society. On the one hand, it must be emphasized that the bulk of this sub-culture is subsidized by the larger society in one way or another. As we have already pointed out, an increasing number of young people do not participate in the labor force. In many cases, the subsidization of youth takes place directly through the parents. Beyond that, however, there is a large and constantly expanding network of subsidizations through the educational system, most of it financed by the state.

At the same time, the youth culture constitutes a huge market. Its peculiar tastes and styles express themselves not only in non-economic behavior but very importantly in patterns of consumption. There are large business interests involved in the marketing of youth clothing and ornamentation, of youth music and its often inordinately expensive technical equipment, of youth art—and, needless to emphasize, of the drugs consumed within the youth culture. This economic market and those who are engaged in doing business in it are involved in an ongoing *interaction* with the youth culture. And, in some instances, some of the youth culture's features are actively manipulated by these vested interests. Whatever may have been the historical origin of the colorful clothing which has now become a kind of youth uniform, it has been vigorously diffused throughout the society by advertising, and has turned out to be immensely profitable to a large number of businesses.

There has been a paradoxical relationship between youth and its sub-cultural consumption patterns. On the one hand, these patterns express what youth wants to be. On the other hand, once they are on the market they can be bought by anyone—including individuals over thirty who would like to identify with youth. As happens inevitably to every area of social life in which advertisement becomes important, the youth culture has become highly subject to the dynamics of *fashion*. That which is truly "with it" changes all the time, at least in part because the fashions are manipulated by those who have an economic interest in them, and thus considerable effort is demanded of the individual who does not wish to be left behind. As a result, the youth culture, which has haughtily disdained the suburban "rat race," has produced its own version of the game of "keeping up with the Joneses."

"STATUS SPHERES," CLASSLESS ECSTASIES AND CONSUMPTION PATTERNS

It is also important to understand the relation of the youth culture to the stratification system. To a considerable degree, the youth culture cuts across class lines. To take up once more Tom Wolfe's helpful term of "status spheres," the youth culture has created symbols and patterns of behavior that are capable of bestowing status upon individuals coming from quite different class backgrounds. In addition, as part of its morality of relentless sincerity (not to say nudity), the youth culture has a strongly egalitarian ethos which has not only made it a locale of quite remarkable racial tolerance but in a real way a kind of classless society. This obliteration of class lines is especially marked in the external manifestations of the sub-culture. Thus young people of all classes can participate in the collective ecstasies of a rock festival (and, as far as is known, this is what actually takes place on these occasions). Class lines begin to be more important when it comes to consumption patterns, since young people of different classes have different amounts of money to spend. We have already referred to the considerable expense involved in obtaining adequate equipment for the reproduction of youth music; not everyone, after all, can afford a top hi-fi system.

But probably the most important class differences are to be found in the areas of values and consciousness. At least in America, it appears that the fullest development of the "new consciousness" of youth has an upper-middle-class location. Thus, in those colleges attended by the youth of the higher classes—rather than the colleges attended by the children of the lower middle class and working class—the youth culture has exhibited its most impressive flowering. This is not the place to speculate on various possible explanations of this relationship. We would, however, like to refer to a previous discussion of differences in child-rearing between classes in American society and to suggest that the most plausible place to look for a sociological explanation of this relationship is there. Not only is upper-middle-class youth more identified with the youth culture, but the latter has been able to win adult sympathy much more in the upper middle class than in the lower strata of American society. Partly, this can be explained by the fact that parents are more likely to be tolerant of the extravagances of their own children than of those of others' children. In any case, upper-middle-class adults have been ready in large numbers to tolerate many, if not all, of the peculiar new ways of the youth culture. Lower-middle-class and working-class people, on the other hand, have been much more inclined to look upon the youth culture as a very dubious phenomenon at best, and a moral abomination at worst. We have recently had occasion to see some of the political implications of this difference.

YOUTH: VOLATILE *CARRIERS* OF A NEW POLITICS AND RELIGION

One aspect of the youth culture that should be emphasized is its volatility. Everything about it makes for rapid change, and indeed invites its being "made" by any number of forces and movements that seek to use it. Its emotionality and its values, as well as its precarious economic structure, all contribute to this. It is important to keep this volatility in mind when looking at recent ideological manifestations of the youth culture, especially in the area of politics and religion. For the last few years, there has existed in the American youth culture what (for lack of a better term) one might call a generally "left mood." It has expressed itself in fairly widespread opposition, ranging from moderate to radical, not only to some current American policies (notably the war in Southeast Asia) but to some of the basic values of the American economic and political system. This has led quite a number of people to view, whether in hope or in anxiety, the youth culture as a potentially "revolutionary" force.

Also, in recent years, there has been a remarkable upsurge of interest in religion (especially in the more occult and esoteric manifestations of religion) in the same sub-culture. A number of people have drawn the conclusion from this that the youth culture is the vanguard of the new age of religion (for example, the well-known writer, Paul Goodman, has spoken of a New Reformation in discussing the youth culture in a recent magazine article). It is possible that the youth culture may indeed be the forerunner or carrier of such political or religious transformations. It is also possible, however, that these trends may change considerably within the not too distant future, precisely because of the aforementioned volatility. It is well to keep this in mind when overly self-assured prognoses are made by some commentators.

YOUTH CULTURE: CONFRONTATION AND CONTINUITY

The elements of conflict between the youth culture and the larger society have been manifest in recent years, not only in America but internationally. The main locale of this conflict has been the university—though it has lately shown signs of extending to the high school. The pattern of confrontation between the university and rebellious students, as it was first enacted at Berkeley some seven years ago, has become, in the minds of many (young and older), the major manifestation of the youth culture.[10] Undoubtedly, this confrontation is of very great importance in our society, and not only important for the future of the university as an institution. It is quite possible, however, to exaggerate the elements of conflict in the relationship between the youth culture and the larger society. There are also important aspects of continuity between the two entities, especially in America. Youth has always been emphasized in America, which, after all, defined itself from the beginning as the "new world," a vigorous and youthful society emerging from the decadent background of the "old world." There has been an ethos of youth in America for a long time—and, indeed, it is as a result of this ethos that so many adults sympathize with youth in at least some of its current aspects. Nor is the identi-

[10] See Daniel Bell and Irving Kristol (eds.), *Confrontation* (New York, Basic Books, 1969).

fication with the young on the part of older people a new phenomenon in America. The middle-aged professor who dresses like a hippie is only repeating the pattern of the middle-aged suburban housewife who dresses like a teenager (and, at least in some places, did so thirty years ago).

COUNTER-CULTURE: A WAY-STATION OR A PERMANENT SETTLEMENT?

Nevertheless, we would not deny the general oppositional motif in the contemporary youth culture. The important question (which we cannot possibly answer here) is whether out of the youth culture is now emerging a permanent *counter-culture* which may eventually contain individuals of various age groups. The youth culture, by its very nature, is a way-station in the life of the individual. Regrettably enough, *everyone,* whatever the length of his hair, eventually gets older. In this respect, many of the manifestations of the youth culture may only be a colorful re-enactment of the venerable American pattern of "sowing wild oats." In other words, society permits the individual to "drop out" for a period of years, and is even willing to subsidize the operation. However, there are indications that for some people the way-station has become a place of permanent settlement. These, of course, are the ones who "drop out" permanently and raise children in this situation. Frequently clustered in communes, or in settlements that are marginal to academic communities, or in the hippie areas of large cities, they usually pursue marginal occupations and ways of life that are emphatically non-middle-class. If this kind of counter-culture maintains itself as a permanent feature of the society, and if it contains sizable numbers of people, this will be a fact of great importance for American society.

READINGS

As we have indicated above, the topic under discussion in this chapter has only recently become a major interest for sociologists. Reliable data are scarce, as are satisfying sociological interpretations. This state of affairs is eloquently expressed by the fact that the authoritative *International Encyclopedia of the Social Sciences,* published in 1968, has no entry under "youth." One of the best-known sociological treatments of youth in general, by an Israeli sociologist strongly influenced by Talcott Parsons, is S. N. Eisenstadt, *From Generation to Generation* (New York, Free Press, 1956), also available in paperback. For a broad sociological interpretation of contemporary culture, including the phenomenon of youth, we would recommend the recent work of a Dutch sociologist, Anton Zijderveld, *The Abstract Society* (Garden City, N.Y., Doubleday, 1970).

Chapter 12

WORK
AND
LEISURE

TO BE AN ADULT means to work. The "seriousness" of life begins when one must work. Childhood and youth, as we have seen, are less than "serious," precisely because they are biographical phases in which the individual is not expected to work. When one is not working, one is assumed to be "playing." Thus, before adulthood, the major activities of the individual are considered to be a form of playing. But no adult works full time either. The adult's life, then, consists of alternating patterns of work and play. Playing, especially in American society, often requires considerable effort and gives remarkably little pleasure. All the same, it is commonly referred to as an activity of our leisure time. In these terms, the life of an adult is organized in rhythms of work and leisure.

NEW FORMS AND NEW PROBLEMS OF WORK AND LEISURE

Work and play are fundamental anthropological categories—that means it is impossible to conceive of man without them. Men have always worked. Men have always played. What has changed in history are the characteristics of each of these two spheres of life and the relation between them. The industrial revolution has produced a fundamental change in this and, as a result, contemporary society has very peculiar forms both of work and of play. One of the most obvious changes has been in the time allocations between these two spheres of human activity. Technological production has progressively reduced the amount of time that most individuals spend at work. Consequently, there has been a very great expansion of leisure time. But there have also been far-reaching changes in the way in which work is experienced and interpreted. Work has increasingly become a "problem" for many individuals.

To say that something is a "problem" is to indicate that people ask questions about what it means. To be sure, such questions have been raised about work by people in pre-industrial societies, but such occasions were very rare compared to the pervasive questions about the "meaning of work" in modern society. In pre-industrial societies, the typical attitude toward work was that it constituted a presumably God-given necessity of human life. It was a matter of fate, destiny, perhaps luck. In many cases, work was connected with religious obligations and rituals. Work was often one of the links that the individual had with the world of the gods. Thus, for example, in classical Hinduism, the proper fulfillment of one's caste duty or *dharma* was the foremost religious obligation of the individual. An essential aspect of *dharma* was the proper carrying out of the occupational tasks belonging to one's particular caste. A classical Hindu saying put it this way: "It is better to fulfill one's own *dharma* poorly than someone else's well." It was within such a religious context that Hindu craftsmen have traditionally prayed to their tools. In other cultures, work was less directly connected with the religious life of the individual. Yet everywhere we find the conception of work as an intrinsic and unavoidable part of human destiny.

To see work as fate, or even as religious obligation, in no way implies that one enjoys it. It is no accident that in the Book of Genesis Adam is *condemned* to labor. What it does mean is that work is not a "problem." One *knows* what it means, therefore one does not ask questions about it.

THE FRAGMENTATION OF WORK

All this has changed with modern industrialism. The vast division of labor brought about by the industrial revolution, which we have had occasion to refer to previously, has had as a consequence that most individuals participate in complex work processes which they cannot grasp in their totality. The classical case of such a process is the assembly line, where each individual worker only performs one minute operation within the total process. He is not concerned with, and need not understand, the steps in the process that lead up to his operation or the steps that follow it. His relationship to the work process, then, is very fragmentary. Most important, he has no relationship—and may actually never see—the final product of his work. Whether or not this makes him unhappy, it almost inevitably leads to a situation in which he must question the meaning of what he is doing.[1]

This transformation in the character of work is most obvious in cases of technological production, as exemplified by the assembly line. Increasingly, however, the same fragmentation of work has been characteristic of occupations further removed from technological production proper. As we have also previously seen, it is characteristic of bureaucracy in a very fundamental way. Today, even scientists often work in teams whose basic structure of work is disturbingly similar to the paradigm of the assembly line. The same is true of lawyers, of high government officials and even of some university teachers. An individual whose job it is to research one small item in a legal case, or to prepare one of twenty sections in a government report, or to teach remedial English to an enormous freshman class, is just as likely to ask questions about the meaning of his work, and perhaps even more so, than the individual whose job it is to do nothing but adjust the nth screw on a piece of machinery.

WORK AS A "VOCATION"

This structural characteristic of work in modern society is combined, in an unfortunate way, with a particular development in the realm of values. Max Weber has shown what happened to the religious concept of "vocation" at the beginning of the modern era.[2] In the Middle Ages (and still in Catholic parlance today), the term referred only to the occupations of the clergy and of monastics. The word "vocation" comes from the Latin verb *vocare,* which means "to call." In other words, the term refers to those occupations to which an individual was supposedly called by God. By comparison with these, other forms of work were "profane," that is, of minor religious and moral significance. Protestantism introduced a radical reinterpretation of the concept

[1] It was Marx who first drew attention to this aspect of work in modern society. He referred to it as the "alienation of labor" and attributed it to capitalism. Most non-Marxist sociologists today accept the basic insight, but trace the "alienation" to technological production rather than to the forms of ownership of the means of production.

[2] In his classic *The Protestant Ethic and the Spirit of Capitalism.*

of vocation. Luther insisted that every lawful occupation was a vocation in the sight of God and that the individual ought to apply to
it the same earnestness that was expected of a priest, a monk or a
nun in the performance of their calling. The Calvinist Reformation
further intensified this understanding. What Weber was interested in
showing was the way in which this reinterpretation of the religious
meaning of work produced a completely new attitude toward economic activity, which he thought was an important causal factor in
the origins of modern capitalism.

Since the Reformation there has taken place a considerable secularization of this concept of vocation, that is, it has been deprived
of its religious significance among most people in modern society.
But the fundamental seriousness with which work is taken under
the aspect of vocation is still very much around. It is still assumed
that work constitutes an essential element in the fulfillment of individual existence. The relationship of this ideological development
to the aforementioned structure of work in modern society is paradoxical: while the industrial revolution has made it increasingly difficult to clearly determine the meaning of work, there is a deeply
instilled notion that work *ought* to have a meaning, indeed to have
a profound meaning for the identity and moral worth of the individual. It is not surprising that, as a result of this paradox, work
should have become a "problem" to many people.

THREE LEVELS OF MAN'S EXPERIENCE OF WORK

Bearing this in mind, it is possible
to distinguish between three types of
work as experienced by the individual. The first type is the one which
can still properly be understood by
the individual as a vocation; that is,
this type refers to work with which the individual can identify and
in the exercise of which he can experience at least a measure of
human fulfillment. At the opposite pole of experience is another
type of work which the individual can only understand as a form of
suffering and as a threat to his self-esteem. Thirdly, between these
two poles is a type of work which the individual experiences as nei-

ther fulfillment nor suffering but as a kind of neutral zone of his life which, while not offering much satisfaction to him, is also humanly tolerable and does not threaten his search for self-fulfillment in other areas of his life. Professionals and higher-echelon executives are typically located on the first level of this occupational hierarchy. The practitioners of such disagreeable occupations as, say, garbage collector or dishwasher are typically located on the bottom level. The great bulk of both white-collar and blue-collar work is to be assigned to the middle level between these two poles.

Conceivably, some such classification could also have been applied to work in pre-industrial societies. What the industrial revolution has done, however, is to greatly expand the middle type of work, especially at the expense of the lowest level. The industrial revolution has progressively tended to eliminate the most odious types of occupations and has made the work milieus of most people in the society at least tolerable. All the same, the question concerning the meaning of work has appeared on all three levels, with different implications but probably with equal urgency. On the top level (no doubt at least partly because of education) we find a variety of often very complex and sophisticated questions about the meaning of a particular occupation: What does it mean to be committed to scholarly excellence in an age of mass education? Is it still possible to maintain the traditional independence of professions such as medicine or the law if one is on a public payroll? What are the social obligations of a business executive? What does it mean to be a social worker? Should social scientists remain politically neutral? Does it still make sense to be a Catholic priest? And so on and so forth.

On the middle level of those enumerated above, the individual is less likely to ask questions about the intrinsic meaning of his work because, by definition, he does not identify himself with it to any appreciable degree. Here, the question typically concerns the relationship of his work to other sectors of his life. Work hours and vacations, as well as retirement age and medical insurance, are important issues. The maintenance and improvement of tolerable conditions at work are also important, as well as job security against the danger that one's work may become obsolete in an age of rapid technological change. Labor unions have become an important institutional means of coping with these problems.

The lowest level of work in our society is probably most similar to what work has been for most people during most of human history—a grinding drudgery. In contemporary society, however, this type of work—with perhaps only a few exceptions—cannot be experienced in the same way that it was experienced in previous periods of history. More precisely, it can no longer be experienced as fate, let alone as religious obligation. Rather, its experience is constantly colored by invidious comparison with the work of others. It is therefore experienced by the individual as an acute affront to his dignity as a person, and even as a violation of his basic human rights. Work, then, is "problematic" on just about all levels of the occupational hierarchy in contemporary society.

VARIOUS APPROACHES TO STUDYING WORK

The Classics

Sociologists have been concerned with the question of work from the beginning of the discipline's history. At least to some extent this was due to the influence of Karl Marx and the effort of most of the classical sociologists to find approaches to modern society alternative to that of Marxism. Marx, in his early, more philosophical writings, had strongly emphasized the crucial importance of labor not only in human history but very fundamentally in terms of what man is. In Marx's later work, and in the ensuing development of Marxist theory, a central place in the analysis of contemporary society was given to economics and economic activity, again pushing the phenomena of work into the forefront of attention. One of Émile Durkheim's major works, *On the Division of Labor in Society* (published in 1893), deals with the relationship of work processes to society. Max Weber, particularly in connection with his concept of rationalization (as previously discussed), repeatedly touches on problems of work. Of the classical sociologists it is probably Thorstein Veblen who gave the most central place to work in his study of contemporary society—*The Theory of the Leisure Class* (1899), *The Theory*

of Business Enterprise (1904) and *The Instinct of Workmanship*
(1914).

American Approaches: Industrial Sociology

All the same, it is probably fair to say that these classical studies
have rather little to do with the very extensive interest in problems
of work in recent American sociology. This interest mainly derives
from two related but distinct developments in American sociology
—the one generally known as industrial sociology, and the other as
the sociology of occupations.

Industrial sociology in America can be dated rather accurately
from 1927, when a far-reaching experiment began at the Hawthorne works of the Western Electric Company in Chicago. For
some time before that date, the company had been engaged in a
number of experiments at Hawthorne designed to study the impact
on the productivity of workers of various changes in the physical
work environment. Particular interest was focused on the nature of
lighting, and a control group of workers had been subjected to various lighting arrangements during their work. Very curious results
emerged from this experimentation. It was found that the productivity of the control group kept climbing quite steadily regardless of
the various changes by which the physical environment was manipulated. Thus the workroom was illuminated with different kinds of
light; the intensity of light was increased or decreased; sometimes
the workers were bathed in brilliant light and sometimes practically
worked in darkness—and all the time their productivity climbed.
Not surprisingly, the engineers in charge of the experiment became
more and more puzzled. It finally dawned on somebody that perhaps some essential cue had been missed all along.

The company then invited Elton Mayo, an Australian industrial
expert connected at that time with the Harvard Business School, to
come in and take over the experiment. Mayo and his associates
quickly came to the conclusion that the essential variable in the situation was not any of the factors that the engineers had been playing around with but was, indeed, the *group* itself—that is, the
group of workers that had been kept together for such a long time
for the sake of the experiment. As a result of the experiment, not

only had an enormous amount of attention been bestowed upon the group by management and by the engineers involved in all this activity but inevitably the members of the group had come to feel much closer ties with each other. Mayo decided that this was the crucial factor in the group's climbing productivity.[3]

The Hawthorne experiments marked a dramatic discovery in the development of the sociology of work (all the more dramatic because it was quite unforeseen at the time the experiments began)— namely, the discovery of the importance of the informal group in industry. Mayo developed this basic insight in a number of works.[4] His interest in all this was not only scholarly but practical. He felt that he had found the clue to a new kind of industrial management that would be both more humane and more efficient. Mayo's work stimulated the development of what came to be called "human relations" in American management. This whole development has been sharply criticized by some as a sophisticated technique for management to manipulate and control workers.[5] Be this as it may, a considerable body of work was produced dealing with the kind of problems that Mayo had first drawn attention to.

After World War II, the number of sociologists interested in these problems greatly increased, and there emerged a distinct sub-discipline in the field, known as industrial sociology.[6] While the center of this research activity remained in the United States, industrial sociology became quite important in Western Europe (particularly in France), and in recent years has even become quite influential in the socialist countries of Eastern Europe. The focus in almost all of these studies has been on the micro-world of work, that is, on the

[3] For a description of the Hawthorne experiments, see Fritz Roethlisberger and William Dickson, *Management and the Worker* (Cambridge, Mass., Harvard University Press, 1939); also, George Homans, *The Human Group* (New York, Harcourt, Brace, 1950).

[4] Elton Mayo, *The Human Problems of an Industrial Civilization* (Boston, Harvard University Graduate School of Business Administration, 1933), and his *The Social Problems of an Industrial Civilization* (Boston, Harvard University Graduate School of Business Administration, 1945).

[5] See Loren Baritz, *The Servants of Power* (Middletown, Conn., Wesleyan University Press, 1960).

[6] For introductions to this field, see Delbert Miller and William Form, *Industrial Sociology* (New York, Harper, 1951), and William Whyte, *Men at Work* (Homewood, Ill., Irwin, 1961).

actual social environment in which work takes place. By the nature of this approach this has brought about a considerable number of individual studies of this or that work situation.[7] There have also been various attempts to integrate these findings into a general theory. These efforts have been very close to the theory of organizations that we have dealt with before.[8] Logically enough, a closely related area of study has been the sociology of labor unions.[9] In most of this work, whether oriented toward management or toward labor, there has been a strong practical bent and an interest in the applicability of the sociological findings.

The Chicago School: The Sociology of Occupations

The so-called sociology of occupations has had a very different origin and outlook. It comes out of the Chicago School of urban sociology, and particularly from the latter's interest in some of the more colorful corners of city life. As we have had occasion to remark before, the Chicago sociologists were animated by a relentless curiosity about every conceivable aspect of social life in their city. One of the results of this was a series of monographs on some less-than-respectable occupations, such as the hobo, the taxi-dance-hall girl and the professional thief.[10] In these studies, the habitat, the customs and the adventures of these marginal social types were described with a loving attention to detail. It may be added in passing that some of these studies have become classical examples of the use of the descriptive method by sociologists—they are master-

[7] For some typical monographs, see Lloyd Warner and J. O. Low, *The Social System of the Modern Factory* (New Haven, Conn., Yale University Press, 1947); Charles Walker and Robert Guest, *The Man on the Assembly Line* (Cambridge, Mass., Harvard University Press, 1952); Ely Chinoy, *Automobile Workers and the American Dream* (Garden City, N.Y., Doubleday, 1955).

[8] See Wilbert Moore, *Industrial Relations and the Social Order* (New York, Macmillan, 1951), and, for a French approach, Georges Friedmann, *The Anatomy of Work* (New York, Free Press, 1961).

[9] See Seymour Lipset, Martin Trow and James Coleman, *Union Democracy* (New York, Free Press, 1956), and Jack Barbash, *The Practice of Unionism* (New York, Harper, 1956).

[10] Nels Anderson, *The Hobo* (Chicago, University of Chicago Press, 1923); Paul Cressy, *The Taxi-Dance Hall* (Chicago, University of Chicago Press, 1932); Edwin Sutherland, *The Professional Thief* (Chicago, University of Chicago Press, 1937).

pieces of careful ethnography. After some time, some of the people from the Chicago School turned their attention to more respectable occupations (perhaps because they were running out of disreputable ones). Following World War II, the sociology of occupations became a recognized discipline, centered at the University of Chicago, and most ably represented by Everett Hughes.[11] Mostly publishing their studies in the *American Journal of Sociology,* Hughes and his associates wrote a number of monographs about a variety of occupations, ranging from medical students to apartment-house janitors.[12]

Again, the preponderant focus of the sociology of occupations has been on the micro-world of work. Its very method—what the Chicago School has called "participant observation"—has made it difficult to move from this level of analysis to the macro-world of institutions that organize work in contemporary society. Wherever this latter level is touched upon, the argument tends to veer off into general organization theory, or else to leave the sphere of sociology altogether and involve itself in questions of economics and political science. Nor have those who have called themselves sociologists of occupations been very much involved in questions of overall occupational mobility such as we discussed previously in connection with stratification—though there has been an interest in the prestige ratings of different occupations and the way in which these have changed over time.

The Structural Approach

Because of the monographic and micro-sociological character of most of this work, it is rather difficult to summarize its overall contribution to sociology and to our understanding of contemporary society. Generally speaking, it may be said that the sociological study of work has focused on three aspects: the structural, the social-psychological and the ideological. Sociologists have made an effort to describe and explain the social structure within which work takes place. As we have indicated, this concern has been mainly with the micro-world of work. Under this heading come

[11] See Everett Hughes, *Men and Their Work* (New York, Free Press, 1958).
[12] See Sigmund Nosow and William Form (eds.), *Man, Work and Society* (New York, Basic Books, 1962).

such questions as: What is the relationship of formal and informal organizations of work? How are informal groupings of workers set up? What are the patterns of leadership, and of resistance to leadership, both in the formal and the informal organizations of work? What are the unwritten rules and mores of particular work situations? Where the sociology of work has gone beyond these questions into the institutional problems of the macro-world, it has tended to ask very much the same questions that we have looked at in our previous discussion of the sociology of organizations. (This is certainly also true of those sociologists who have studied labor unions and professional organizations.) An interesting problem on this level is that of conflict and compromise between different occupational groups competing with each other.

The Social-psychological Approach

The social-psychological aspects of the sociology of work can be summed up in one question: What does work (or a particular type of work) do to the people engaged in it? Put in more proper sociological language: What processes of socialization are let loose in particular work situations? In dealing with this question the concept of *career* has been given a particular meaning.[13] The term "career," as used in ordinary usage, already refers to the passage of an individual through predetermined stages. In the sociology of occupations this has been given a psychological twist, and career now refers to a series of *psychological* stages. Thus sociologists have studied the changes in outlook, and perhaps even personality, that a medical student undergoes in the course of his training. But it has also been possible to apply this concept to the "careers" of hospital patients and prison inmates.[14] The general insight here is that as an individual goes through the stages of his external career in an occupation (or, for that matter, in any other institutional timetable), there is a corresponding internal career during which certain things happen within his own consciousness.

Thus, for example, a medical student in the course of his studies not only learns (one hopes) the body of knowledge and the techni-

[13] *Ibid.,* pp. 284ff.
[14] Julius Roth, *Timetables* (Indianapolis, Bobbs-Merrill, 1963).

cal skills that are required for the practice of medicine. The medical student also *becomes a doctor*. This involves considerable changes in norms and opinions about various matters, but finally it also involves a change in identity (more precisely, in self-identification). In the end, ideally, this process is completed when the individual can be awakened in the middle of the night and, upon being asked who he is, will reply with automatic self-assurance, "I am a doctor." Obviously, there will not be this degree of self-identification in the case of occupations that are less filled with meaning to the individual. Thus an individual awakened in the middle of the night is less likely to reply to the aforementioned question, "I'm a salesgirl at Woolworth's." Almost all occupational careers, however, let loose socialization processes of one kind or another and of varying intensity. One pole here is represented by those occupations with which an individual identifies with pride. Equally significant for sociological analysis, however, is the other pole, in which the individual relates to his occupation as a kind of stigma. As we have pointed out before, most occupations in contemporary society are located somewhere between these two poles.

The Ideological Approach

Finally, the sociology of work concerns itself with the ideologies of different occupations. In some cases, these are very sophisticated.[15] Thus the upper echelons of management in the American business community have developed an ideology that involves far-reaching propositions concerning economics, politics and even the nature of man. Other occupations have developed more limited ideologies, limited in scope to whatever their particular vested interests may be. Thus, for example, the ideology of dental technicians need not cover any more ground than is necessary to protect their status as against that of the dentist, in the shadow of whose much greater status they must maintain themselves. Finally, there are such ideologies as that of the burlesque dancer who maintains that she is an artist, and the garbage collector who defines himself as a front-line

[15] See, for example, Francis Sutton *et al., The American Business Creed* (Cambridge, Mass., Harvard University Press, 1956); also, Nosow and Form, *op. cit.,* pp. 403ff.

fighter in the urban crisis. Not surprisingly, the study of occupational ideologies can be used as an exercise for the sociological analysis of confidence games and one-upmanship of the most colorful kind.

THE SOCIOLOGY OF LEISURE

To reiterate: Adult life consists of a rhythm between work and leisure. Between these two aspects of social life, sociologists have overwhelmingly concerned themselves with the former. But there has been a certain amount of sociological study of leisure, and even some tentative beginnings of a sub-discipline calling itself the sociology of leisure.[16] If there is such a thing as the sociology of leisure, then, undoubtedly, its father is, once more, Thorstein Veblen, especially through his aforementioned book on what he called the "leisure class." [17] The term, however, is indicative of what has happened since Veblen's work.

In 1899, when Veblen wrote, he was dealing explicitly with an upper class and its patterns of leisure. Since then, leisure has become a mass phenomenon. Nevertheless, some of Veblen's ideas on leisure are still applicable today. Probably the most influential concept deriving from this work of Veblen's is that of *conspicuous consumption*. By this Veblen meant consumption whose purpose is not to satisfy particular needs of the consumer but rather to serve as a symbol of the consumer's status—and since the symbol was to be widely visible to others, the consumption had to be very noticeable also. What Veblen was writing about under this heading were the extravagances of the rich during the so-called Gilded Age of American capitalism. It remains true today also, however, and in all social classes, that leisure is the time for conspicuous consumption. Nor does this term necessarily have to be understood in a negative sense. In their leisure, individuals engage in activities that are de-

[16] See Eric Larrabee and Rolf Meyersohn (eds.), *Mass Leisure* (New York, Free Press, 1958); Nels Anderson, *Work and Leisure* (New York, Free Press, 1961); Sebastian DeGrazia, *Of Time, Work and Leisure* (New York, 20th Century Fund, 1962).

[17] Thorstein Veblen, *The Theory of the Leisure Class* (New York, Macmillan, 1899).

signed to tell the world who they really are. In this sense, taking up the study of a foreign language or becoming an expert in trout fishing is no more and no less conspicuous consumption than the purchase of an expensive sports car or devotion to a valuable stamp collection.

WHAT SHOULD I DO WITH MY LEISURE?—A MODERN PROBLEM

To say this is to put one's finger on one of the essential sociological relations between work and leisure. For most people in modern society, as we have indicated before, work no longer serves to fulfill their personal aspirations or to provide for them a plausible way to identify themselves. Therefore these fundamental human needs have to be met in places and times other than those of work. A major structural presupposition of such a state of affairs is the great division of labor that has been brought about by the industrial revolution, and the institutional segregation of work that we have had occasion to mention a number of times. A further presupposition, however, is that the individual is given a considerable degree of liberty in how he is to organize his leisure time. This too is an innovation of modern society. We may assume that there never existed a human society in which people worked all the time. There have always been occasions when people did something else besides work. In most preindustrial societies, however, these occasions were also highly institutionalized. That is, the activities that were undertaken at such times were also highly structured by society. While play is a universal human phenomenon, leisure in our modern sense is not. In preindustrial societies, most play activities were institutionally structured through ritual and ceremony.[18] With the advent of modern society (for reasons that probably have to do with the decline of religion), this institutionalization of the work-free times of social life became much weaker. As a result, the individual was increasingly left to his own resources in organizing this part of his life. He was

[18] See Roger Caillois, *Man, Play and Games* (New York, Free Press, 1961).

made free to shape at least a great part of his leisure time in accordance with his own desires—or, if one prefers, he was condemned
to this.

Modern society is characterized by a fundamental institutional
cleavage which contemporary German sociologists have called the
cleavage between the *public and private spheres* of social life.[19]
The institutions of the public sphere (notably, those of the economy
and the state) continue to be firmly structured. This is much less
true of the private sphere. The most important relation of most individuals to the public sphere is through their work. Conversely,
the private sphere is experienced (or inhabited) during leisure time.

The new freedom provided by the private sphere can be experienced both as opportunity and as oppression. In the first case, individuals might feel liberated to undertake activities of every conceivable sort and to indulge in their own "creativity" as far as their
resources will permit. Oppression begins precisely when individuals
sense that their resources are limited. This is obviously the case
when one thinks of economic resources. Thus an individual may
feel that he could most truly fulfill himself by sailing around the
Mediterranean in a yacht, or by flying a plane, or by owning a Pi-
casso original. In these instances, lack of funds may decisively crip-
ple this individual's quest for self-fulfillment. Resources may be
limited in other ways, though. Thus another individual may feel
that he can most authentically fulfill himself by having five affairs
going simultaneously. *This* quest for fulfillment may be abruptly
stopped by physical collapse. But perhaps the most depressing experience of limitation in all of this may have to do with limited resources of the mind and the imagination. The advertising man who
identifies himself as "really a very creative person," and who is
writing the great American novel of the century on the sly, may
discover that no one agrees with his own estimation of this opus.
Or he may even conclude himself that he has nothing to say—or
that he can't write. The freedom to shape one's own leisure time
and to use it for fulfillment of important personal needs is thus a
double-edged sword.

[19] Notably Arnold Gehlen, Helmut Schelsky and Juergen Habermas. The relevant works are not available in English at the time of writing.

NEW STRUCTURES FOR LEISURE: "PROGRAMS" AND CONSUMPTION

Perhaps one can speak of mercies of society alongside those of nature. We might take it as such a mercy that modern society, after having opened up the private sphere for all these terrible options, then proceeded to develop certain new institutional programs. These pre-empted some of these options and gave the individual an opportunity to be relieved of the necessity of relying on his own "creativity." Arnold Gehlen, one of the aforementioned German sociologists, has used the term *secondary institutions* to describe this phenomenon. The term refers to all those social agencies and programs which serve to structure (or, if one prefers, to restructure) the private sphere, which modern society originally left distressingly unstructured.

The word "program" should be taken seriously here. At work, the individual is presented with very firm programs. During work hours it is very clear what he ought to be doing and how he ought to go about it. Both ends and means are usually clearly defined. Needless to say, this does not mean that the individual likes these programs, but at least he is freed from the obligation to invent them. The private sphere, as it first emerged in modern society, was bereft of such programs. The secondary institutions provide them anew. They tell the individual what to do in his leisure time, and they offer assistance to him in his quest for private fulfillment and self-identification.

Some of these programs have to do with consumption, some do not. Leisure has become a very important area of consumption, and thus an important area for economic organization. A short time spent in front of an American television screen will quickly convince anyone of this fact. If one wants to, and has the money, one can spend all one's leisure in the pursuit of consumption. In this connection (as advertisers know very well), it is important to stress that the value of such consumption for the individual lies not only in the actual objects or services that are consumed but in their "image," that is, the relationship that they have to the imagination. To own a certain type of car is, at least partially, to define oneself as a certain kind of person. The same is true of a great range of material objects of consumption. The same is also true, however, of a large number of services that one can purchase—services provided by agencies ranging from a symphony orchestra to a psychotherapist. Music and psychotherapy, whatever else they may be, are *also* purchasable commodities; indeed, their consumption may be very conspicuous and intimately related to the individual's efforts to establish his status. It would be superficial, however, if one only looked on such activities in terms of what Erving Goffman calls "impression management." The individual engaging in these activities may not only wish to impress others but to define himself in a very serious way. Thus the intended end product of this consumption may be deeply significant statements of personal identity such as, "I could not live without Mozart," or "I have finally come to understand that I detest women."

Leisure is thus the arena of a multitude of social activities. Some, as we have seen, are linked to consumption. Others are not. Some are highly organized. Others are not. For example, the individual may be a fanatical photography fan. This may involve him in an endless and ruinous sequence of purchases of photographic equipment of various sorts. It may put him on the mailing list of a whole set of companies making and selling photographic equipment. It may also lead him to join clubs and organizations whose members concern themselves with photography. But there are leisure-time activities of a different nature. For example, an individual filling his leisure time with a consuming interest in music can also spend a great deal of money in acquiring hi-fi equipment and records, and he can join any number of organizations whose program has to do with music in one way or another. He may also, however, acquire nothing more than a beat-up old guitar, which he may play either in blissful solitude or in the company of a few friends.

Closely related to the sociology of leisure have been studies in mass culture [20] and mass communications.[21] The former has been

[20] See Bernard Rosenberg and David White (eds.), *Mass Culture* (New York, Free Press, 1957).

[21] See Wilbur Schramm (ed.), *The Process and Effects of Mass Communication* (Urbana, Ill., University of Illinois Press, 1954).

very much related to the concerns of the sociology of leisure and
has concerned itself with such questions as the kind of people who
frequent museums, the social content of popular literature or the
ideology promoted by advertising. A comparatively small number
of sociologists have occupied themselves with questions of this sort.
The sociological study of mass communications, on the other hand,
has become a sizable enterprise. Some of its studies have been quite
technical and limited in scope, but there have been some important
investigations into the role of the mass media in contemporary society. One important area of inquiry here has been the relative importance of mass media and of face-to-face relations in the formation of opinions and values. One significant result of these studies
appears to be a general consensus that the mass media act directly
upon the individual in only relatively few cases. The more usual
impact is through the mediation of immediate face-to-face social
relationships.

LEISURE: A STUDY OF GROWING INTEREST

Some general trends of the occupational system of modern society are
very clear, and their continuation in
the future is very likely. Probably
the most fundamental trend directly
related to the development of mod-
ern technology is the expansion of the white-collar sector of the occupational system. This is very likely to continue, and the spread of
automation is accelerating the process. Very probably, then, there
will be a continuing shrinkage of work time for most individuals,
and a concomitant expansion of leisure time. American labor statistics show a continuing trend through which an ever-expanding
segment of the labor force is engaged in activities geared to the leisure-time market, such as travel, entertainment, hobbies, adult education, therapeutic activities of various sorts—and, last but not
least, the mass media of communication, through which all of these
are propagated. It is thus very likely that the sociology of leisure
and, more generally, the sociology of the secondary institutions of
the private sphere will become an increasingly important concern
for sociological inquiry.

READINGS

Probably the best course for outside reading would be to have a look at some case studies in the sociology of work and/or leisure. For this purpose the reader may turn to the following collections: Sigmund Nosow and William Form (eds.), *Man, Work and Society* (New York, Basic Books, 1962); Peter Berger (ed.), *The Human Shape of Work* (New York, Macmillan, 1964); Eric Larrabee and Rolf Meyersohn (eds.), *Mass Leisure* (New York, Free Press, 1958). Alternatively, the opportunity may be taken to read a sociological classic: Thorstein Veblen, *The Theory of the Leisure Class* (New York, Macmillan, 1899), also available in paperback.

Chapter 13

POWER

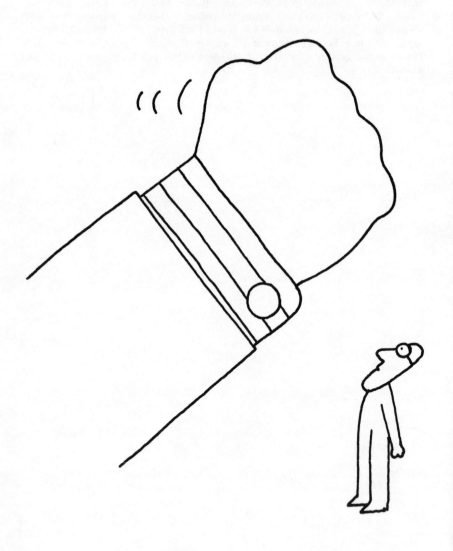

DOING THINGS I DON'T REALLY WANT TO DO: THE EXPERIENCE OF POWER

Everyday life is full of experiences of power and of the differences in power between people. This is very much so in the micro-world of the individual. Within the family, in school or at work the individual continuously realizes that he cannot do everything he wants to do; and most of the time, the obstacles to the realization of his wishes are other people. Conversely, the individual knows which other people he can get to do things that *they* do not want to do, using means that range from physical force to gentle cajoling. These microscopic manifestations of power can, of course, be very significant to the individual—overwhelmingly so to the child. The adult, however, has his most significant experiences of power through a variety of encounters with the institutions of the macro-world. A dominant place among these institutions is occupied by the state or government, the tentacles of which appear to reach into every aspect of everyday life.

WHO ARE *THOSE PEOPLE?*

Especially in the lower strata of society, this experience of power is well expressed in the category of "them." It is "them" who, behind the scenes, make the real decisions that affect the individual's life. "They" are really running things. "They" are pulling the strings. "They" really know what is going on. The social territory covered by this category is not identical with the area of political institutions, but they occupy a pre-eminent place in it. From city hall to Washington, there are various embodiments of "them" who confront the individual with exhibitions of power that very often seem to him to be arbitrary and even mysterious. As one goes up in the stratification system, this experience of power against powerlessness diminishes somewhat. At any rate, middle-class individuals tend to have more organized notions as to who "they" are (which does not mean at all that the notions are accurate), and there may even be some idea as to how it might be

possible to get back at "them." Even here, though, there continues
to be a quality of opaqueness about power relations in the larger
society. Specifically, there is a great deal of uncertainty as to how
the formally established institutions of the political order relate to
other institutions, especially those of the economy. Which are the
labor unions that have most influence in city hall? What economic
interests are represented by which state legislators? Which aspects of
American foreign policy are dictated by corporation interests? It is
questions such as these which make clear that the category of
"them" is not just limited to the lower strata. Very few sociologists
have had the opportunity to penetrate those top levels of the society
at which power is really a matter of "us" rather than "them." All
the same, we may have the sneaking suspicion that, even at those
rarefied heights, there may be occasional doubts about just who belongs with "us" and whether there may not be some sinister forces
lurking as a potential "them" in the background.

POLITICAL
SCIENTISTS AND
SOCIOLOGISTS:
CONVERGING
APPROACHES

The scientific discipline that has
made political institutions its special
area of interest is political science.
Until very recently, however, political scientists, especially in America,
have done one of two things: either
they have concentrated their attention (and in this they are similar to
Constitutional lawyers) on the formal structures of the political
order—comparing, for example, the peculiarities of the American
political system with those of British or French democracy—or
they have concentrated on the behavior of people with regard to
their formal political institutions—accumulating, in this area, a
large body of data about such phenomena as voting behavior and
participation in political parties. Sociologists, by the very genius of
their discipline, have, by contrast, tended to look at those phenomena of power that may be discerned *behind* or *beneath* the formal
political institutions. The fundamental assumption in this is that
the latter do not exhaust the phenomena of power in a society. Indeed,

one of the crucial sociological problems is the relationship of power as "officially" defined and the various "unofficial" manifestations of power. Thus a distinct sub-discipline has developed, known as political sociology.[1]

Especially in recent years, there has been a coming together of the work of political sociologists and sociologically inclined political scientists. But, in any case, power is not a new concern in sociology. It was a central question of sociological thought from the discipline's inception, and it is not easy to see how this could have been otherwise. In classical sociology, it was two figures in particular who made the question of power a central concern for their sociological theory. These two were Max Weber and Vilfredo Pareto.

WEBER'S ANALYSIS

It is probably fair to say that the basic categories for the sociological analysis of power are still those that were originally constructed by Weber.[2] The key categories, which together constitute an analytic framework of their own, are *power, authority and legitimacy.*

FIRST: POWER EVEN AGAINST RESISTANCE

Power is defined by Weber as the probability that an individual or a group will be able to carry out its will even against resistance. This is regardless of the means by which such resistance is overcome. The matter of resistance is very important here. It serves to differentiate phenomena of power from what is generally called "leadership." The difference becomes most ob-

[1] For an overview, see S. N. Eisenstadt (ed.), *Political Sociology* (New York, Basic Books, 1971). For some basic statements in the sub-discipline, see Harold Lasswell and Abraham Kaplan, *Power and Society* (New Haven, Conn., Yale University Press, 1950); William Kornhauser, *The Politics of Mass Society* (New York, Free Press, 1959); Seymour Lipset, *Political Man* (Garden City, N.Y., Doubleday, 1960).

[2] Max Weber, *The Theory of Social and Economic Organization* (New York, Oxford University Press, 1947), pp. 152ff. and pp. 324ff.

vious in terms of everyday life. Almost all human groups have
leaders of one sort or another. Suppose that a group of students in
a dormitory are discussing how they should spend the evening. Various ideas will be put forth. It is likely that in such a group there
will be one or two individuals whose ideas will count more than
those of the others. Indeed, it is even likely that the ideas proposed
by the others are actually put forth as suggestions (President Nixon
would call them "options") to the leaders. In the end, in most cases,
the decision of the leaders will be the one that really sets the group
in motion. It does not make very much sense to call such a process
an expression of power. An entirely different social situation arises
when, say, one member of the group stubbornly sticks to his own
idea against the decision made by the leaders. At that point, subtly
(or not so subtly, as the case may be), the recalcitrant group member may be presented with an "or else" proposition. He will then either bow to the decision made by the leadership "or else" he may
have to face various real or imagined disagreeable consequences—
which may range from getting beaten up or being expelled from
the group to being given a hard time verbally. At this point it does
make sense to speak of power. The phrase "real or imagined," in
connection with the consequences of continued resistance, points to
the variety of means that may underlie the exercise of power. Some
of these may be very real indeed, including, in the last resort, employment of physical force. It is quite possible, however, that
power rests on means of enforcement that lie only in the imagination. A little boy may have his way on the playground because he
is supported by his big brother. He may also have his way because
he can threaten to call in his big brother, who in fact is sitting just
around the corner. But it is also possible that he may have his way
by invoking a big brother who does not exist. Sociologically speaking, all three cases are instances of successfully exercised power.
The same goes for power on the macro-level. Here, too, there may
be real big brothers, or big brothers who exist only in the minds of
people. The derisive comment attributed to Stalin on an occasion
when someone mentioned the power of the Catholic Church—
"How many divisions does the Pope have?"—showed a remarkable
lack of sociological sophistication on the part of the Russian dicta-

tor. Needless to say, the Pope has no divisions at all. But his power is very great—*over those who believe in it*. We shall come back to this point presently.

PREVENTING DEVIANCE AND CARRYING OUT DECISIONS: SOCIAL CONTROL AND POWER

The category of power is, of course, closely related to that of social control, which we have discussed previously. In both cases we are dealing with phenomena that involve societal coercion against recalcitrant individuals or groups. There is an important difference, though. Social control is, as it were, a negative category. It refers to societal mechanisms that are designed to prevent deviant or disruptive conduct. Power has more positive implications: it is not just a matter of preventing someone from doing what is not desired by the society but rather a question of carrying out the will of an individual or a group. What is more, the category of social control suggests some sort of unified social system which tries to keep individuals and groups within its bounds. The category of power, on the other hand, suggests conflict. The will to power of one individual can clash with that of another, and the same is true of groups, institutions or entire societies. Thus, when the police put a criminal in jail, it makes sense to speak of social control. But when two criminal syndicates are fighting over a territory, it makes a lot of sense to speak of a power clash, but very little sense to try to subsume this phenomenon under the category of social control. For this very reason, the category of social control has been favored by those sociologists who tend to look upon society as a functioning system, while those sociologists who have emphasized conflict in society have tended to use the term "power."

Be this as it may, just as it is impossible to conceive of a functioning society without social controls, it is impossible to imagine a society of any sort without the presence of power—and this means power with the Weberian stipulation "or else." This statement is not altogether accurate. There have, of course, been visions of society

in which there will be no more differences in power between people
and in which the structures of power will disappear in favor of a
freely arrived at consensus. Such a vision can be realized in small
groups. Some may believe in the possibility of its realization on a
larger societal scale in the future. So far, there are no empirical instances of this. All societies that we know of in human history have
contained structures of power and have been full of struggles over
this power. Most sociologists are likely to be skeptical over the idea
that this may change in the foreseeable future.

THE "PROBABILITY" THAT POWER WILL PREVAIL

One other term in Weber's definition
of power should be emphasized.
This is the term "probability." No
exercise of power, however awesome, is an absolutely sure thing.
There is always the chance that one
day the "or else" will be put to the test—and at that point it is always possible that the test cannot be met. But it is equally clear
that such absolute certainty, while unattainable, is also unneces-
sary. For most practical purposes, for those who wish to exercise
power it is enough that they can operate in the realm of probability. All the same, the term suggests something quite important
about power, namely, its intrinsic precariousness. This is true in the
micro-world as much as in the macro-world. Every playground
bully may one day find his match. So may every dictator. Neither
one can be absolutely certain as to how long this day of reckoning
can be postponed. This may be a depressing thought for bullies
and dictators; it is a cheering one for almost everybody else.

SECOND: THE HABIT OF OBEDIENCE AND AUTHORITY

Authority is again defined by Weber in terms of this kind of probability —namely, it is the probability that a specific order will be obeyed by specific individuals or groups. The essential difference between power and authority is the continuity of the latter.[3] Power, even at its most overwhelming, can be a sudden and momentary thing: an order is given, it is obeyed despite resistance and that may well be the end of it. Such exercise of power obviously cannot have any continuing effect on a society. To have such an effect it is necessary that power be exercised in a durable and systematic form. This means that people become habituated to this exercise of power, or, in other words, that a durable discipline is imposed upon people's conduct. At that point, power becomes not just a momentary domination or the general threat that such domination may be imposed, but it becomes an orderly exercise by which specific people get into the habit of obeying specific commands.

Once more, of course, this is not a sure thing. As history makes perfectly clear, authority may one day collapse (that is, be successfully resisted or overthrown), even after very prolonged duration. Authority, like power itself, is precarious. Yet, if authority has been successfully imposed upon a particular human group over a long period of time, the probability of its self-maintenance increases. The reason for this is habit. Habit is an important factor precisely when an old authority has been overthrown and a new one seeks to establish itself in its place. Thus revolutionary governments are extremely tenuous in their hold on power in the period immediately following their takeover. Naturally, it is important what they do during this period. But even if they do nothing else

[3] A. M. Henderson and Talcott Parsons, who first translated this part of Weber's work, used the term "imperative control" for Weber's *Herrschaft*, adding in a footnote that, for most purposes, "authority" (which includes the notion of legitimacy) would be the less awkward term. We have followed this less awkward usage here.

but simply hold on to power (that is, in Weber's terms, if they continue to exercise authority), their chance of survival increases with time; people get used to them. Anyone who wishes to use his power, whatever that may be based upon, in order to have durable effects on a society faces the basic problem of transforming this power into authority.

THIRD: LEGITIMACY

Habituation is not the only factor by which power becomes durable authority. Another crucial factor is *legitimacy*. By legitimacy Weber means the belief held by people that the authority over them is not only a simple fact but is a fact charged with moral content. In other words, when we say that a particular authority is "legitimate," we mean that people believe that its exercise of power is just, that those who hold the power do so rightfully. The process by which legitimacy is acquired is called *legitimation*. Unless an authority can successfully legitimate itself, its survival is unlikely. An authority devoid of legitimacy must constantly reaffirm its power by the use of physical force. This is very uneconomical. The normal business of a society cannot proceed very well if everybody in that society has constantly to be hit over the head. If only for such practical reasons, those who hold power are likely to try to enlist the acceptance of at least a majority of the people over whom this power is exercised. The continuous use of physical force, however, is not only uneconomical, it is also self-defeating. It breeds resistance. More precisely, it breeds resistance *unless* it can cloak itself in legitimacy in the eyes of at least a majority of the population. Only at that point can it be used effectively against whatever minority continues to resist.

Legitimacy very clearly is in the mind. To return to the previous example of Stalin's question about the number of divisions available to the Pope, legitimacy exists only as long as there are those who believe in it. It too, therefore, is of a fundamentally precarious nature. It too, however, has a capacity to grow with time. Hans Kelsen, an Austrian legal philosopher, has coined the suggestive phrase "the normative power of facticity." By facticity is meant here the simple facts of a political situation. The term "normative" is synonymous with Weber's term "legitimate." In other words, what Kelsen is saying is that facts *generate* legitimacy. The underlying mechanism of this is, once again, that of habituation. Thus, although legitimacy is clearly in the mind, it can be brought about not just by persuasion or propaganda but by forcing people to come to terms with certain facts. For example, people in American society who are opposed to racial integration can be subjected to some kind of liberal propaganda that tells them this would be a good thing for them. It is very possible that such propaganda has a way of influencing some of them. However, it has been found in a number of areas (for example, in housing projects and in the military) that the most persuasive way of changing people's minds about racial integration is to simply change the facts. Thus a prejudiced white person who is compelled by the situation to interact with blacks is under pressure to revise his point of view. The evidence seems to indicate that, under such pressure, he is much more likely to do so than under the impact of propaganda only. The relationship between power and legitimacy is thus a complicated one. On the one hand, the continuing and successful exercise of power depends on legitimacy. On the other hand, such exercise of power produces legitimacy. For example, with regard to civil wars (in Indochina and elsewhere), some commentators have argued that it is essential "to win the hearts and minds of the people"—that is, to convince people that one side in the struggle is legitimate, the other not. Other commentators have said that the important thing is to win battles, with each victory convincing people that one side has the power to win in the end. It is important to understand that these two views are by no means contradictory. Political institutions are maintained in power through a subtle interplay between the hard facts of power and the shifting ways in which this power is perceived and judged in the minds of people.

LEGITIMATIONS FOR AUTHORITY

Weber differentiated between various types of authority in terms of differences in legitimacy. He distinguishes between three major types: *traditional, charismatic* and *legal-rational*. In each case, the basic question can be put as follows: On what basis do those in authority have the right to give commands to the population under their sway? In a traditional type of authority, this question is simply answered in terms of precedent. In other words, legitimacy rests upon the fact that things have always been done this way. For example, why does the King of Egypt, and only he, have the right to marry his sister? Answer: Because kings of Egypt have always done this. Charismatic authority, by contrast, rests upon the extraordinary claims made on behalf of those who exercise it. By virtue of this extraordinary quality, charismatic leaders abrogate or modify tradition. The reiterated phrase of Jesus in the New Testament, "You have heard it said—but I say unto you . . . ," constitutes a claim to charismatic authority in pure form. Question: By what right does this man make such extraordinary statements? Answer: He has the right because God is speaking through him. Charismatic authority always appears in counter-position to some traditional authority. It challenges the latter, either seeking to modify it or, in the extreme case, to overthrow it.

Charismatic authority is intrinsically revolutionary. It breaks through the habituations on which traditional power rests. By the same token, charismatic authority is extremely precarious and it has little lasting power. It can only assert itself in an atmosphere of intense excitement. Probably by the very nature of man, such excitement cannot last. When it begins to ebb, charismatic authority must be modified or be succeeded by some other form of authority. Legal-rational authority, finally, is based upon law and rationally explicable procedures. Question: By what right can the governor collect this tax? Answer: He has the right by virtue of a law passed by the state legislature on such and such a date. Unlike the first two types, this form of authority does not cloak itself in mystery. Each exercise of power is, as it were, backed up by specific legal provisions. At least in principle, these provisions can be rationally explained, and so can the social purpose behind them. This third type of authority is the most common one in the modern world, and its appropriate administrative form is bureaucracy, as we have previously discussed.

UNINTENDED CONSEQUENCES AND THE IRONY OF HISTORY

In connection with this typology of political forms, Weber developed a theory of political and social change. He saw charisma and rationalization as the two great revolutionary forces of history. The implications of this, however, go considerably beyond the topic of power and its institutions, and we will return to it in the chapter on change. But there is yet another aspect of Weber's approach to political matters that we would emphasize here, and that is the aspect of the *unintended consequences of political action*. All human actions in society, whatever their meanings and motives, are ventures into the unknown. Consequences can be rationally weighed, but they can never be foreseen with absolute certainty. This general fact, however, becomes accentuated in the area of political action. All exercises in power are precarious, volatile and predictable in their consequences to only a very limited degree. The American embroilment in Vietnam may serve as a distressingly timely illustration of this. There can be little doubt that the American government would not have embarked on this adventure if its later course could have been foreseen. It is even more instructive to recall why the American intervention began in the first place—to wit, as part of the intention of the Kennedy administration to show that "counter-insurgency" wars could be fought successfully with limited means and without leading to nuclear confrontations between the great powers. It is true that the war in Vietnam has not (or, at least, not yet) led to a nuclear confrontation. It seems, though, that in regard to "counter-insurgency" wars it has shown almost exactly the opposite of what the strategists of the Kennedy administration intended to show.

This unpredictability has always been simultaneously the great attraction of power, its adventure and its potential tragedy. Because of this, Weber saw a pervasively tragic quality in all political action. His notion of the unintended consequences of such action provided him with a deeply ironic view of history.[4]

PARETO: ELITES OF LIONS AND FOXES

Pareto's approach to power is dominated by a simple and pervasive dichotomy of rulers and ruled. The former, Pareto called the elite.[5] Power, for Pareto, is a harsh and inevitable reality of human life. It is inevitable and it makes little sense to moralize about it. The task of the sociologist is to contemplate it with detachment and without illusions. In this approach to power, Pareto stands in a classical tradition of Italian political thought that goes back at least as far as Machiavelli, though it has elements that link it strongly to Roman antiquity. A somewhat similar approach to political sociology was worked out by Gaetano Mosca, another Italian scholar who was a contemporary of Pareto.[6] The two had an intense quarrel, each claiming that the other had taken from him some essential theoretical elements. Whatever may be the merits in this quarrel, there can be little doubt that Pareto was by far the more important thinker, especially in terms of the development of sociological thought about power.

Pareto distinguishes between two types of elites. Following Machiavelli, he calls one the *lions* and the other the *foxes*. The two have very different motivations and psychological characteristics —or, as he calls it, they are based on different *residues*. By the term "residues" Pareto means recurring constellations of motives in human history. He has a complicated and slightly bizarre list of those, which need not interest us here. For the purposes of his political sociology, only the first two kinds (or, as he calls it,

[4] This tragic sense of politics is eloquently expressed in Weber's essay "Politics as a Vocation," in Hans Gerth and C. Wright Mills (eds.), *From Max Weber* (New York, Oxford University Press, 1946).

[5] Vilfredo Pareto, *The Mind and Society,* Vol. IV (New York, Dover, 1963).

[6] Gaetano Mosca, *The Ruling Class* (New York, McGraw-Hill, 1939).

"classes") of residues are significant because they relate to the two types of elites.

Elites of lions are characterized by the residues Pareto calls "the persistence of aggregates." This can be characterized as a fundamentally conservative impulse, a mind-set that is concerned with the preservation of things as they are, addicted to forceful action and not overly given to reflection. By contrast, elites of foxes are based on another class of residues which, according to Pareto, are those of the "instinct for combination." This represents a mind-set that is less rigid intellectually, more innovative and reflective but much less given to decisive action. Pareto's reasoning in all of this is quite complex and burdened with an often irritating terminology. But what he is basically saying about these types of rulers is this: lions essentially rule by force, foxes by cunning. These respective characteristics are not just tactics developed under the pressure of immediate necessities, but they are general predispositions that are deeply rooted in the consciousness of these groups. To use the imagery evoked by Pareto's own terminology: once this or that type of residues has become firmly sedimented in the consciousness of a social group, it becomes extremely difficult for this group to act in a way that is contrary to the "program" dictated by the residues in question. In other words, every elite tends to become heavy-handed and increasingly inflexible in its response to new situations.

THE CIRCULATION OF ELITES AND DECADENCE

Because of this dynamic, both types of elites eventually fail to cope with certain situations which must eventually arise. Therefore they lose their grip on power, and the way is open for another elite to take their place. Typically, this will be an elite of the *other* type. This succession of ruling groups Pareto called *the circulation of elites,* and he gave to it the status of something like a law of history. As in the case of Weber, there is profound irony in this view, because the very strengths that brought a particular elite to power eventually cause its downfall. Thus an elite of lions originally came to power by virtue of its capacity for forceful and decisive action. Sooner or later, however, a situation arises in which such action is self-defeating. What is needed now is the cool application of reflection and the skills of diplomatic manipulation. But these are precisely the qualities which this type of elite lacks. Instead, the only course followed is that which is in accordance with the old "program," namely, forceful action. The result is a helpless giant, violently thrashing about and eventually being brought to a fall. Conversely, an elite of foxes succeeds in remaining on top of the situation as long as its peculiar gifts of cunning are required. Sooner or later, however, the need arises to cut through all the subtle manipulations and to act with decisive force. Again, this particular type of elite lacks the qualities that make for such action. It continues to exercise diplomacy at a moment when machine guns are required. It is then likely to be replaced by a group which does have the capacity to use machine guns at the correct moment.

The circulation of elites is fostered by another well-nigh inevitable process, namely, the onset of *decadence* in any elite that has been in power over a long period. This process applies to both of the previously mentioned types of elites. It means, quite simply, that the original vigor of the group in question becomes weakened through the enjoyment of the privileges of power. In other words, all elites, whether they were originally based on force or on cunning, eventually become flabby. This flabbiness impedes both action and thought, thus weakening both types of elites equally. The future always belongs to the lean ones who have discipline and keep their wits about them. There is, indeed, one measure of defense that elites can undertake. This is to remain at least partially open to new recruits from the lower strata. In other words, elites have a better chance of survival if occasionally they permit an infusion of "new blood" within their own ranks. This will be especially therapeutic if the new recruits represent the *other* class of residues that is lacking in the elite in power. (That is, every elite of lions should make provisions to let in a few foxes and vice versa.) Such a procedure represents a kind of controlled circulation of elites which allows mobility to certain individuals without making it necessary for the whole system to change. Such a situation is not easily achieved precisely because of the increasing flabbiness and inertia of elites that have been in power for a long time. Such an elite becomes set in its ways, ingrown and lacking in either the consciousness or the will to take the steps that are necessary for its own survival.

PARETO AND WEBER VERSUS MARX

Pareto was deeply impressed by the sway of irrational forces over social life. As with Weber, this led him to an ironic and tragic view of history in general and political history in particular. But he was well aware of the fact that individuals and groups also act out of rational motives. This is when, to use his term, they act to push forward their own *interests*. The conscious motives in a struggle for power are usually the advancement of such rational interests. Nevertheless, the irrational forces that grow out of the dumb predispositions that Pareto called residues keep cutting across rational conduct and often frustrate the very interests that are at issue. Social life, and particularly that sector of it that revolves around the exercise of power, is therefore an inextricable tangle of rationality and irrationality, of interests and habits, of lucid planning and blind passion.

Both Weber and Pareto, in the development of their thoughts on power as well as in their work in sociological theory generally, were very much aware of Marx. At many points in the work of both men, Marx figured, as it were, as the invisible partner. This is particularly important to understand in their political sociology.

Marx's ideas concerning political power were directly related to his ideas concerning the class struggle, which we had occasion to mention before. For Marx, political power is always an instrument of the dominant class.[7] Since the Marxian concept of class is fundamentally an economic one (that is, classes are defined in terms of

[7] Compare especially the so-called early writings: Karl Marx, *Early Writings* (London, Watts, 1963); also his *Selected Writings in Sociology and Social Philosophy* (New York, McGraw-Hill, 1964) and *Economic and Philosophic Manuscripts of 1844* (London, International Publishers, 1964).

their relationship to the means of production), this means that Marx sees political relations as a reflection of underlying economic relations. Political power is the result of and a reflection of economic power. The state and its legal system are only a veneer that superficially covers a structure of class interests. Thus Marx could speak of the state of his time as an "executive committee of the bourgeoisie." This same way of looking at political power has continued to be a guiding principle for Marxist thought since Marx.

As we have seen earlier, Weber, in his attempt to arrive at a more differentiated view of society than Marxism provided, separated the concept of social class from that of political class. He did this in order to emphasize that power had its own dynamic that could not simply be reduced to the dynamics of economic interests. Political institutions have a logic of their own. Also—and this becomes particularly clear in his concept of legitimacy—Weber emphasized the importance of norms and values in the realm of political behavior. Despite the greatly different theoretical orientation, Pareto is rather similar to Weber in emphasizing the complexity with which rational and irrational factors relate to each other in society. Both Weber and Pareto differ from Marx by emphasizing the irrational aspects of power, that is, by pointing out that rational interests (whether of a class character or any other) cannot adequately explain what goes on in this realm of social life.

POWER IN AMERICAN COMMUNITIES, BUSINESS "POWER STRUCTURE" OR PLURALISTIC FACTORS?

In American sociology there was for a long time a considerable reluctance to deal with problems of power, or even to use the term. We mentioned this a little earlier in comparing the concepts of power and social control (the latter having been coined by an American sociologist). The probable reason for this is the ideology of American democracy which assumes that political power expresses a popular consensus and therefore is reluctant to think of the political sphere as an arena of struggle between power interests that have no broad democratic legitimation. During the earlier period of American sociology, the only notable exception to this allergy to questions of power was Thorstein Veblen, who delighted in stripping away the veneer of democratic legitimations from the real motives of different groups. But even Veblen spoke less of power than of manipulation. In his various analyses of the business system, Veblen stressed not so much its ability to coerce as to bamboozle the public. If Pareto's work constantly evokes the image of a Machiavellian prince, then Veblen's rather suggests the figure of the confidence man. Perhaps there is something very American about this shift in imagery.

Today, sociological interpretations of power in America are sharply divided. In this we face a situation rather similar to the one we looked at during our previous discussion of stratification. Once more, we cannot take it upon ourselves here to adjudicate between these different approaches; we can only report on them and make clear what differences there are in one's picture of the situation, depending on which approach one takes.

There is in contemporary American sociology a strong radical or critical position which, in some of its representatives, is strongly influenced by Marxism. This position strongly debunks the democratic explanations of what goes on in the political arena and emphasizes various forces of hidden or invisible power. Usually in this view, the economic elite in American society is seen as the crucial power factor. As against this, there are more conventional views of the situation. They usually concede some of the points made by the radicals but emphasize the at least relative potency of the democratic processes in the society and the complexity of power relations. This latter approach is more prevalent among political scientists than among sociologists, though it has its strong representatives in the latter discipline as well. It should be added that most sociologists do not concern themselves with questions of power and so cannot easily be put in either category. Among political sociologists proper, it is quite difficult to say at this time how these two broad camps are numerically distributed.

The debate has been taking place both on a micro-scopic and on a macro-scopic level. More precisely, it has concerned the question of power both in the local community and the national society. On the first level, an important book was published in 1953 that inaugurated a controversy that is still going on. This was a study of the power structure of a large Southern city (called in the book by a pseudonym but generally thought to be Atlanta) by Floyd Hunter.[8] Hunter had actually been engaged in social work in the community that he subsequently studied sociologically, and he had been impressed by the fact that, apparently, the basic decisions in the community were made by a small group of people. His research purpose was to locate this group more precisely. The method he used was very similar to that of a police detective going about the solution of a crime. Hunter kept asking people questions as to their thinking and experience concerning power relations in the community. He then put together the jigsaw puzzle of these answers until he had assembled a complete picture to his satisfaction. The result of the study was that a very small group of people was found to make the major decisions in the community. Business figures were central to this group, although some of its members were not businessmen (for example, lawyers, elected politicians or labor leaders). This decision-making group Hunter called the *power structure,* a term that subsequently gained general currency, especially in radical circles. (It should be mentioned here that neither Hunter nor his 1953 book could be called radical in themselves; it was others who drew the radical implications from the study and its viewpoint.)

Hunter's study was very sharply criticized by other sociologists. One element of criticism concerned his method. It was suggested that his method might provide a fairly good notion of the *imagery* of power existing in a particular community but that it could not get at the actual power relations. In other words, the method only allowed one to say what people *thought* the power structure to be, but it is always possible that people are very much mistaken about such things. Subsequently, a number of community power studies were made with the aim of disproving Hunter's findings. One that became quite influential was undertaken by Robert Dahl in New Haven.[9] Dahl (a political scientist) claimed to find a much more

[8] Floyd Hunter, *Community Power Structure* (Chapel Hill, N.C., University of North Carolina Press, 1953).

[9] Robert Dahl, *Who Governs?* (New Haven, Conn., Yale University Press, 1961).

complex and differentiated power structure than the one alleged in Hunter's study. Compared with Hunter's vision of a more or less unified elite in the community, Dahl's approach suggests a much more pluralistic situation. Business interests are indeed very important in the community, but they have to reckon with various other forces that have a social base and social strength of their own. Most important, the formal political process which, in Hunter's analysis, appears mainly as a mechanism to carry out the interests of the elite is given by Dahl the character of an independent factor.

This approach has also been sharply criticized by the other side. One telling criticism, leveled particularly against Dahl, has been that his conception of power is too much limited by a local perspective. In other words, he arrives at his more pluralistic picture because he concentrates on local issues where, in fact, there is more of a pluralistic interplay of interest groups. It is suggested that the carriers of national power are generally not interested in such local issues and therefore stay in the background.

THE NATIONAL LEVEL: A BUSINESS "POWER ELITE" OR A MULTI-FACTOR HYPOTHESIS?

There has been quite general agreement on both sides of the aforementioned divide that it is not possible to argue directly from power on the community level to power on the national level. Clearly, different structures are involved, and it may be assumed that their respective mechanisms of power differ also. Hunter himself tried to extend his approach to the national level.[10] He employed the same method that he had previously used in his community study, beginning with interviews of supposedly leading national organizations. The method, already sharply attacked on the community level, was generally criticized as being quite inadequate for a determination of national power relations.

The most important book for the debate over national power in

[10] Floyd Hunter, *Top Leadership, U.S.A.* (Chapel Hill, N.C., University of North Carolina Press, 1959).

America was the study of the so-called power elite by C. Wright Mills, which was first published in 1956.[11] Mills argued that America is ruled by an elite that is divided into three major components: an economic, a political and a military component. The economic component represents the top strata of big business and corporation management. The political component consists of key figures in the formal apparatus of government, especially but not exclusively on the federal level. The military component, of course, is composed of the top echelon of the armed services. While Mills took some pains to disavow a simplistic or conspiratorial view of the power elite, it is quite clear from his analysis that the economic component of the elite is a decisive one. To this extent at least, Mills's analysis of power in contemporary America runs along familiar Marxist lines. A particularly important part of his thesis concerns the rise of the military to a pre-eminent position in the American power structure since World War II, a new and important element in the situation. Mills maintained that the leadership in these three elite groups is increasingly interchangeable and, in fact, interchanged—so that what emerges is a system of interlocking directorates. Top corporation officials go into top government positions; generals retire from the military and take positions in private business. All three groups mix with each other in a variety of both informal and official contacts. The general trend, therefore, is toward cohesion and impermeability at the top of American society.

Since its publication, Mills's book has had a vast influence far beyond the confines of the social sciences. It became one of the intellectual underpinnings of the view that America today is dominated by the "military-industrial complex," and it has become a basic text for political radicalism in America. Recently, a number of other studies have followed in Mills's footsteps and have further elaborated on his view of the power structure of American society.[12]

Mills's book was greeted by a storm of criticism at the time of its

[11] C. Wright Mills, *The Power Elite* (New York, Oxford University Press, 1956).

[12] See, for example, Gabriel Kolko, *Wealth and Power in America* (New York, Praeger, 1962).

publication, and the point of view that Mills represents has been criticized by a variety of people. Within sociology, the most comprehensive statement of a position contrary to that of Mills is represented by a work by Arnold Rose published in 1967.[13] Rose criticizes Mills for a high selectivity in the evidence chosen to present his picture of the power elite. Rose asserts that Mills fails to see that there is in fact a variety of interest groups within the power structure. Each group does indeed push interests of its own, but these are usually limited in scope and frequently conflict with the interests of other elements within the power structure. Against what he calls Mills's "economic elite dominance hypothesis," Rose proposes his own "multi-influence hypothesis," which essentially confirms a pluralistic model of political relations in American society. One can say that the Mills-Rose dichotomy of interpretation replicates on the national level what the Hunter-Dahl debate represents on the level of the local community.

A SPECTRUM WITH THREE MAJOR POSITIONS

We do not wish to oversimplify the debate. There are a number of positions that do not fall clearly into either of the two aforementioned camps. More or less intermediate between them is the notion that a new elite has emerged which is coextensive with the technical and professional staffs that run the major institutions of the society. The economist John Galbraith has called this group the *technostructure*. The idea here is that a modern society cannot get along without this technical elite and that, therefore, its members are increasingly powerful.[14] In a curious way, this position is a continuation of the theory of the "managerial revolution" which we briefly looked at in our discussion of bureaucracy.

Also relevant to the discussion of power in American society are a few studies of the upper class as such. The foremost sociologist

[13] Arnold Rose, *The Power Structure* (New York, Oxford University Press, 1967).

[14] John Galbraith, *The New Industrial State* (Boston, Houghton-Mifflin, 1967).

engaged in these has been Digby Baltzell.[15] Baltzell also began his investigations on the local level, with a study of the old upper class of Philadelphia. He then extended his inquiries to the national scale, and in 1964 published a study of what he called the "Protestant establishment," a perhaps not altogether happy term to refer to a national upper class. Baltzell's major thesis is that the latter has increasingly hardened in its relation to potential recruits. He argues that it has been in the process of conversion from an "aristocracy" (something which Baltzell, incidentally, regards as not only inevitable but desirable in a society) to a "caste," that is, an increasingly closed and impenetrable social group. If one applies Pareto's perspective of the circulation of elites to Baltzell's argument, one might conclude that the American elite is in the process of falling exactly into the trap of exclusiveness that Pareto regarded as a major cause for the downfall of power groups.

At the risk of some oversimplification, we might summarize the present thinking in American sociology on this topic in the following way: three major pictures of power in American society are being presented by different sociologists and other social scientists. First, there is the picture of a fairly cohesive elite which is mainly dominated by its economic component of top businessmen and corporation executives. This picture may or may not be described in strictly Marxist terms, but it is most congenial to a Marxist view of capitalist society. This is the view generally held by radicals within sociology, and is, of course, congenial to people whose political stance is one of radical opposition to the political and economic status quo in American society. Secondly, there is the picture of a more variegated elite which is not necessarily dominated by its economic component. Those who maintain the importance of the so-called technostructure generally arrive at this picture. While it is more complex in its view of power relations than the first position, it is similar to the first approach in deprecating the influence or even the reality of the democratic processes that determine power in the "official" view of American society. Finally, there is the picture of a pluralistic power structure within which democratic proc-

[15] Digby Baltzell, *Philadelphia Gentlemen* (New York, Free Press, 1958) and *The Protestant Establishment* (New York, Random House, 1964).

esses and democratically elected officials constitute at least one of several powerful elements. This view, of course, is most congenial to political positions that not only believe in the desirability of the "official" definitions of political reality in America but also think that these definitions correspond to the empirical reality to a high degree. Obviously, the lines between these three positions are not always sharp, and there are individual interpretations of the situation that cut across these lines.

READINGS

We would suggest that the reader turn here to two major and contradictory sociological interpretations of power in contemporary American society: C. Wright Mills, *The Power Elite* (New York, Oxford University Press, 1956) and Arnold Rose, *The Power Structure* (New York, Oxford University Press, 1967). Both books are available in paperback. A very influential book in the Mills line, which the reader may also consult, is William Domhoff, *Who Rules America?* (Englewood Cliffs, N.J., Prentice-Hall, 1967), also available in paperback.

Chapter 14

DEVIANCE

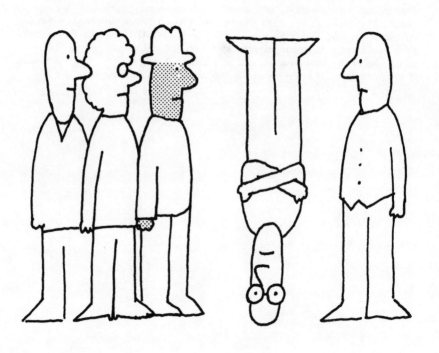

DEVIANCE AND *MORAL* DIFFERENCES

From childhood on, everyday life contains many experiences of people who, in one way or another, are different. There is the little black child in a class of whites; there is the girl who stands out as a wallflower at the party; there are the physically handicapped and the psychologically disturbed. There is another kind of difference, however. There is the boy who expresses disgust while the rest of the group are laughing at a dirty joke; there is the dove in an office full of hawks—or, for that matter, there is the hawk at a cocktail party of doves. These differences are (or seem to be) unlike the previously mentioned ones because they constitute a deliberate denial of the values or norms of the group. Being black, shy or crippled is a condition that is imposed upon the individual. Being a prude or a political nonconformist, on the other hand, is (or appears to be) the result of an act of choice. It is this second kind of difference that we will be concerned with in this chapter.

The term generally used today by sociologists for this kind of difference is *deviance*. Deviance has been defined and explained in different ways, as we will see. But there is widespread agreement among sociologists about the basic concept: deviance always refers to conduct that is in violation of the *rules* constructed by a given society or group. In other words, the concept of deviance implies a *moral* difference. It refers to the refusal or perhaps inability of an individual or group to abide by the moral norms that prevail in the social context in question.

THE RANGE OF "NORMAL" CONDUCT

Social order is maintained by enforcing compliance with the social norms and rules that are thought to ensure the effective operation of a particular society. As we have seen, there are a variety of devices of social control, varying from physical force to mild psychological pressure, that are supposed to protect and enforce these norms and rules. In the background of any system of social control there is a set of assumptions concerning the range of conduct that is deemed permissible—that is, against which social controls will *not* be applied. The scope and character of this permissible zone of conduct vary from society to society. Everywhere it is the kind of conduct that is considered to be "normal." Whatever may be the latitude with which "normality" is defined, there will be a certain point beyond which an individual cannot go without being considered "abnormal." It is safe to say that nearly everyone goes beyond this point occasionally. The individual who does so habitually is considered to be a deviant (though obviously people who have not had the benefit of an introductory sociology course will probably call him other names—none of them flattering).

What this means in terms of the real social experience of people can best be seen by looking at ordinary, everyday situations. Each situation in which people interact socially is made up of typical expectations to which individuals are expected to respond in a typical way. The deviant announces his presence by failing to respond as typically expected. Imagine a male newcomer being introduced at an American party. There are a few people of both sexes already present in the room. The typical expectation is that once the man has been introduced by name to the other individuals who are present, he will make the rounds, shake everyone's hand and sit down. If he does just that, he will be responding in a typical way. But suppose that, having done all this, he walks over to one of the women at the party, kneels down before her, folds his hands, touches the floor with his forehead and says, "You are very beautiful. Allow me to pay homage to your beauty." Chances are (even in a very sophisticated milieu) that everyone, and particularly the woman so honored, will be slightly alarmed. If it is established that the character on his knees is not the native of some exotic Oriental country but actually comes from Brooklyn, the alarm will deepen. Depending upon his subsequent behavior, he may be classified in a number of different ways. It may be concluded that he is simply a jerk trying to make an impression. Or it may develop that he is expressing some bizarre convictions of his own as to the proper forms of interaction between people—he may belong to some fringe group that wishes to restore the codes of medieval chivalry, or he may have decided all by himself that this is his authentic style as discovered in a marathon sensitivity training session. On the other hand, people might decide that he is simply psychotic. Whatever the outcome, the individual's act has placed him in everyone's mind in the general category of deviant, though the precise sub-category may remain to be decided upon.

"THAT WAS UNREAL"— DEVIANCE FROM *TYPICAL* BEHAVIOR

The typical is that which is thought of as normal. Deviance from typicality is always alarming because it puts in question what people conceive of as normality. Therefore, even before it is taken as a moral offense, it is, as it were, an offense against reality. People's notions about normality give order to their experience. They separate "the real" from what is "unreal." Probably because of the very nature of human existence, all such definitions of reality are precarious. Therefore deviance (especially if it is gross and continual) must be dealt with not only in order to protect the moral rules of society but, even more importantly, in order to protect the sense of reality of the members of society.

THE RELATIVITY AND SOCIAL DEFINITION OF NORMALITY

Clearly, what is deviant, and what is not, is relative. The behavior of our overly chivalrous character might be perfectly normal in another culture or, for that matter, in an earlier period of our own culture. What is considered to be normality in one society may be classified as rank madness in another, and vice versa. As Pascal put it in a classic statement: "What is truth on one side of the Pyrenees is error on the other." In other words, deviance in France need not necessarily be deviance in Spain, and the other way around.

As soon as one recognizes the relativity of social conceptions of normality, and therefore of deviance, one arrives at a simple but very important insight: deviance is "in the mind." Put differently: deviance is a matter of social definition. We may here once more recall the famous statement of W. I. Thomas: "If people define a situation as real, it is real in its consequences." Normality and deviance are important components of "reality" in this sense. Thus, to paraphrase Thomas, if a society defines a certain type of conduct as deviant, then those who engage in it will have to suffer the consequence of being considered deviants whether they like this or not. Societies are always nervous about their definitions of reality. When an individual appears to refuse deliberately to acknowledge the reality as socially defined, he is considered dangerous. Nor can the sociologist deny that in fact he *is* dangerous, given the assumptions of the society in question. This is particularly the case when the deviance has no "excuse." If in our previous example it could be established that the individual engaging in this aberrant behavior comes from Outer Mongolia, or has just been released from psychiatric care, these facts might be considered as valid "excuses." But in the absence of such explanations, his conduct can only be considered a willful and inexcusable affront against the taken-for-granted reality of social life.

THE "RELIABILITY" OF DEFINITIONS OF REALITY: DIMINISHED BY SOCIAL CHANGE AND PLURALISM

It also follows that the concept of deviance has meaning only if one is speaking about a social situation in which there exists a fairly high degree of consensus as to what the rules of social life are supposed to be. The more stable this consensus, the more "reliable" are the designations of deviance—"reliable" in the minds of the designators, that is. In areas of social life in which no such consensus exists, it is literally impossible to be deviant. In such areas, there are no typical expectations, or it has not yet been established what these expectations should be, and therefore almost anything goes. One may say facetiously that there is no fun in being bad when no one knows any more what it means to be good. Philosophers have long maintained that vice is parasitical upon virtue. In a somewhat different frame of reference, sociologists can say that deviance is dependent upon conformity. In a situation in which almost all men are clean-shaven, an individual can say something by growing a beard. But in a situation in which the hirsute adornment of the male face ranges all the way from meticulous nakedness through sideburns, mustaches and goatees to flourishing jungles of matted hair, the significance of either having or not having a beard becomes very blurred. At this point one can no longer speak of deviance.

In times of rapid social change, or in situations in which there is a plurality of standards, social expectations become uncertain and deprived of the strength of consensus. In consequence, people become confused as to what is "normal" and what is not. In such situations, there are rapid changes in the definitions of reality. Behavior that was thought to be deviant yesterday becomes accepted today, and vice versa. This, more or less, is our situation today in many areas of social life. It has a curious consequence. Previously at least it was fairly clear who was deviant and who was not, and it was mainly the deviant who had to be nervous. Now, when all these dividing lines have become unstable and hazy, *everyone* tends to be nervous because everyone has reason to worry that his own "normality" may be radically questioned tomorrow. Madness lurks around every corner, and those who specialize in exorcising its terrors (therapists of every description) run a booming business.

As we have had occasion to see before, sociologists frequently get into jurisdictional disputes with other social sciences. In the area under consideration in this chapter, the other social science in question is criminology, which sometimes (especially in America) has been regarded as a part of sociology but which, nevertheless, has a long, independent history of its own.[1] As regularly happens with jurisdictional disputes, whether between unions or sciences, the conflict is carried on around problems of definition. Here, the problem is just how to define crime and how to distinguish crime

[1] See, for example, John Gillin, *Criminology and Penology* (New York, Appleton-Century, 1945), pp. 217ff.

from other forms of deviance. The usual way in which this problem has been resolved is to define crime as a particular form of deviance which involves violations of codified law. Let us return to our previous example. However deviant the behavior of our character may be, it is clearly not criminal. There is no law or statute which prohibits males from kneeling down and making declarations of admiration to females at social gatherings. But suppose that our character, having made his declaration, would then go on to assault sexually the object of his admiration. At that point, he would clearly cross the line between deviance and crime. The police could be called, and he could be charged (depending upon the degree of his success) with offenses ranging from disorderly conduct through assault to rape. However these various categories of social action may be defined, it is clear that the category of deviance covers a broader territory than that of crime and that consequently the latter may be considered as being a special case of the former.

CAUSES OF DEVIANCE

Biological Theories

How have sociologists gone about explaining and interpreting the phenomenon of deviance? There is a long tradition (scientific or pseudoscientific, according to one's point of view) which traces deviant or anti-social behavior back to biological causes. This approach maintains that deviants are born, not made. In the history of criminology (which, in its earlier stages, was considered to be a branch of medicine), an outstanding representative of this approach was the nineteenth-century Italian physician, Cesare Lombroso. Lombroso developed a complex description of what he called the "born criminal," who, he claimed, could be recognized by a variety of physical (especially facial) characteristics. In a certain wing of the medical faculty of the University of Rome, the visitor may still today admire a long gallery of portraits of magnificently ugly delinquents put there at the time to illustrate Lombroso's theories. Very few, if any, students of crime would today adhere to Lombroso's views. But there are still some in contemporary American social

science who stress the genetically based aspects of all human behavior, including that behavior which is termed deviant or criminal.[2] Sociologists, with their professional aversion to explanations
of social conduct in terms of heredity, have generally shied away
from such theories.

Psychological Causes: Faulty Parent-Child Relationship

On the other hand, sociologists have been much more open to
psychological explanations of deviant behavior, perhaps partly because these very commonly overlap with sociological ones. These
theories explain deviance in terms of this or that psychological mal-
function or disturbance. They resemble the aforementioned biological theories in that they view deviance as a disease to be looked at
from an essentially medical point of view. The difference between
the two lies at least partly in how the prospects for treatment are
considered. There is, after all, nothing one can do about the physical structure of an individual's face—all that Lombroso could
really do was to hang all these ugly pictures on the wall for his own
disinterested pleasure and for the instruction of policemen. At least
since the advent of psychoanalysis, however, it has been generally
assumed that most psychological disturbances can be treated. This
latter assumption is very common throughout that part of the literature that approaches deviants from a psychological point of view.

The overlapping between psychological and sociological theories
in this approach is also due to psychoanalysis. All the way back to
Freud, psychological pathology was assumed to be related to faulty
relationships between parents and children, especially in the early
years of life. If nothing else, then, such psychological explanations
relate to the sociology of family life and therefore are more congenial to sociologists than theories that explain deviance in purely
biological terms.

A well-known example of such an approach is the study of juve-

[2] See W. H. Sheldon *et al., Varieties of Delinquent Behavior* (New York,
Harper, 1949); F. F. Kallman, *Heredity in Health and Mental Disorders* (New
York, Norton, 1953).

nile delinquents by the Gluecks.[3] The Gluecks made a careful comparison of 500 delinquents and 500 non-delinquents, matched by
neighborhood, age, intelligence and national descent. They claimed
in their findings that a close and affectionate relationship with their
parents was one of the features most often distinguishing non-delinquents from delinquents. Overly lax, overly strict or erratic parental attitudes were found to contribute to delinquency. On the other
hand, a generally "firm but kind" attitude by parents was found to
inhibit delinquent tendencies.

Albert Cohen, one of the best-known sociological experts in the
area of juvenile delinquency, has tried to combine the psychological approach with more conventional sociological forms of analysis.[4] In discussing the causes for juvenile delinquency, Cohen
placed himself in the middle between those explanations that account for juvenile delinquency in terms of a specific sub-culture
and those that explain the phenomenon in terms of the psychological peculiarities of individuals. Some sociologists had been maintaining that, particularly in lower-class areas, there was a specific
sub-culture that gave birth to delinquent behavior. Cohen rejected
this theory on the grounds that there were many individuals ex-
posed to this sub-culture who did not themselves become delinquents. At the same time, he rejected the explanation of delinquency in terms of individual psychological factors only, arguing
that many individuals with similar psychological constellations, especially if they were located in low delinquent areas, did not become delinquents but expressed their psychological disturbance in
other ways. Only a combination of these two factors—sub-culture
and individual psychological predisposition—can, according to
Cohen, explain the phenomenon. Despite this modification of a
psychological approach, however, Cohen strongly emphasizes psychological factors and uses clinical psychiatric materials to make
his point.

[3] Sheldon and Eleanor Glueck, *Predicting Delinquency and Crime* (Cambridge, Mass., Harvard University Press, 1959). For a similar approach, see W.
and Joan McCord, *Origins of Crime* (New York, Columbia University Press,
1959).

[4] Albert Cohen, *Delinquent Boys* (New York, Free Press, 1955).

Sociological Causes: The "Ecology" of the City

If we now turn to more exclusively sociological theories of deviance, we find a considerable variety of approaches. Some of the earliest sociological research on deviance in America came out of the Chicago School, which we have had occasion to mention before in a number of different areas. In line with that school's approach to urban sociology, its first interest in what later came to be called deviance (the Chicago sociologists themselves preferred the term "social disorganization") dealt with the spatial distribution of these phenomena within the city.[5] The interest here was to relate various deviant patterns (such as crime, juvenile delinquency, alcoholism, mental illness or suicide) to the "ecology" of the city. The early findings indicated a remarkable consistency of rates of incidence of these phenomena in a particular neighborhood, even if the ethnic composition of that neighborhood changed. Thus it was found that for most of these phenomena a slum neighborhood constituted very fertile ground, regardless of the particular population that occupied the geographical area at any given time. As the place of residence of a particular group became more distant from these slum neighborhoods, however, it was found that incidence rates began to differ appreciably for each ethnic or racial group. Thus, within the work of the Chicago School itself, there occurred pretty early a tendency to move away from purely spatial analyses of these phenomena.

Sociological Causes: The "Sub-culture" Approach

The notion of sub-culture clearly goes beyond the spatial dimension. While sub-cultures, especially in urban areas, generally do have a particular geographical location or at least focus, the term suggests a much more complex phenomenon. As we have seen earlier, the fascination of the Chicago sociologists with the most bizarre corners of urban life led them to intense investigations of various types of sub-cultures such as, for example, the sub-cultures of particular occupational groups. Some of them were very much interested in ethnic sub-cultures, a subject of particular prominence

[5] See, for example, Clifford Shaw and Henry McKay, *Juvenile Delinquency and Urban Areas* (Chicago, University of Chicago Press, 1942).

during the last remaining period when there was mass immigration from Europe to America. The classical study of Polish immigration by W. I. Thomas and Florian Znaniecki discussed "social disorganization" in the context of the difficulties of assimilation of immigrants into American life.[6] Thomas followed up this interest with a number of investigations into juvenile delinquency in Chicago among Poles and other groups as well. In the same tradition, the Chicago School produced a number of classical studies of deviant sub-cultures, such as those of the hobo, the juvenile gang and the professional thief.[7] Many of these studies have by now attained the status of sociological classics and have had a great influence on subsequent work in this area. Their approach, however, has not been without its critics. We have already mentioned Cohen's criticism of the entire notion that deviance and delinquency can be explained exclusively in sub-cultural terms. Another difficulty is contained in the very term "social disorganization." The term is perhaps appropriate to certain types of behavior subsumed under it —for example, alcoholism. It is ironic, though, to reflect that this term was supposed to refer to crime—and that was in Chicago in the 1920's! Many of these phenomena are indeed highly organized, except that the organization is not that of the "official" society.

FUNCTIONS OF DEVIANCE: REAFFIRMING SOLIDARITY AND COMPENSATORY BEHAVIOR

Sociologists in the structural-functionalist tradition have given an important place to the consideration of deviance. The basic question around which any functionalist discussion revolves can be stated with a little oversimplification like this: Is deviance harmful to society? The same question can be stated in more sophisticated terms: Is deviance always functionally disruptive? Or is it possible that deviance may have its own societal functions? This

[6] W. I. Thomas and Florian Znaniecki, *The Polish Peasant in Europe and America* (Chicago, University of Chicago Press, 1919–1921).

[7] Nels Anderson, *The Hobo* (Chicago, University of Chicago Press, 1923); F. Thrasher, *The Gang* (Chicago, University of Chicago Press, 1927); Edwin Sutherland, *The Professional Thief* (Chicago, University of Chicago Press, 1937).

basic question can be traced back to Émile Durkheim, who has been quite correctly called "the father of functionalism." In one of Durkheim's earliest works we find the following sentence which rather elegantly sums up his point of view: "Crime brings together upright consciences and concentrates them." [8] What does this mean? Deviance (or, as Durkheim called it, "social pathology") is a necessity of society. Essentially, it provides a badly needed scapegoat for society. The presence of the deviant allows the group to draw together and reaffirm not only its social but its moral identity. Deviance is opposed, and thereby the group is strengthened. In other words, deviance is highly functional for the maintenance and reaffirmation of solidarity. Durkheim quite consistently carried over this idea into the sociological explanation not only of crime but also of punishment. Criticizing the liberal penologists who (then, as now) argued that the purpose of legal punishment was the rehabilitation of the offender, Durkheim maintained that, on the contrary, the purpose of punishment was to reaffirm the moral authority of society. In other words, Durkheim understood deviance in terms of the functioning of society, and he felt that this (rather than an inquiry into individual motives) was the proper focus for any sociological approach to this subject. It is interesting, incidentally, that George Herbert Mead, who operated from very different premises, came to similar conclusions, as the following quotation shows: "The criminal . . . is responsible for a sense of solidarity, aroused among those whose attitude would otherwise be centered upon interests quite divergent from each other." [9]

Both major figures in contemporary functionalism in American sociology, Talcott Parsons and Robert Merton, have discussed deviance in essentially similar terms.[10] They agree that deviant behavior is most likely to occur when the norms governing conduct in any given setting seem to be contradictory. Merton especially has tried to explain all deviant behavior in terms of social structure. He

[8] Émile Durkheim, *The Division of Labor in Society* (New York, Free Press, 1947), p. 102.

[9] George Herbert Mead, "The Psychology of Punitive Justice," *American Journal of Sociology,* XXIII (1928):602.

[10] Talcott Parsons, *The Social System* (New York, Free Press, 1951); Robert Merton, *Social Theory and Social Structure* (New York, Free Press, 1957). Also, see the introduction to Robert Merton and Robert Nisbet (eds.), *Contemporary Social Problems* (New York, Harcourt Brace, 1966).

suggests that all forms of deviant behavior result from differentials in the access to the success goals of a society by legitimate means. In other words, when certain individuals or groups are unable to obtain success (as defined in the society) by socially approved means, they will be driven to turn to compensatory behavior that lacks social approval. Deviance thus occurs as a result of a discrepancy between the aspirations which society has socialized into its members and the ways that society has provided for realizing such aspirations. Merton uses the Durkheimian concept of anomie to refer to such a situation. It can easily be seen that such an explanation seems plausible when applied to contemporary urban America. There is a strong and widely diffused emphasis on the goals of material gain and high status, but not everyone is given similar means to achieve these goals legitimately. There are great differentials in terms of age and sex, but particularly in terms of social class as well as ethnic and racial position. Among those who are deprived of ready access to the road toward success because of these factors, there is a high probability of deviant behavior. The following quotation neatly sums up Merton's point of view:

> It is only when a system of cultural values extols, virtually above all else, certain *common* success-goals for the population at large while the social structure rigorously restricts or completely closes access to approved modes of reaching these goals for *a considerable part of the same population,* that deviant behavior ensues on a large scale.[11]

Merton's approach in this area has been very productive in that it suggested a linkage between the Durkheimian concept of anomie and the analysis of social class. A number of empirical investigations followed up Merton's suggestion. Thus Cloward and Ohlin interpreted delinquency as the consequence of unsuccessful efforts to achieve goals of the society (especially money and power) by legitimate means.[12] A number of investigations related the anomic consequences of certain class positions to mental illness.[13] The reader

[11] Merton, *op. cit.,* p. 146.

[12] R. Cloward and L. Ohlin, *Delinquency and Opportunity* (New York, Free Press, 1960).

[13] A. Hollingshead and F. Redlich, *Social Class and Mental Illness* (New York, Wiley, 1958); J. Myers and B. Roberts, *Family and Class Dynamics in Mental Illness* (New York, Wiley, 1959).

who recalls our previous discussion of stratification will readily see that this linkage leads to a number of serious problems of interpretation. The basic problem here is the predominance of middle-class norms in American society generally, and therefore the temptation to consider as deviant precisely those forms of conduct that deviate from middle-class norms. On the one hand, it can be argued that this constitutes class bias on the part of the sociologist. On the other hand, however, it can be maintained that since, in fact, middle-class norms are dominant in American society in this manner, it is perfectly valid for the sociologist to take this dominance as his empirical starting point and to define deviance accordingly.

DEVIANCE AND THE "CULTURE OF POVERTY": IS DEVIANCE CLASSLESS?

In recent years, there has been extensive use of the concept of a "culture of poverty" (a term widely used by the anthropologist Oscar Lewis), both in social-scientific literature and in political debate. The notion itself is really not new, and in terms of American sociology could be traced back all the way to such early investigations as the aforementioned one of Polish immigrants by Thomas and Znaniecki. It is also part of this tradition to trace various types of deviance to the cultural traits peculiar to the lower classes. For example, Walter Miller (also an anthropologist) came to the conclusion, after several years of work with gangs in a high-delinquency section of Boston, that lower-class delinquency is derived directly from the distinctive attributes of lower-class culture rather than being a reaction against middle-class expectations.[14] Thus the cultural traits of toughness, smartness and excitement are taken as factors conducive to delinquency. Middle-class delinquency is then interpreted as being mainly a diffusion of some of these lower-class values to the middle class. Since some of these diffused styles (for example, clothes, habits or speech) are rejected by middle-class parents, middle-class young see them as an expression of personal independence. The de-

[14] Walter Miller, "Lower Class Culture as a Generating Milieu of Gang Delinquency," *Journal of Social Issues*, XIV (1959):5ff.

linquent aspects of lower-class culture are then interpreted in a similar way by the middle-class young to whom they are diffused.

This approach has been challenged both on empirical and theoretical grounds. A number of studies have produced findings to the effect that delinquency, *if properly measured,* is distributed fairly evenly throughout the class system. Middle-class children may simply be delinquent in slightly different ways from lower-class children—for that matter, the same relationship pertains to adults.[15] As far as the young are concerned, Bloch and Niederhoffer have suggested that there is a similar "ganging process" among adolescents at all class levels in our society (and in other societies as well) and that the specific manifestations of this merely vary by class level.[16] This particular approach has behind it a considerable tradition in criminology proper, as in Sutherland's theory of "differential association" for the explanation of individual delinquent and criminal careers.[17]

This entire approach, however, has also been challenged on fundamental theoretical grounds. As one might expect, the focus of this theoretical criticism has been the class bias in the definition of deviance. Even in view of the admitted predominance of middle-class norms in American society, is it scientifically valid to base the entire analysis of the phenomenon upon this fact? Could not even the concept of lower-class culture be taken as the starting point of a very different kind of analysis in which adherence to these cultural traits would *not* be taken as deviance? Indeed, within the context of lower-class culture, could it not be said that *middle-class* norms constitute a kind of deviance? Thus it might perhaps be admissible to describe a drug-taking and car-stealing youth in suburbia as being engaged in deviance. But can the same thing be said in a

---

[15] F. Nye, J. Short and V. Olson, "Socio-Economic Status and Delinquent Behavior," *American Journal of Sociology,* LXIII (1958):381ff.; H. Reiss and A. Rhodes, "The Distribution of Juvenile Delinquency in the Class Structure," *American Sociological Review,* XXVI (1961):720ff.

[16] H. Bloch and H. Niederhoffer, *The Gang* (New York, Philosophic Press, 1958). Also, see discussion of gangs in S. N. Eisenstadt, *From Generation to Generation* (New York, Free Press, 1956).

[17] E. Sutherland, *Principles of Criminology* (Philadelphia, Lippincott, 1939); E. Sutherland and D. Cressey, *Principles of Criminology* (New York, Lippincott, 1960).

slum? Or could it not rather be said that, in the social context of the slum, a church-going, law-abiding and college-motivated youth could very well be described as a deviant?

PROBLEMS IN TERMINOLOGY

The very headings under which sociology has dealt with the subjects under consideration in this chapter already invite critical analysis. "Social disorganization"—as we have already remarked in the case of crime, this is a singularly unconvincing category to apply to some of these phenomena. "Social pathology"—is it really legitimate to apply medical categories to social phenomena? Or does this not perhaps constitute a too ready acceptance of the prevailing norms as being "healthy"? "Social problems"—*whose* problems? The deviant's? Or those agencies of society that are supposed to keep them under control? To be sure, the criminal is the problem of the policeman. But from the criminal's point of view, it is precisely the policeman who is the problem. The term "deviance" was indeed brought into usage in order to avoid this kind of bias. As we have seen, however, the terminological change does not do away with the theoretical problem.

These criticisms are not too recent either. As early as 1943, in an article entitled "The Professional Ideology of Social Pathologists," C. Wright Mills launched a broadside attack against the assumptions generally held in this field.[18] The focus of Mills's attack was precisely the middle-class myopia of the sociologists in question. At the time, Mills's article did not attract too much attention, but as Mills's other work became widely known in the 1960's, this article also began to exert considerable influence.

[18] C. Wright Mills, *Power, Politics and People* (New York, Ballantine Books, 1963), pp. 525ff.

STIGMA AND "LABELING" THEORY

We have previously mentioned, in another context, the ground-breaking work of Erving Goffman in his sociological analysis of a mental hospital.[19] Goffman's sovereign disregard for the point of view of the psychiatrists (the "management" of that situation—or, for that matter, its "policemen") stimulated a large number of sociologists to take a fresh look at this whole field. Goffman's most direct contribution to the study of deviance to date is his little book, suggestively entitled *Stigma—Notes on the Management of Spoiled Identity*.[20] It may be said that Goffman's approach represents a return to an important tradition in American social psychology that, like so many others, has its roots in the Chicago School of the 1920's. Deviance is here understood as simply one way in which people define a situation. Its "reality" depends upon the power of the people who do the defining to impose their definition upon others. Stigmatization is a process which one group of people inflicts upon another. The definition will "stick," depending upon the power of the definers. In that case, those who are thus defined, the stigmatized, will have to come to terms both socially and psychologically with their "spoiled identity." Needless to say, this is neither a pleasant nor an easy task.

Along the directions pointed by Mills and Goffman, a new approach to deviance has emerged in recent years. Under the name "labeling theory," this approach is becoming increasingly influential, and by now may even be the dominant approach in the field.[21] The best-known representative of this new school is Howard Becker.[22]

[19] Erving Goffman, *Asylums* (Garden City, N.Y., Doubleday-Anchor, 1961).

[20] Erving Goffman, *Stigma* (Englewood Cliffs, N.J., Prentice-Hall, 1963).

[21] For an overview, see Earl Rubington and Martin Weinberg (eds.), *Deviance* (New York, Macmillan, 1968). Pioneering work in this approach was undertaken by Edwin Lemert in the 1950's.

[22] Howard Becker, *Outsiders* (New York, Free Press, 1963).

DEVIANCE: FROM WHOSE POINT OF VIEW?

Becker and others working along the same lines try as resolutely as possible to free themselves of the various evaluative approaches with which the field has been previously afflicted. Not only do they wish to do away with middle-class bias in the approach to these phenomena but also with such bias as may come from a psychiatric or juridical point of view. Put simply: they want to clearly differentiate the approach of the sociologist from that of social worker, the psychiatrist or the law-enforcement officer. Deviance is a label attached to certain people or acts as the result of social processes (hence, of course, the name of the theory). The image deliberately suggests the arbitrariness and relativity of such a process. There are no universal criteria for what is labeled as deviant. What is deviance today may be normality tomorrow, and vice versa. Moreover, the term suggests the power relations that are invariably at play. Thus one individual may wish to stick the label of deviant on another but may lack the power to do so.

There are, then, no intrinsic features that differentiate deviants from other people or deviant acts from other acts. For example, if a woman appears on Fifth Avenue in the nude, she is likely to be arrested for indecent exposure. Such nudity is labeled as deviant behavior at this time, and the person who engages in it is not only labeled but persecuted as a deviant. However, if a woman appears in the same state on a theatrical stage, she is (at least in New York) likely to be applauded. The same act, possibly engaged in by the same person, is labeled one thing in this situation and another in that. If one speaks of deviance, therefore, one must always ask, "Deviant from whose point of view?" There are some groups who are outraged by prostitution, homosexuality or drugs. There are even still some who are outraged by the consumption of alcohol. Others not only accept but even propagate these forms of behavior. The same sociological description can be extended to acts or views that are labeled deviant in the political or religious areas of life.

WHO HAS THE POWER TO SUCCESSFULLY LABEL?

This concept of deviance inevitably focuses on conflict. The conflict is between relatively small and powerless persons or groups, on the one hand, and large, powerful and relatively well-organized social interests, on the other. Who wins in such conflicts is not determined by any intrinsic qualities of the individuals or acts in question but by their relative power in the overall social situation. Becker states this very well:

> From this point of view, deviance is *not* a quality of the act a person commits, but rather a consequence of the application by others of rules and sanctions to "an offender." The deviant is one to whom that label has successfully been applied; deviant behavior is behavior that people so label.[23]

This approach is interesting far beyond the limits of the relatively narrow scope of phenomena that it was primarily designed to deal with. It brings out quite dramatically the precarious character not only of the idea of normality but of the very fabric of "reality" as defined in a society. It is important to see that this applies not only to statements of norms but also to what is taken to be statements of facts. To say that somebody is a "criminal" or a "delinquent" is quite clearly a normative statement—if not on the part of the sociologist, then certainly on the part of the society that institutionalizes such stigmatization. Essentially, what such a statement says is that the individual or the act is to be condemned. But labeling theory goes beyond this. It also deals with such phenomena as homosexuality, or mental illness, or retardation in these terms. The final questions that are raised by this approach, therefore, concern not so much that which is labeled "abnormal" as that which is regarded as "normal" in a society. What is sexual normality? What is mental health? What is normal intelligence? Whatever the representatives of other disciplines (such as medicine, law or moral philoso-

[23] *Ibid.,* p. 9.

phy) may say, these sociologists answer very simply: These things are what they are defined as being by society.

It will readily be seen that this approach will be particularly congenial to people or groups that wish to challenge the normative status quo in this or that area of social life. In recent years, for example, groups that have sought to defend the rights of homosexuals to engage in their deviant practices or who have sought to legalize the use of certain hallucinogenic drugs have found theoretical allies in the sociological literature just discussed.

READINGS

For a general introduction, we suggest Mark Lefton, James Skipper and Charles McCaghy (eds.), *Approaches to Deviance* (New York, Appleton-Century-Crofts, 1968), also in paperback.

For an introduction tending toward "labeling theory": Earl Rubington and Martin Weinberg (eds.), *Deviance* (New York, Macmillan, 1968), also in paperback.

For good insights and lively reading: Erving Goffman, *Stigma* (Englewood Cliffs, N.J., Prentice-Hall, 1963), also in paperback. And also Ned Polsly, *Hustlers, Beats and Others* (Garden City, N.Y., Doubleday-Anchor, 1969), also in paperback.

Chapter 15

CHANGE

EXPERIENCING CHANGE AND RESPONDING TO IT

Sociology is hardly required to point out that change is one of the fundamental experiences of human life. The natural environment in which men live is constantly subject to change, some of it seasonal, some seemingly permanent. Our own bodies change all the time (after a certain age, alas, rarely for the better), and so do the bodies of those we associate with. The material artifacts with which we surround ourselves are equally subject to change. But the social fabric of life changes as well. And when people are disturbed about change, much of the time it is events and movements in the social sphere that they are referring to. Neighborhoods change as specific groups move in or out, and the neighborhood becomes "better" or "worse," depending upon one's point of view. Entire communities change as, for instance, in the wake of economic or technological readjustments. Specific institutions change, sometimes drastically altering their character (for example, what is happening today in the university as an institution). And, indeed, entire national societies change, at times slowly, at times in cataclysmic transformations.

Different individuals react differently to experiences of change. Some are exhilarated by change, regarding it as a challenge or as a spur to their own creativity. Others are deeply troubled or frightened by it, seeing it as a disorganizing and destructive force and seeking to contain it in some arresting order. No doubt there are psychological differences between individuals involved in these different reactions. Clearly, there are also differences that have to do with age. For the young individual, who still sees his life stretching out before him into the future as an open possibility, change tends to have positive implications. For the older person, who sees an increasing portion of his life behind him and whose overriding concern is to safeguard those gains that he has been able to make, change tends to be seen more as threat than as promise. Very probably, some of the fundamental human reactions to change have a timeless quality about them; very probably they were not very different in, say, ancient Egypt from what they are today. But in re-

cent times all processes of change have accelerated to an unprece-
dented degree, mainly as a result of modern technology.
Transformations that in earlier times took many decades, if not
centuries, now unfold in the span of just a few years. Thus, more
than ever, change is today a pervasive experience of nearly everyone.

SOCIAL CHANGE AS AN INTELLECTUAL AND POLITICAL PROBLEM: THE URGE TO CONTAIN OR CHANNEL

The experience of social change is at the very core of sociology as a discipline. As we have seen in an earlier chapter, sociology developed as an intellectual response to cata-clysmic social change. In Europe, it was the response to the catastrophic upheavals brought about by the French Revolution and its enduring aftermath. In America, it was the response to the vast and rapid trans-formations of society that followed in the wake of the Civil War and the industrial revolution. In both cases, sociology was more than simply an effort to understand these changes.

Behind the wish to understand was also the deeply felt need either to contain the changes within certain limits deemed to be reasonable or to take charge of them for the purpose of channeling
them in a desired direction. The former motive characterizes sociologists with a conservative bent, the latter those sociologists whose
orientation may be described as progressive or radical. In either
case, social change presents itself as a problem in a double sense:
social change is an intellectual problem in that it is a challenge to
understanding; social change is also a political problem in that it
demands practical actions. Depending upon their view of the nature of their science, sociologists have differed in the manner in
which they have linked the intellectual and the political problem.
To Max Weber, for instance, who strongly believed that sociological
understanding must be separated from value judgments, the relationship between these two was only indirect. To Marxists, on the

other hand, who believe in the unity of theory and practice, the relationship is very intimate. It is important to see, however, that even sociologists who believe that the scientist must approach these questions in detachment from practical action are providing ideas and interpretations that have political consequences—if not for themselves, then for others.

DOES CHANGE HAVE A PURPOSE? COMTE, SPENCER AND MARX

During the early period in the development of sociology, there were attempts at constructing all-embracing theories that would not only explain the change that was occurring but predict the direction that change would take in the future. In other words, these theories were teleological in character; that is, they asserted that the processes of change had a purpose or moving force that could be grasped by means of sociological inquiry. The work of Auguste Comte, the founder of sociology, is typical of this kind of approach.[1] Comte, although conservative and anti-revolutionary in orientation, was nevertheless deeply imbued with the idea of progress that had been the major fruit of the eighteenth-century Enlightenment. By virtue of some allegedly inevitable laws of history, society was moving forward and upward through clearly discernible stages. Comte's central notion about this is formulated in his so-called law of the three stages. Following the two earlier stages in which man's thought was dominated first by mythology and then by theological and philosophical ideas, man is now about to enter the third stage that Comte characterized as "positive." In this stage the dominant role is to be played by scientific reason—and, needless to say, the sociologist is to play a crucial role at this point. It is not an exaggeration to say that, in Comte's view, sociology was understood as a kind of religion of progress, with the sociologist playing the role of priest.

Evolutionary theory and Marxism were two other early attempts

[1] For a very useful discussion of Comte's theory of social change, see Raymond Aron, *Main Currents in Sociological Thought,* Vol. I (New York, Basic Books, 1965).

to provide overall categories within which both present and future processes of social change could be understood. Herbert Spencer was the most important representative of the former approach in the early history of sociology.[2] Here, the Darwinian notions about the dynamics of evolution are directly applied to society and its changes. As in the biological sphere, social change too is dominated by the conflicts and adaptations that result in "natural selection." The purpose of evolution, biological or social, is the "survival of the fittest." In the case of Marx, as we have seen earlier, just about all social change is explained in terms of the varying constellations of class struggle.[3] There are certain similarities between the Spencerian and the Marxian views of social change. In both cases, there is an emphasis on conflict, struggle and, as it were, blind instinct as moving forces of history. This makes both theories appear grim when compared to the more benign interpretations coming from the idea of progress in its Enlightenment form.

There is also in both theories the important assumption that most of the participants in the drama of history are not aware of the real roles they are playing, a notion that Marx aptly caught in his concept of "false consciousness"—the consciousness of people who are systematically unaware of their real social position and thus of the part they are playing in the societal drama. But Marx was much more specific (or, if you prefer, imprudent) than Spencer in making very precise predictions as to the future course of society. The laws of the class struggle were inexorable, and therefore certain future manifestations of it were inevitable. Marx thought that the development of capitalism would inevitably lead to a deepening struggle between the exploiting bourgeoisie and the exploited proletariat. The former would get ever richer and fewer in number, the latter ever poorer and more numerous. Inevitably, the point would be reached when the vast masses of wretched proletarians would rise and overthrow the whole system. The proletarian revolution was an inevitable event in the future, although its timing could not be exactly predicted and was, indeed, subject to influence

2 See Jay Rumney, *Herbert Spencer's Sociology* (New York, Atherton, 1966).

3 Both the most succinct and the most influential statement of the Marxist theory of social change is *The Communist Manifesto* of 1848. This is available in many English editions.

by the actions of revolutionary groups. (It is clear that unless Marx had believed in the last of these propositions, his theory could not have provided any rationale for revolutionary activity.) The socialist society that was to emerge from the revolution was also inevitable, though Marx was reluctant (perhaps quite understandably) to describe its features in any detailed way.

During the classical age in the development of the discipline, sociologists generally avoided theories of such scope. Instead, there was a shift to less all-embracing or teleological analyses.

CLASSICAL THEORISTS: DURKHEIM'S CHANGE FROM "MECHANICAL" TO "ORGANIC" SOLIDARITY

For Durkheim, a key factor in social change was the division of labor.[4] But Durkheim was not so much interested here in establishing a grand theory of social change as in illuminating specific changes that characterized the emergence of modern society. He maintained that as the division of labor becomes progressively complex (a process sharply accelerated by the coming of industrialism) there takes place a change in the fundamental bonds that tie people together in society. These bonds are what Durkheim had in mind when he used the term "solidarity." He then maintained that the change is one from *mechanical* to *organic solidarity*. The terms used by Durkheim are rather unfortunate because they arouse images and associations that are not directly relevant to understanding his point. That point, however, is important: mechanical solidarity prevails in situations where the ties between people living together in a society are total both in scope and strength. Organic solidarity, on the other hand, dominates in situations where ties between people are partial and less committing. In a primitive society, in which mechanical solidarity prevails, there is never any doubt as to whom an individual belongs with. All members of the solidary group in question (say, a tribe) belong to each other in what might be called a

[4] Émile Durkheim, *The Division of Labor in Society* (New York, Free Press, 1947).

total way. Individuals are tied to each other not by some specific, partial interests or aspects of their social life but in the totality of their social existence. Such ties are, of course, very strong indeed and can only be broken at grave psychological peril for the individual.

By contrast, in a modern society, characterized by organic solidarity, ties between people are far less secure. There is considerable doubt, very often, as to just who is part of the group with whom an individual feels solidarity. The common situation in a modern society is that the individual relates to most of his fellow men in very partial and functional ways. For example, two men doing business with each other relate to each other only *as* businessmen. Typically, they have no interest in each other beyond this very limited relation. Such ties are much more easily broken. The contract, as it developed in modern law, is a typical expression of a society run under the principle of organic solidarity. To be sure, any contract, even the most trivial business contract, entails a kind of social tie between the people who are parties to it. There are mutual rights and obligations, and at least to the extent that these are honored there is a solidary relationship between the individuals in question. However, it is intrinsic to the very notion of a contract that the rights and obligations refer to the subject matter of the contract *and to nothing else*. There are, indeed, exceptions, even in modern society, to this kind of partial or functional relationship. Thus relations within the family are not supposed to be, and rarely are, of this kind. Not only would it be a very rare occurrence, but it would generally be regarded as a moral perversion if, for instance, parents made a contract with their children under which the children, in exchange for present provision of room, board and educational expenses, would contract to be subject to parental discipline for a specified number of years and to guarantee economic support to their parents after the latter attained a specified age. The principles of organic solidarity thus never hold absolute sway in any society, and probably could not by the very nature of social life. All the same, *most* human relationships in a modern society are of this general type.

INCREASING ANOMIE AND THE FRAGMENTING OF "COLLECTIVE CONSCIOUSNESS"

We have previously referred to Durkheim's concept of anomie—the state of an individual, or a group, that feels deprived of secure and meaningful relations with other people. A central proposition of Durkheim's sociological analysis of the modern world was that anomie was a widespread and ever-threatening fact in the modern world because of the nature of social relationships in it. In a society dominated by mechanical solidarity, it is much more difficult for an individual or a group to fall into a state of anomie. For better or for worse (and it should be emphasized that very often it is for worse from the point of view of the people concerned), the individual knows exactly where he belongs, and there is no ambiguity about either his rights or his obligations in his solidary group.

Situations dominated by organic solidarity, on the other hand, are much more fragile in their capacity to provide for every individual a comprehensively and enduringly meaningful context for life. As social relations become fragmented, so do the common meanings (or, as Durkheim would say, the "collective consciousness") that provide a meaningful context for the individual's life. Merely functional relations with people change as the functional requirements of the situation change. They are, almost by definition, of a transitory kind. Therefore the individual finds, quite literally, that most of his human relationships are less than reliable. Anomie becomes an ever-present possibility, if not probability.

FROM
GEMEINSCHAFT
TO
GESELLSCHAFT

A strikingly parallel formulation of this problem was arrived at independently about the same time by a German sociologist, Ferdinand Toennies.[5] Toennies distinguished between two fundamental forms of social life, which he called *Gemeinschaft* and *Gesellschaft*. These two terms can be translated as, respectively, "community" and "society," but they are usually left in their German original in English sociological literature in order to retain the specific meaning which Toennies gave to these terms. The two terms correspond very closely to the two types of solidarity as analyzed by Durkheim. *Gemeinschaft* is a group in which the relations between people are direct, profound and all-embracing. By contrast, a *Gesellschaft* is a group in which the relations between people are largely indirect, of superficial quality and relating to only parts of the lives or personalities of those concerned. Modern society is characterized by a global transition from *Gemeinschaft* to *Gesellschaft* forms. The prevailing condition of modern man, therefore, is one of uprootedness and lack of profound social ties— precisely the condition that Durkheim characterized as anomie.

There is, however, an important difference in what might be called the "mood" of Durkheim's and Toennies's approaches to this question. Toennies, a conservative, influenced by the Romantic tradition in German social thought, greatly deplored the transition that he was describing. The move from *Gemeinschaft* to *Gesellschaft* appears as one of degeneration and, perhaps, even dehumanization. Life in a *Gemeinschaft* setting is perceived as more whole, more humanly satisfying than life under the *Gesellschaft* conditions of modern life. Durkheim, on the other hand, was very much what today would be called a liberal, and strongly adverse to any form of Romantic conservatism. While he was indeed aware of the anomic threats produced by life in a modern society, he nevertheless

[5] Ferdinand Toennies, *Community and Society* (East Lansing, Mich., Michigan State University Press, 1957).

fundamentally affirmed the latter as an advance. If the threat of anomie is one side of the modern coin, then the other is the greater possibility that exists for individual liberty. The threat of anomie, and even its relatively frequent occurrence, may be regarded as a price worth paying for the greater degree of freedom possible under modern conditions. This basic difference in viewpoint between Durkheim and Toennies, even when they are looking at the same facts, is of continuing importance in sociology today. There is wide agreement among sociologists of every ideological or political stripe as to some of the fundamental characteristics of modern society. There are very far-reaching differences, however, in the way in which these facts are evaluated.

MAX WEBER: THE THEORY OF CHARISMA AND RATIONALIZATION

Of the classical sociologists, it was probably Weber whose views of social change had the most permanent effect on later thinking about this subject among sociologists. This is particularly so with regard to Weber's theories of *charisma* and *rationalization*.[6]

We have already come across the concept of charisma when we discussed Weber's approach to political sociology. Charismatic authority, in contrast to traditional or legal-rational authority, is based upon the extraordinary claims made by an individual or a group, claims that are self-validating and that do not rest either upon tradition or on law. What we must now look at is Weber's view of what happens to charisma, specifically his notion of the *routinization of charisma*, which is one of his fundamental contributions to the analysis of social change.

Charismatic authority, by its very nature, is revolutionary and innovative. It sets itself up *against* whatever structures preceded it, be they structures of tradition or of law. This is typically expressed

[6] See Max Weber, *The Theory of Social and Economic Organization* (New York, Oxford University Press, 1947), pp. 358ff.; Hans Gerth and C. Wright Mills (eds.), *From Max Weber* (New York, Oxford University Press, 1958), pp. 196ff.

in the statement of Jesus in the New Testament: "You have heard it said, *but* I say to you . . ." In this "but" lies the clue to the revolutionary significance of charisma. It is subversive of existing structures in the most profound way possible, namely, by denying their previously accepted legitimacy. Charisma subverts, disrupts, explodes existing institutional structures whether religious, political or anything else. Charismatic leaders, therefore, are among the most dangerous of men. Often enough, to be sure, they are suppressed by the forces that wish to preserve the status quo. Wherever charismatic movements are successful, however, they bring about a revolution in the order of institutions. Either they create new institutional structures or they drastically change the existing ones.

Weber maintained that through most of human history charisma was a very important revolutionary force. In saying this, he did not deny other forces making for far-reaching social change such as, for example, changes in technology or economic relations. But wherever society underwent abrupt and far-reaching change, there is good reason to guess that charisma was somewhere involved in the events that brought about the change. Weber's theory of charisma is of particular importance, however, because of its propositions concerning the fate of charismatic authority *after* its success. It is in this part of the theory that we once more come across Weber's profoundly ironic view of human affairs.

The key proposition can be simply stated: *charisma never lasts.* Or, as Weber put it, charisma only exists *in statu nascendi*—that is, it only exists in the state of being born. As soon as charisma becomes established as authority, it begins to disintegrate and to begin changing into something else. Charisma then, while an important revolutionary force, cannot sustain itself as social reality once its revolution has succeeded.

CHARACTERISTICS OF CHARISMATIC MOVEMENTS AND THE SECOND GENERATION PROBLEM

There are a number of reasons for this. Charismatic movements tend toward loose and informal organization. For instance, in terms of their economic organization, charismatic movements favor such methods of sustenance as begging or robbery. Neither of these is conducive to the reliable economic maintenance of successful institutions. As long as the charismatic movement is new and has not yet firmly established its authority, its loose organization is actually an advantage. Authority is invested in the charismatic leader as an individual, or perhaps extended to a small group of lieutenants that surround him. Any more formal organization would rob the charismatic leader of the immediacy and the dynamic quality of his leadership. If the charismatic movement attains success, however, these informal arrangements become progressively less viable, because now the charismatic leadership faces the basic problems of administration. A successful charismatic movement in the area of religion can now no longer exist as a wildly excited band of enthusiasts but must make provisions to meet the religious and perhaps other social needs of a large population that looks to it for continuing sustenance. Even more clearly, a charismatic movement in the sphere of politics must, after its success, find forms of administration that will secure an orderly and durable government over the population that it now controls. In neither case will the old charismatic arrangements serve any longer.

The history of twentieth-century revolutions is full of illustrations of this process. The Russian Revolution went through a period of intense charismatic fervor. It lasted, though probably with diminishing strength even then, while Lenin was alive. After Lenin's death, the revolution and its major organizational embodiment, the Communist party, "hardened" into the forms that subsequently came to be known as Stalinism. Mao Tse-tung saw this process as a basic threat to his own revolution in China. He identified the threat with party bureaucracy. The so-called Cultural Revolution was Mao's attempt to revive the revolutionary charisma of an earlier period and to pit the enthusiasm of youth against the party bureaucrats. In Cuba, Castro has continued to try to rule on the basis of a charisma born during the years of revolutionary struggle. As one (sympathetic) observer commented, Cuba has been ruled out of the pocket of Castro's fatigue jacket—the pocket into which he has the habit of stuffing the notes he takes while moving about the country by car or helicopter. Such habits of government have greatly endeared Castro to a large number of Cubans. But some (again, quite sympathetic) observers have wondered if some of Cuba's difficulties may not be related to this charismatic style of administration.

But there is a deeper reason for the transitory nature of charismatic authority. It becomes clear when we look at Weber's suggestion that the demise of charismatic authority can usually be dated in a rather precise way—at the time when the first generation of followers has died. Why should this be? The answer probably lies in some fundamental traits of human nature. Charisma is, by definition, extraordinary, tremendously exciting, disruptive of all the structures that used to determine the everyday life of people. Charismatic movements typically operate at an extremely high pitch of emotional intensity. Very likely, human beings cannot sustain for very long this kind of excitement. This is probably even true of most people who were originally caught in the turmoil of a charismatic movement and constituted its first followers. But as long as the original generation of followers is still alive, the charismatic authority can sustain itself, if not on their present excitement then at least on the memory of the great experiences in these people's past. All this changes drastically when a new generation that was not present at the inception of the movement comes into being and grows into positions of leadership in whatever structure the movement has set up. By now, the original leader or leaders are dead. The second generation has not, in its own life, participated in the great events that saw the beginning of the movement. They only know these events through the stories of their elders. Most fundamentally, however, that which to the first generation was truly extraordinary now, in the second generation, becomes part of the ordinary fabric of social life. After all, the second generation has grown up with these stories, and it cannot be expected to react to them with the same breathless excitement. For the second generation, the great events of the charismatic revolution are "old hat," a more than slightly boring hangup of the parental generation. This is exactly what the term "routinization" refers to—those things that once were extraordinary have now become routine. Weber's German term makes that point even more clearly. The German word for which routinization is a very apt translation is *Veralltaeglichung*— literally, "rendering into everyday." It means that something which once broke the structures of everyday life now has become itself one of the structures. When this happens, charismatic authority inevitably loses its old legitimacy and must find new ways to maintain the institutional structures it has created. With this change, the revolutionary impulse of the charismatic movement begins to die.

ROUTINIZATION: TRADITIONALIZATION AND RATIONALIZATION

In line with Weber's three-fold typology of authority, he argues that the routinization of charisma can take two distinct directions. Charisma can be traditionalized, that is, transformed into traditional authority. Or charisma can be rationalized, that is, transformed into legal-rational forms of authority. A recurrent form of the traditionalization of charisma, very widespread in human history, is the establishment of a dynasty among the descendants of the charismatic leader. The quality of authority that was previously unique and extraordinary in terms of an individual now becomes transmitted through natural procreation. It is then no longer necessary that the descendants lay claim to extraordinary qualities for themselves as individuals; the quality has, so to speak, entered their bloodstream. It is then quite possible that, say, the grandson of a charismatic leader turns out to be a most undistinguished specimen of humanity and, nevertheless, retains his authority.

RATIONALIZA-
TION: THE CASE
OF THE
CATHOLIC
CHURCH

The more important form of the routinization of charisma in modern times is that of rationalization. The prototypical case of this for Weber was the Catholic Church. He describes the process as one in which *charisma of person* is changed into *charisma of office*. The development of the Christian priesthood (and then of the episcopate and finally the papacy) illustrates this very clearly. In the apostolic age, authority in the Christian Church was vested in the Apostles (all of whom, except Paul, had been personal witnesses to the great events in the life of Jesus) and their directly designated lieutenants. The charisma, though clearly in a less intensive way than in the case of Jesus himself, was still tied to specific persons *as* persons. With the successful establishment of a Christian Church covering a wide territory and administering a growing population of Christians, this type of authority became progressively less viable.

As a professional priesthood came to be established, authority in the Church was more and more clearly vested in the office of the priest rather than in any personal qualities of his. The priest had the authority to perform certain acts (notably to administer "valid" sacraments) not because he was some extraordinary person but because he was ordained to his office by the proper ecclesiastical procedures. It followed (this point was clearly established when the Church condemned the so-called Donatist heresy) that a priest could, as a person, be a morally altogether despicable character— but *nevertheless* carry out the functions of his priestly office in a valid manner.

This same conception was also extended to bishops and popes. It reached a kind of climax in the doctrine of papal infallibility. This doctrine maintained that the pope was infallible in matters of faith and/or morals when he speaks *ex cathedra*. The term literally means, "from the throne"—that is, when he speaks *as pope*. The doctrine never maintained that the pope was infallible in any other matters, or even that in those specific matters he was infallible as an individual. His infallibility derived exclusively from his office as pope, an office that Catholics believe to be under special divine protection. It also followed that a pope, with all these powers appertaining to his office, might be a most fallible person, or indeed a wicked one. Few Catholic historians would disagree with the notion that, for example, Alexander Borgia was one of the most wicked people in Renaissance Italy, and if the Catholic view of the universe is true, he is very probably in hell right now. This does not change the fact that Alexander Borgia was a real pope, with all the authority vested in that office. It was perhaps fortunate that Pope Alexander, busy as he was waging wars, poisoning cardinals and entertaining in the brothel he had set up in a wing of the Vatican, did not find the time to make any pronouncements *ex cathedra* on such (to him) uninteresting matters as faith or morals. This very omission, however, can quite logically be taken by Catholics as another case in point of the special divine protection from which the office of the papacy benefits.

RATIONALIZATION: THE PERMANENT REVOLUTION?

If charisma is for Weber the first great revolutionary force in history, the other is rationalization. We have also come across this term when we discussed Weber's analysis of bureaucracy. For Weber, rationalization was the great transforming force in the modern world. It is the process by which, in more and more areas of social life, means and ends are linked through rationally designed and rationally comprehensible procedures. Bureaucracy, as we have seen, is the major institutional expression of a rationalized society. Rationalization, in common with charisma, has a fundamentally revolutionizing impetus. Like charisma, it is inimical to tradition; it subverts established institutional orders; it radically, and often abruptly, changes long-established patterns of social life. Unlike charisma, however, rationalization does not carry within it the seed of its own destruction. Rationality cannot be routinized. Indeed, rationalization *is* rou-

tinization. Thus, in Weber's view, the revolutionary transformations brought about by rationalization have an enduring character
that charisma can never bring about. Put differently: Weber saw the
revolution of modernity as a permanent one.

WHAT ABOUT MAN'S NON-RATIONAL NEEDS?

The bureaucratic necessities of a modern technological society further guarantee this permanence. This does not mean, though, that Weber saw all processes of change coming to an end in the rationalized procedures of modern bureaucratic society. He saw and foresaw that the very rationalization of social life would give birth to new eruptions of irrationality. Again, this very probably has profound roots in the very constitution of man. There are profound psychic needs or impulses in man that resist total absorption in the rational structures of the modern world (and these emphatically include the structures of the modern mind). Invariably, these irrational impulses will erupt, either in direct opposition to the rational order of institutions or in subterranean enclaves that survive in the midst of these institutions.

In the development of American sociology, the major interest has been in very specific aspects of change. For example, the interest has been in the types of social change involved in urbanization, in immigration, or, particularly in recent years, in modernization. While there have been many attempts to explain, and sometimes predict, the changes taking place in these areas, there has been a shying away from more general approaches. Even those sociologists who have theorized about change have tended to develop concepts that remain close to empirical material in specific areas and that were directly applicable to the description and explanation of such materials. William Ogburn was one of the foremost earlier American sociologists interested in social change.[7] But Ogburn, while having theoretical interests, did not produce sweeping theories of social

[7] William Ogburn, *Social Change* (New York, Viking, 1950). The work was originally published in 1922.

change comparable to the European ones just discussed. One of Ogburn's concepts has had continuing and widespread use. This is the concept of *cultural lag*. It refers to a situation in which there is discrepancy between different processes of change. For example, there can be a situation in which there has occurred a drastic transformation of the economy and technology of a society while its family institutions or its moral values still retain their traditional forms. In this case, there exists a lag between these areas of social life. Ogburn's concept has been useful in drawing attention to the complexity of change processes and to the fact that not all areas of social life change at the same time or in the same way.

SOROKIN'S SENSATE, IDEATIONAL AND IDEALISTIC CULTURES

One important figure in this area is Pitirim Sorokin, a Russian scholar who came to America in the 1920's and who did most of his work in sociology in this country.[8] Sorokin's approach to social change may, with some modifications, be described as a strongly idealist one, in the sense that he gives a very important place to ideas as causal factors in social change. Sorokin understands social change in terms of a succession of overall views of reality pertaining in a particular society. He distinguishes between three major types of such views, and societies are characterized in terms of the predominance of one of these types. He calls these the sensate, the ideational and the idealistic types. They are distinguished by the different ways in which truth is conceived of. In other words, the basic dynamic of change is cultural, meaning by culture the integration of definitions of reality. Social change must always be understood in conjunction with these cultural processes. A sensate culture is one in which truth or reality is fundamentally defined on the basis of sense ex-

[8] Sorokin was a prolific writer, but his major contribution to the topic under discussion here is his *Social and Cultural Dynamics* (Englewood Cliffs, N.J., Bedminster, 1962). The four volumes of this work originally appeared between 1937 and 1941.

perience. An ideational culture is one in which allegedly spiritual principles predominate (that is, essentially a culture determined by religious views of the world). An idealistic culture combines important elements of the previous two types, but it integrates them in an essentially rational view of the world. Sorokin thought that modern society was increasingly based on a sensate culture, and he inclined to the view that this constituted a kind of degeneration.

An important aspect of Sorokin's theory of social change is what he called the "principle of limits": all processes of change occur within certain limits, which are presumably set by human nature itself. Therefore there is a periodic recurrence of basic social constellations. However much societies may change, there are definite limits to the range of changes. In the end, very few things in social life are really new. In this notion of the periodicity or cyclical character of social change Sorokin is quite similar to Pareto, whom we discussed in an earlier chapter.

PARSONS'S PATTERN VARIABLES: FROM PARTICULARISM TO UNIVERSALISM; FROM AFFECTIVITY TO AFFECTIVE NEUTRALITY

Talcott Parsons, the broadest theorist among contemporary American sociologists, has emphasized the impossibility of a general theory of social change at the present stage of our knowledge. He has, however, taken a number of steps in this direction.[9] Parsons's emphasis, as always, is on society seen as an ongoing system. Social change takes place as a result of the system's efforts to maintain itself from within and to defend itself against outside influences. An important place in the causation of social change is given to what might be termed the misfortunes of socialization—that is, various flaws in the socialization of individuals and groups

---

[9] Talcott Parsons, *The Social System* (New York, Free Press, 1951), pp. 480ff.

which bring about an imperfect adjustment of personalities to the requirements of the social system and thus produce imbalances and instabilities in the latter.

One of Parsons's most influential theoretical contributions has been his conception of the so-called *pattern variables*.[10] These are a set of twin concepts representing alternatives in the basic orientation of a society or an institution. For example, one pair of twin pattern variables is that of particularism and universalism. Under a particularistic pattern of social relations, individuals derive their status from qualities that are ascribed to them by virtue of membership in a particular group. By contrast, a universalistic pattern applies certain criteria of status to all affected individuals without discrimination in terms of previous group membership. For example, in a particularistic type of political administration, it is assumed that an individual's application will be favorably acted upon by an official who is the individual's relative. By contrast, in an administration operating under universalistic principles (the typical case in modern bureaucracies), it is assumed that all applicants will be judged by the same criteria of eligibility, regardless of their personal family relations, or lack of such, with the official who is responsible for this matter.

Another twin pair of pattern variables is that of affectivity and affective neutrality. Social relations marked by affectivity are assumed to be based upon, or, at any rate, to involve, strong emotional ties between individuals. A pattern of affective neutrality, on the other hand, assumes that certain ties will be maintained in the absence of such emotionality. For example, it is assumed in Western societies today that relationships within the immediate family are marked by affectivity. By contrast, businessmen entering into a contract with each other are assumed to do so in a state of affective neutrality. In either instance, the intrusion of the other pattern would be regarded as inappropriate and, at least in the first case, as contrary to moral norms: it would be taken as both improper and immoral if a husband and a wife started out viewing their marriage as nothing but a contract mutually guaranteeing certain sexual and

[10] *Ibid.*, pp. 58ff.

economic privileges, to be carried out in cold detachment from any emotional relationship. It might not be regarded as immoral, but it would be both improper and illegal if the two aforementioned businessmen took the position that they will only abide by *their* contract as long as they stay in love with each other. Parsons's pattern variables, which we will not fully enumerate here, have shown their usefulness in a number of areas. In terms of social change, Parsons and various students of his have been able to show that change entails important shifts in the way a society is organized, in terms of the pattern variables. These concepts are particularly useful in describing the transition from pre-modern to modern social structures, a transition that involves specific shifts in the pattern variables. To take the two just mentioned, modernization typically entails a shift from particularism to universalism, as well as from affectivity to affective neutrality, in a wide spectrum of social relations. This shift, as described by Parsons, is very similar to the transitions analyzed by Toennies and Durkheim.

In recent years, Parsons has increasingly used evolutionary language to refer to social change.[11] In line with this evolutionary perspective, Parsons has placed growing emphasis on the process of *differentiation* in social change. The term refers to an increasing division of labor between institutions. For example, while economic and political institutions coalesced in feudal society, modern society (at least under capitalism) has increasingly differentiated these two spheres of social life and organized them in separate institutional structures. The immense complexity of modern society is largely ascribed by Parsons to these processes of institutional differentiation and to their consequences in the realm of both culture and personality.

[11] See, for example, his little volume on comparative sociology, *Societies* (Englewood Cliffs, N.J., Prentice-Hall, 1966).

OTHER AMERICAN APPROACHES

A number of other American sociologists have attempted to view social change in essentially systemic ways, that is, by looking at society as a system engaged in differentiating, adapting and maintaining itself. A close student and collaborator of Parsons, Neil Smelser, has tried to develop Parsonian ideas of social change toward a general theory of modernization.[12] A similar attempt, though on a much more ambitious scale, has been that of Marion Levy, who tried to analyze the functionally necessary patterns of a modern society.[13] A work that has recently attracted considerable attention is by Amitai Etzioni.[14] Etzioni is much more independent of the Parsonian or structural-functional approach than either Smelser or Levy, but he also takes a fundamentally systemic view of social change. Etzioni's basic question concerns what he calls the "active orientation": How is it that certain societies can be described as active while others seem to be inert or stagnating? Etzioni seeks to answer this question by analyzing both power and the organization of knowledge in a society. Activation occurs under conditions where the power structure and the organization of knowledge (which includes norms and values) appear in specific combinations.

We have had occasion to remark before that there has taken place in America, in recent years, a resurgence of what is termed radical sociology both by its adherents and its opponents. This development can be dated rather precisely with the virulent attack by C. Wright Mills on the prevailing sociological approaches (including the Parsonian one) in 1959.[15] Since then, this movement has taken a number of different forms, some more explicitly Marxist than others. A recent statement of the major presuppositions of at least

[12] Neil Smelser, *Essays in Sociological Explanation* (Englewood Cliffs, N.J., Prentice-Hall, 1968).

[13] Marion Levy, *Modernization and the Structure of Societies* (Princeton, N.J., Princeton University Press, 1966).

[14] Amitai Etzioni, *The Active Society* (New York, Free Press, 1968).

[15] C. Wright Mills, *The Sociological Imagination* (New York, Oxford University Press, 1959). Also, see Irving Horowitz (ed.), *The New Sociology* (New York, Oxford University Press, 1965).

an important segment of this movement is the work of Alvin Gouldner.[16] The approach of the new radical sociology to social change can be seen on two levels. On the more general level, it consists of a new emphasis on power and conflict in society, an approach that puts these sociologists in strong contradiction not only to Parsons but to any functionalist or systemic orientation. On a more concrete empirical level, the new radical sociology tends to view at least many, if not most, current processes of change as being the result of the tensions or "contradictions" of the capitalist society, both domestically and in its international relations. Thus such varied phenomena of social change as American military and political policies in the Third World, the racial conflict within the United States and the "alienation" of segments of American youth from established norms and career patterns are viewed together in a comprehensive scheme as intrinsic manifestations of a capitalism in crisis. (It may be added that most of these analysts fervently hope that the crisis will be terminal.) On both levels, the new radical sociology represents a return of Marxist perspectives, even though probably only a minority in this group would identify themselves with Marxism without reservations.

"WHERE WE'RE AT": ADVANCED INDUSTRIAL, POST-INDUSTRIAL OR "LATE CAPITALIST" SOCIETY?

The different perspectives on change now prevailing among American sociologists can be rather conveniently distinguished from each other in terms of their views as to where our society is at this particular time of its history. These views are already expressed in the overarching concepts that are employed by different sociologists to describe our society.

A widely used concept of this sort is that of *advanced industrial society*.[17] This concept is very widely used, not only in America but

[16] Alvin Gouldner, *The Coming Crisis of Western Sociology* (New York, Basic Books, 1970).

[17] See, for example, Raymond Aron, *The Industrial Society* (New York, Praeger, 1967).

in Western Europe, by what could be called mainstream sociologists. The basic meaning of the concept is that societies at a certain level of industrial development will tend to develop specific social structures that are appropriate to this level. There is the further implication that societies of this type (such as America and Russia) will tend to resemble each other sociologically in, at any rate, a considerable number of their institutions. This implication is sometimes called the *convergence thesis*. There is, however, an additional implication, namely, that many of the processes of change our society is now undergoing are *not* due to the peculiar qualities of capitalism but are endemic to advanced industrial societies of any type of economic organization and, more specifically, are shared with socialist societies at a comparable stage of industrial development. It should come as no surprise that this last implication is profoundly repulsive to radical sociologists, so that the very term "advanced industrial society" has become something of a dirty word in their dictionary.

Some observers of the social scene in change have gone one step further and describe our society as a *post-industrial society*. This term has been in favor not only among sociologists but particularly among so-called futurologists, that is, a rather heterogeneous group of social scientists who make it their business to forecast future trends.[18] The meaning of this concept is that while our society is still dependent on industrial production, an increasing portion of its population is engaged in occupations that are far removed from such production. The *problem* of production has been solved with the attainment of a phenomenal rate of economic growth—in other words, continuing productivity can be taken for granted. It is consumption now that becomes problematic—not only consumption in the narrow sense of material goods but in an enlarged sense of all social and cultural activities taking place on the basis of our gigantic production machine. This concept has been adopted by some mainstream sociologists, and it has even had some appeal to those interested in what is sometimes called the contemporary "cultural revolution." It is quite uncongenial to most radical sociologists be-

[18] See Herman Kahn and Anthony Wiener, *The Year 2000* (New York, Macmillan, 1967).

cause, like the first concept, it seems to them to blur the important difference between capitalism and its socialist alternatives.

Within the camp of radical sociology itself, the favored concept is that of *late capitalist society*. In a procedure that Herbert Marcuse (not himself a sociologist) has made popular, all the important tensions of contemporary American society are explained as necessary consequences of capitalism.[19] The concept is congenial to a Marxist view of social change because it emphasizes the importance of the type of economic organization (in this case, capitalism) and, by the adjective "late," tacitly includes the prognosis of impending revolution.

POSITIVE AND NEGATIVE JUDGMENTS ABOUT MODERNITY

In concluding, we want to return once more to the difference in what we called "mood" between the classical approaches of Durkheim and Toennies to modern society. These differences are still very much with us today, and to some extent they cut across political lines. Mainstream American sociology can be called Durkheimian in the sense that it is fundamentally disposed to accept modernity as a necessary and at least partly desirable phenomenon. There are very few sociologists today who continue Toennies's conservative and Romantic reaction against modernity, if only for the reason that there are very few conservative sociologists. Within the context of radical sociology, there is an interesting split in this regard. The more explicitly Marxist sociologists, whatever other differences they may have with mainstream sociologists, share with the latter a fundamentally positive attitude toward modernity. The socialist society they seek is still marked by the structures made familiar by modern institutions—except that the society will now be under a different form of management. There is also a trend within radical sociology, however, that reacts against modernity in a general way and is

[19] See Herbert Marcuse, *One-Dimensional Man* (Boston, Beacon, 1954).

interested in the possibility of regenerating pre-modern social and cultural patterns. Youth-culture and counter-culture influences are clearly discernible in this approach. It finds a logical expression in a strong interest in Third World societies—that is, in societies that are still relatively free of the alleged evils of modernity.

R E A D I N G S

We would suggest that the reader at this point read two contradictory inter-pretations of the present condition of modern society:

Aron, Raymond, *The Industrial Society* (New York, Praeger, 1967).

Marcuse, Herbert, *One-Dimensional Man* (Boston, Beacon, 1954), available in paperback.

Chapter 16

OLD AGE, ILLNESS AND DEATH

EXPERIENCING THE LIMITS OF EVERYDAY LIFE

It is possible to conceive of human experience as being divided into a day side and a night side. The day side of experience is the world of everyday life which, even where it includes unhappiness, is clear and reliable in its structures. The night side contains experiences that are uncanny, sometimes terrifying, and which put in question the firm reality of everyday life. It is the world of dreams, of visions, of those twilight experiences of other possibilities of being that ancient man used to look upon as encounters with the divine and which we generally assign to the jurisdiction of psychiatry. The human experience most obviously belonging to this night side is the experience of death—which not only terminates the world of everyday life for whomever passes through it but which, for those who are witnesses of the death of another, appears as the ultimate threat to whatever is firm and lucid in everyday life. Old age and illness are less dramatic in their threat to the structure of ordinary living. Yet, even at their best, old age and illness constitute signals of death. For this reason, they evoke very special reactions, both on the part of individuals and of society.

Old age, illness and death are experiences *in* everyday life. But by their very nature they are also experiences that point toward the limits of everyday life—to use the term coined by the philosopher Karl Jaspers, they are *borderline experiences*. For this reason, it has always been important for human societies to provide special institutional arrangements that would somehow contain these experiences and prevent them from disrupting the basic structures of social life. This has always been so. The problem of institutional containment, however, is especially difficult in modern society, and doubly so in American society. Particularly in the latter, there has been established a cult of youth, of health and of life. To be youthful, to be healthy and to be full of vital energies is widely looked upon not simply as the happy condition of those favored by nature with these qualities but as, in some way, a moral duty for *everyone*. Consequently, to be old, to be ill or to be facing death appears not only as misfortune but in some fashion as moral failure.

One visible result of this attitude has been that old age, illness and death (in ascending order) are, as far as is possible, hidden away. The modern family has less place for the old than older forms of kinship organization. Those who are seriously ill go through this experience in hospitals that are quite rigidly segregated from other sectors of social life. The hospital is also the socially designated location for dying.

THE BUDDHA-LIKE EXPERIENCES OF YOUTH TODAY

According to legend, the Buddha's father, an Indian prince, wanted to shield the young Buddha from all experiences that would be profoundly distressing—and especially from having to witness old age, illness or death. Therefore the prince arranged the boy's life in so careful a way that these human experiences would never come into view. The legend goes on to tell about the day when these protective arrangements accidentally broke down and the Buddha saw in succession an old beggar, a leper and a corpse being taken out for cremation. This massive confrontation with what we have called the night side of human life was so shocking to the Buddha that it motivated him to leave his father's palace, go out into the wilderness and search for an answer to the agonizing question of human suffering. One may assume that, in ancient India, it must have been difficult even for a prince to arrange such a protected life for his son. It is then somewhat startling to reflect that to see very little of old age, hardly anything of serious illness and probably nothing of death is a perfectly normal condition for most middle-class children in modern society.

The first two of these three experiences—old age and illness—have been widely studied by sociologists. Indeed, they have become the subject matter of two sub-disciplines: social gerontology and medical sociology.[1] Most of the work in these sub-disciplines has

---

[1] For overviews of work in social gerontology, see the following: Clark Tibbitts (ed.), *Handbook of Social Gerontology* (Chicago, University of Chicago Press, 1960); Ernest Burgess (ed.), *Aging in Western Societies* (Chicago, University of Chicago Press, 1960); Richard William *et al.* (eds.), *Processes of Aging*

been very practical in orientation. It has obvious relevance for public welfare and health policies, and very often has actually been sponsored and subsidized by agencies with these concerns. We shall not try in this chapter to give an overview of these findings, however great may be their interest for the specialist. But there are considerably broader implications to these topics and it is these that we propose to look at.

GETTING "OLD": MORE OF US ARE DOING IT

The process of aging is a universal biological fact. But who it is that is looked upon as aged or old is a matter of societal definition. As the result of modern medicine and nutrition, a basic fact about our society (as we have already seen in an earlier context) is the increasing longevity of people. Today, people live longer than they ever have before in human history. This has had the consequence of pushing up the age at which people are considered, or consider themselves, to be old. In, say, the Middle Ages, when the life expectancy was somewhere in the thirties, a person who reached the age of fifty could, quite logically, be considered old. Today, when life expectancy is steadily pushing upward in the seventies, no one laughs when, for example, a man in his forties is described as "a young politician" or "a young executive." It is important to recognize this historical relativity in the social definition of old age.

A further consequence of this situation is that there are more of the aged around (by whatever definition). At the turn of the century, 4 percent of the American population was over sixty-five. In 1965, this figure was over 9 percent. It is very likely to keep on increasing, since the birth rate is tending to decline and the life expectancy to rise. All over the world, these demographic trends are

(New York, Atherton, 1963). For an excellent introduction to the topic see Yonina Talmon, "Aging: Social Aspects," in *International Encyclopedia of the Social Sciences,* Vol. I (New York, Macmillan, 1968), pp. 186ff. For a broad cross-cultural approach to age groups, see S. N. Eisenstadt, *From Generation to Generation* (New York, Free Press, 1956).

directly related to the degree of industrial development as well as to public-health policies. Where there is high industrial development and vigorous public-health policies on the part of the government, the proportion of the aged in the general population increases. This is expressed by the so-called "index of aging," which is computed as the number of people over sixty over the number of children under fifteen. In 1950, for example, this index was 10.2 for Brazil, 21.8 for Japan, 45.40 for the United States and 64.0 for Sweden. Both the factors of industrial development and of public-health policies are relevant to these discrepancies.[2]

BECOMING OBSOLETE; THE LOSS OF STATUS; ANOMIE

The economic effect of these changes is ambivalent. On the one hand, in an industrial economy there is a tendency for the aged to become obsolete in the labor force. There tends to be a general oversupply of labor, and the elimination of the aged from active work is very convenient economically. On the other hand, affluence permits generous economic provisions for the aged, both in terms of public programs and as a result of private initiative. In this situation, it is possible for the individual to make provisions for his old age in a manner quite impossible in a society with little or no economic surplus.

It is quite debatable whether the aged are treated worse or not in contemporary American society. There can be little question that their purely economic fate is much brighter today. Economic survival, though, is not everything. There is a good deal of romanticism concerning the allegedly better position of the aged in earlier periods of Western history. This romanticism evokes an idyllic picture of grandfather and grandmother sitting near the fireplace and telling wonderful stories to the children. This picture leaves out the brutality with which old people were very frequently dealt with in the past. But one thing is quite clear: very widely, old age means a loss of status in contemporary society. Among most men and many

[2] Henry Sheldon, "The Changing Demographic Profile," in Tibbitts, *op. cit.*, p. 28.

women, this loss of status is the direct result of retirement. Among housewives it is due to a loss of functions after their children have grown up and left the home. Because of earlier marriage and child-bearing, and increasing longevity, the so-called "post-parental period" (that is, the period in which the children have left the house of their parents) tends to become ever longer. This loss of status becomes particularly painful because it is generally coupled with declining income and declining health.

Thus old age is looked upon as a "social problem" today, both for society and for the individual. Various policies for the aged recur as a political problem. For the individual, old age is, above all, a problem of meaning in life. Studies of the aged report again and again widespread feelings of loneliness and meaninglessness. In Durkheim's sense, then, old age is full of the threat of anomie.

GETTING "SICK": BECOMING DEPENDENT AGAIN

Like aging, illness is also a relative matter; that is, it is subject to social definition. This is very clear in the case of mental illness. What is considered madness in one society may be looked upon as a perfectly normal condition in another. But social definition also extends to physical illness. Chronic obesity and indigestion, for example, are commonly regarded as calling for medical treatment today, while even very recently they might just have been accepted as belonging to the physical attributes of a particular individual. Generally speaking, the advance of modern medicine has had the result of expanding the definition of illness and of serious illness. That is, not only has the general concept of illness expanded but illnesses which were previously regarded as not meriting much attention are now taken with much greater seriousness.

In our society there is a vast institutional complex dealing with illness. Most of the sociology of medicine has been concerned with the way in which this institutional complex works.[3] But the phe-

[3] For overviews of work in the sociology of medicine, see Dorrian Apple (ed.), *Sociological Studies of Health and Sickness* (New York, McGraw-Hill, 1960); Howard Freeman *et al.* (eds.), *Handbook of Medical Sociology* (Englewood Cliffs, N.J., Prentice-Hall, 1963).

nomenon of illness has sociological implications that go beyond this particular institutional setting.

"Being ill" is to be in a very specific social situation. Talcott Parsons has coined the suggestive term "sick roles" to refer to this.[4] The term suggests that society has constructed specific roles to be played by sick people, that is, by people who are socially defined as sick. Complementary to these, of course, are the roles to be played by people who have to deal with the sick. One basic characteristic of the sick role in contemporary society is a change from independence to dependency. Varying with the degree of sickness, the sick person is no longer considered as an independent actor in society but as someone who is dependent upon others. This dependency of the sick person puts him back, in an often disturbing way, into the condition of early childhood. The sick role therefore entails what psychologists have called "infantilization." Sometimes, indeed, this may be pleasurable to the individual, or perhaps even sought by him. More commonly, though, it is an experience of shock and dismay. The latter are particularly likely, of course, in cases of serious or chronic illnesses and when the illness requires hospitalization.

Sociologists in the symbolic-interactionist tradition have used the term "career" to describe the process by which a sick role is learned. There takes place a specific socialization or re-socialization process with specific stages in which the individual "graduates" to his new status as a sick person. Often this involves "bargaining" with medical personnel and with others such as family members as to the exact meaning of the new status.[5]

BEING LABELED AND BEING STIGMATIZED

All of this can again be plausibly subsumed under the heading of anomie. Recently, some sociologists have even dealt with illness as a form of deviance, to be understood in terms of labeling theory as we have discussed it before. This can most readily be done in the case of mental illness, since its social

[4] Talcott Parsons, *The Social System* (New York, Free Press, 1951), pp. 285ff.
[5] See, for example, Julius Roth, *Timetables* (Indianapolis, Bobbs-Merrill, 1963), which deals with the "career" of being a TB patient.

relativity is most obvious.[6] Thomas Scheff, for example, in a way strongly influenced by Erving Goffman, has dealt with mental illness entirely in terms of its social definition as a deviant condition. In other words, the mentally ill are those who are so labeled by society (at least from a sociological point of view). But there has also been a serious attempt to analyze physical illness in these terms. One sociologist who has pushed this approach very far is Eliot Freidson.[7] Freidson distinguishes between illnesses that have a stigma attached to them and those that do not—for example, respectively, syphilis and pneumonia. In the former case, being ill clearly involves some imputation of moral irresponsibility. But society is not always that logical. Thus being blind or crippled, or even having cancer, also entails various forms of stigmatization—although, clearly, the individual afflicted with these conditions could not possibly be regarded as responsible for his state. The stigmatization at least involves placing the victim in a separate social category in order to ease the psychological difficulties of those having to deal with him. At that point, the finer moral distinctions may become rather irrelevant for the person in this situation.

In the broadest sense, in a society dominated by a cult of youth and health, both old age and illness are necessarily stigmatized, at least to a degree. They are therefore conditions of which the victim is likely to be ashamed, even if not exactly guilty. The process of stigmatization becomes crystal clear in the attitude of contemporary society toward dying and toward death.

In the proximity of death, all social roles are put under severe strain. As a result, special patterns of conduct emerge that are not altogether different from those characteristic of soldiers at war.[8] For this reason, there emerges what David Sudnow has called "the social organization of dying." [9] An important part of this are the socially prevailing notions of how one is supposed to die "prop-

---

[6] See Thomas Scheff, *Being Mentally Ill* (Chicago, Aldine, 1966). Some support for this view has even come from a few psychiatrists. See Thomas Szasz, *The Myth of Mental Illness* (New York, Hoeber-Harper, 1961).

[7] Eliot Freidson, *The Sociology of Medicine* (New York, Dodd, Mead, 1967).

[8] See, for example, Renée Fox, *Experiment Perilous* (New York, Free Press, 1959), a sociological study of the conduct of patients and medical personnel in a critical-care hospital ward.

[9] David Sudnow, *Passing On* (Englewood Cliffs, N.J., Prentice-Hall, 1967).

erly." These notions are held both by the patients and by the medical personnel in charge of them. Not infrequently, there are conflicts between them about this.

THE AWARENESS OF DEATH

A crucial question is how the situation of an individual who is about to die is defined by those around him as well as by himself. This has been studied in great detail by two sociologists, Barney Glaser and Anselm Strauss.[10] These two authors have distinguished between three types of situations, which they call "closed awareness," "suspicion awareness" and "open awareness." The first term refers to a situation in which the patient does not know that he is about to die and in which the others around him try to keep this knowledge from him. The second term refers to a situation in which the patient begins to suspect what his real condition is. Finally, the third term refers to those cases in which all concerned are fully aware of what is happening and in which, therefore, there is no attempt at hiding the truth from the patient. In each of these three situations, there are specific rituals governing the conduct of the participants. It is the third situation that puts the most stress on everyone, since the patient is now openly accorded the status of a dying person. It follows that the normal expectations of social life no longer prevail. The patient himself must "live up" to the expectations of this status and, in a complementary way, so must the others around him. By contrast, from the viewpoint of those who have to deal with a patient, it is the first situation that is most comfortable, because it permits everyone to act as if there is nothing out of the ordinary that is about to happen. It is not surprising that, for this reason, in American hospitals very frequently patients about to die are not informed of their true condition by the medical personnel in charge of them.

[10] Barney Glaser and Anselm Strauss, *Awareness of Dying* (Chicago, Aldine, 1965).

DEALING WITH THE DEAD   However the situation of dying may be defined and dealt with, death, once it has occurred, is an inescapable fact. What is more, it is a fact that most powerfully puts in question the everyday fabric of social life. Again, this is not peculiar to contemporary society. The ceremonialism surrounding funerals has always been a response to this mighty threat to the taken-for-granted patterns of social life. In all societies, it has been an occasion to reaffirm the fundamental meanings of society and its solidarity in the face of this ultimate threat. Cultural anthropologists have often emphasized this function of funeral ceremonialism.[11] In almost all human societies, these fundamental meanings have been religious. In contemporary society, at least partially because of the decline in religious beliefs, there has been considerable difficulty in making such affirmations. Therefore there has been a tendency to organize funerals in such a way as to camouflage the stark facts of death as much as possible.[12] This tendency to camouflage death has gone furthest in America. It is very clearly expressed in the terminology that is used. The corpse is referred to as "the loved one"; death as having "passed away"; the coffin as a "casket"; the undertaker as a "funeral director" or "mortician." The practices of the funeral, from the décor of "funeral chapels" (or, even more drastically, "funeral homes") to the cosmetic procedures applied to corpses, all serve to mitigate the harsh facts of death. To some extent, this is undoubtedly the result of a greater sensitivity for the feelings of mourners, which may be related (as it is always done by morticians) to the humane ideas prevailing in our society. Very probably, however, these attempts at camouflaging death also express a deep-seated inability to cope with the fact. In a society that glorifies vitality in all its aspects, death is necessarily a meaningless event.

[11] See Bronislaw Malinowski, *Magic, Science and Religion* (New York, Free Press, 1948).

[12] See Geoffrey Gorer, *Death, Grief and Mourning* (Garden City, N.Y., Doubleday, 1965). In a more popular vein, see Jessica Mitford, *The American Way of Death* (New York, Simon & Schuster, 1963).

As we have seen, society provides the individual with definitions of reality from cradle to grave. There is also the need for society to provide comprehensive definitions of the overall meaning of an individual's biography, and particularly those situations in his biography in which he is confronted with acute pain and terror. To some extent it may be said that social life always takes place in a context of "closed awareness," that is, in a context in which people pretend that the fact of death is not quite real or, at least, very far away. If this were not so, the ordinary patterns of life would be overwhelmed with anxiety. Since the borderline situations are inevitable, there must be ways of being ready for them. In other words, in one way or another, every society must have some way of answering the fundamentally searching question: "What is it all about?" Through most of human history, it has been the social function of religion to provide the answer.

READINGS

We would suggest further reading on the relation of borderline situations to the quest for meaning, which will lead the reader into the questions of the following chapter. We recommend one of the following three books:

Fox, Renée, *Experiment Perilous* (New York, Free Press, 1959).

Glaser, Barney, and Anselm Strauss, *Awareness of Dying* (Chicago, Aldine, 1965).

Sudnow, David, *Passing On* (Englewood Cliffs, N.J., Prentice-Hall, 1967).

Chapter 17

VALUES
AND
ULTIMATE
MEANINGS

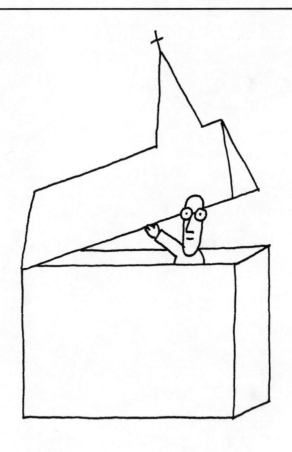

WHAT IS LIFE ALL ABOUT? COLLECTIVE AND INDIVIDUAL JUDGMENTS

Values have been the hidden theme of this book. Directly or indirectly, values have been involved in almost every area of social life that we have looked at. Socialization has been described as the initiation of every new generation into the world of its elders, a world in which values play a central part. Beginning with language, we have tried to show how social institutions are dependent on common ways of looking at life and how social control consists primarily in the internalization of these institutionalized patterns of thought. Stratification, whatever its economic determinants, crucially involves division over values between different strata. In the sphere of power, the same hidden theme re-emerged in the problem of legitimacy. We have seen how deviance, whatever its physical or psychological bases, turns out to be something "in the mind." Finally, in the preceding chapter, we have looked at those borderline situations of social life in which the question, "What is it all about?" becomes an urgent concern.

Values, of course, have been a subject of interest to philosophy and ethics for a very long time. But for our present purposes we can be satisfied with a simple definition of the term: values are notions as to what constitute right, as against wrong, actions. In other words, values are moral judgments about actions. Sometimes such judgments are made by isolated individuals standing in opposition to their own society. Most of the time, however, these judgments are collective, that is, are held in common by most of the members of a particular group or society. It is values in this latter sense that sociology is mainly interested in.

WHAT IS THE *MEANING?* HOW DO PEOPLE MAKE SENSE OF AND DEFINE REALITY?

It is largely due to Max Weber that sociologists have become aware of the importance of paying attention to the meaning of social actions. If one is to understand what goes on in a particular social situation, then one must understand how the participants in that situation make sense of it, what their motives and intentions are and how they judge the moral implications of what they and others are doing. In that case, values may be understood as a special category of meaning. We would suggest slightly different terms here. We would use once more a term we have previously employed, though without going into its full implications. This is the term *"definition of reality."* [1] Just as individuals participating in a social situation jointly define what that situation means, so entire societies will produce definitions of the overall reality of human life, and these definitions of reality serve as the taken-for-granted context of *all* social situations in that society. For example, a particular social situation may be defined by its participants as a classroom situation. This definition, however, is based upon much broader definitions of reality. Thus it takes for granted that there is an institution of higher learning of which this classroom is a particular case in point; that there are bodies of knowledge worth transmitting; and that the transmitter, in this situation, has the proper credentials for doing so; that the participants in the situation have motives and purposes that are meaningfully related to the activity now going on; and so forth.

---

[1] In this usage we deliberately want to recall W. I. Thomas's concept of the definition of the situation, but in a broader theoretical context derived from the work of Alfred Schutz. See especially Vol. I of the latter's *Collected Papers* (The Hague, Nijhoff, 1962).

WHAT "OUGHT TO BE" AND WHAT "IS"—BOTH ARE DEFINED

Definitions of reality may be both *normative* and *cognitive*. The former assert what reality *ought to be*, the latter what reality *is*. Most social situations, in one way or another, involve both these types of definition; that is, most social situations are determined both by norms and by "knowledge" (meaning, by the latter word, *whatever passes for knowledge* in this particular group). These two types of definitions of reality are closely related to each other. For example, one of the most ancient and most widespread social norms concerns the incest taboo, or, putting it positively, the permissible limits of marriage. Thus a particular society may hold the norm that one *may not* marry a first cousin. Implied in this norm is the knowledge of what a first cousin *is*. Most contemporary Americans probably know. But there are societies in which the norm asserts that one may not marry a *fifth* cousin. Not only would most of us have a hard time thinking of any fifth cousins of our own, but we would be, in all likelihood, incapable of even explaining what a fifth cousin is theoretically. In other words, we would be lacking the knowledge that is required as a basis for the norm. To take another example, most societies have certain norms concerning property. It is forbidden to steal, that is, to take from another what is his own. But what *is* his own? Societies differ widely in answering this question. Individual property may be limited to land, or it may exclude land. Property may include or exclude material artifacts, animals or even other human beings. And it is even possible (as modern copyright laws assume) that an individual's property may extend to the realm of ideas. In order to be able to follow the norm of not stealing, it is necessary to have knowledge of the definition of property.

NORMS IN SOCIETY: HOW DO RELIGIOUS NORMS RELATE TO ECONOMICS?

Although Weber was interested in the meaning of social action in the broadest sense of the term, the normative dimension of society occupies a central place in his work. His classical study of the relationship between Protestantism and capitalism illustrates this very clearly.[2] Weber's original interest was in economics, and more specifically, in the origins of modern capitalism. In order to pursue this interest, he found it necessary to investigate the motives and orientations of people engaged in economic activity. He subsequently came to the conclusion that Protestantism supplied certain values that proved to be of great importance in motivating people to the kind of economic activity that capitalism requires. This complex of values Weber termed "inner-worldly asceticism." The term (which points to a shift from another world to this world in Christian conceptions of self-discipline) covers such virtues as striving for success, hard work, rational planning, honesty and frugality.

It is important to point out that Weber was not satisfied in establishing that Protestantism favored these norms. He was further concerned to discover the relation between these norms and some of the fundamental religious propositions emerging from the Reformation. This led him into theological domains rarely frequented by students of economics. Weber analyzed the Lutheran doctrine of vocation, which insisted that any lawful work in the world was as pleasing to God as the work of a priest, a monk or a nun. And he showed how this reinterpretation of an old Christian value gave a tremendous spur to the serious pursuit of economic goals. In the most famous (and most hotly debated) part of his argument, Weber also tried to show how these norms were particularly related to the concepts of salvation that emerged in Calvinism. The original Calvinist doctrine of so-called double predestination (which said that

[2] Max Weber, *The Protestant Ethnic and the Spirit of Capitalism* (New York, Scribner, 1958).

God had predestined the greater part of humanity to eternal damnation and a small minority to eternal salvation, and that neither group could do anything to change its lot) was progressively unbearable psychologically to those who believed in it. The early Calvinists, in the first flush of charismatic excitement, were willing to live with such a notion—which means that they were at least theoretically prepared to accept that they themselves, despite all their good works and piety, might be among the damned. Later generations of Calvinists preferred to look for some method that would tell them which of the two groups they belonged to. One method was the deduction of divine election from what looked like divine blessings upon one's work. In other words, out of the innermost logic of a particular religious psychology came a set of norms that encouraged the striving for economic success.

Throughout his vast work in the comparative sociology of religion, Weber steadfastly pursued the same question: How do different religious traditions generate norms that relate to economic activity? [3] The economic history of Western Europe differed from that of India or China at least partly because it was dominated by different norms originating in differing religious traditions. The general point in all of this is that economic activity (and that applies equally to other areas of activity in social life) can never be understood by itself and without reference to the normative assumptions of those engaged in it. This approach to economic questions ran directly counter to the belief of classical economists (still held by many today) that there is some kind of "natural" way for people to act economically. It is presumably "natural" to desire physical survival and the satisfaction of physical appetites. But there is nothing "natural" in the innumerable social arrangements that men have developed in the course of their history in order to achieve these goals. Each of these social arrangements is dependent upon specific norms that will motivate people to act in accordance with its institutional patterns. Indeed, some of these norms can aptly be described as quite "unnatural"— as, for example, the kind of asceticism that demands self-denial and

[3] See especially Max Weber, *The Religion of China* (New York, Free Press, 1951) and *The Religion of India* (New York, Free Press, 1958).

even self-sacrifice from people. It is taken as a virtue in modern society (and, incidentally, in its socialist as well as its capitalist versions) for a person to work hard for goals that lie far in a future that, quite conceivably, he may never live to see, and for him to go on working even when his immediate needs are satisfied. From the viewpoint of, say, a Latin American peasant, such an attitude is incomprehensible, if not downright crazy. If one takes a literal view of what would be more "natural," one would probably have to side with the peasant.

One recurring question in this area is that of the *relation of norms and interests*, meaning by the latter term those concrete material purposes of social action that have nothing to do (seemingly) with values. We can translate this problem into the terminology of much current debate by saying that it concerns the relation between people's real motives and their moral rhetoric.

THE MARXIST STRUCTURE OF SOCIETY AND THE MIDDLE-CLASS FAMILY

The basic terms of the discussion about this were set by Karl Marx.[4] These terms, occasionally with some modifications, are still employed today in Marxist analyses. The basic concepts in this type of analysis are those of *sub-structure* and *super-structure*. The sub-structure is the sphere of material activity and interests which, for Marx and his followers, is above all that of the struggle between classes. The super-structure, in turn, contains both ideas and institutions that are the direct outgrowth of these "underlying" forces. The entire sphere of norms clearly falls within the super-structure. Thus, in any Marxist analysis of a problem involving the normative dimension of human society, the normal procedure is to deduce the norms from whatever "real" interests "underlie" them. Some Marxists have modified this scheme somewhat by conceding that, at times at least, the super-structure may have a certain autonomy of its own.

[4] See Karl Marx, *Selected Writings in Sociology and Social Philosophy* (New York, McGraw-Hill, 1964).

In terms of our particular problem, this means that at times norms may be developed according to some logic other than the logic of material interests. Nevertheless, the basic Marxist procedure in such cases continues to be that of looking upon norms in the role of dependent variables, determined more or less directly by the "underlying" interests (usually class interests).

For example, a Marxist sociologist analyzing the moral values of American family life will try first of all to determine the class position of the people involved in this particular type of family. Suppose he establishes to his own satisfaction that he is dealing with a middle-class (or, in his terms, bourgeois) group. He will then try to relate the moral ideas in question to the actual class interests of these people. Thus he may argue that notions of marital fidelity are the direct outgrowth of bourgeois interests in property. Or he may argue that this particular morality is designed to produce barriers between the middle class and the lower class it is exploiting. Or if, as has lately been the fashion among Marxists, he tries to combine Marx and Freud in his analysis, he may argue that middle-class morality is "repressive" (that is, stifles normal sexual impulses) in order to produce individuals who will function in a properly "uptight" manner in the capitalist system.

ARE MOST OF OUR MOTIVATIONS *UN*CONSCIOUS?

A strangely similar scheme of interpretation, though quite different in its theoretical implications, is that of Vilfredo Pareto.[5] The key concepts in Pareto's scheme are *residues* and *derivations*. Residues are recurring constellations of human motives which, presumably, are based on biological human nature as such. Derivations are the usually misleading reasons that people give for their actions. In order to understand what people are doing, it is not enough to observe their actions, and certainly not advisable to listen to their explanations of these actions. Instead, according to Pareto, the sociologist must penetrate to the sphere of residues, that

[5] Vilfredo Pareto, *The Mind and Society*, Vol. II (New York, Dover, 1963).

is, of the real motives that underlie both what people do and what they say. Pareto has a long list of types of residues, and one could imagine a number of different approaches he might have taken to the question of contemporary American family morals. Since sexuality is considered as one type of residues, it might be possible to interpret whatever derivations exist in this area as being simply expressions of the dominant sexual interests in the situation. In that case, a Paretian analysis would be very similar to a Freudian one. The similarity with Marx clearly lies in the tendency to view norms as being nothing but embellishments (Freud would say "sublimations" or "rationalizations") of the actual motives which, very often, are unconscious to the individual. The difference is equally clear. For Marx, the underlying motives are almost invariably related to the economic and social interests of class. For Pareto, these motives are based on a much more variegated "substructure" and are ultimately related to a human nature which Pareto conceived of as a constant—that is, as something that remains the same through all the fluctuations of history.

DO OUR ACTIONS EXPRESS NORMS?

At the other end of the pole, as it were, from the Marxian or Paretian approaches is that of Pitirim Sorokin.[6] As we have seen in an earlier chapter, Sorokin views society and the changes through which society goes as essentially an expression of varying ideas of "truth." In other words, norms are here given a determinant role which is almost exactly the opposite of the part assigned to them in the Marxian or Paretian scenario. In this view, it makes no sense to reduce morality or any other normative ideas to some allegedly underlying factors. On the contrary, human conduct in society must be seen as essentially an expression of norms. Such a view is much closer than the aforementioned ones to the way in which people in society usually look upon their own actions themselves, and, of course, is also congenial to the views of ethicists or moral philosophers.

[6] Pitirim Sorokin, *Social and Cultural Dynamics* (Englewood Cliffs, N.J., Bedminster, 1962).

ELECTIVE AFFINITY: DO IDEAS "FIND" GROUPS OR GROUPS FIND IDEAS?

Max Weber, particularly with his notion of "elective affinity" that we have had occasion to mention previously, stands between these two poles.[7] *Neither* norms *nor* interests are seen here as being invariably in a determining role. Both norms and interests can have independent origins and independent logics of development. They "come together" in particular situations in history. Such "coming together" may be put in different ways. One may say that the norms, because of a particular constellation of historical accidents, "find" social groups that will serve as their distributors; or one could describe the same process by saying that certain social groups discover, and then adopt, those norms that are convenient to their interests. No general rule can be made about the sequence of events in such situations. Each one must be investigated separately. The sociologist cannot, therefore, assume from the beginning that a particular morality is simply the expression of "underlying" interests, but neither can he start from the assumption that such interests are not present and that the conduct of people in a particular group is simply an expression of their moral ideas.

PARSONS'S "CULTURE," "PERSONALITY" AND "SOCIAL" SYSTEMS

Any functionalist approach to these questions is more likely to be closer to Weber's than to either of the two polar types of explanation. In this school, it is probably Talcott Parsons who has developed the most finely calibrated approach to analyses of norms.[8] Norms are assigned by Parsons to what he calls the "culture system." This is the repository of all symbols, ideas, values and beliefs in a particular society.

[7] See, for example, Hans Gerth and C. Wright Mills, *From Max Weber* (New York, Oxford University Press, 1958), pp. 284ff.

[8] Talcott Parsons, *The Social System* (New York, Free Press, 1951), especially pp. 326 ff.

The culture system has its own logic which cannot be simply re-duced to the logic of another system. It relates, in a variety of ways, to the two other systems which, according to Parsons, are necessary for the analysis of human conduct. These other two are the social system (essentially what all sociologists mean by society) and the personality system (which is the way in which individuals are psychologically structured). Each of these systems has its own set of functions and functional requirements which relate to each other in an exceedingly complex way. In this way, Parsons, like Weber, manages to avoid explanations of norms and interests by a one-sided causation.

YOUTH AND COUNTER-CULTURE: NORMATIVE CONFLICT WITH ESTABLISHED NORMS

It makes very much sense to look at important developments in contemporary society in terms of normative conflict.[9] This is particularly clear in America. The phenomena of the youth culture and the counter-culture can be understood in terms of their conflict with the established normative systems of middle-class society. Similar confrontations between opposing normative beliefs are also taking place in Western Europe and, indeed, in the socialist societies within the Soviet orbit. Throughout the so-called Third World, the process of modernization involves head-on collisions between new norms and the old normative patterns of traditional society.[10] In all these cases, the clash on the normative level is linked to a variety of class or other group interests. It is probably safe to say that the sociological analysis of these normative developments will be one of the principal tasks of the discipline in the years to come.

[9] See, for example, Anton Zijderveld, *The Abstract Society* (Garden City, N.Y., Doubleday, 1970).
[10] See, for example, C. E. Black, *The Dynamics of Modernization* (New York, Harper & Row, 1967).

"WHAT IS" COGNITIVE DIMENSIONS AND THE SOCIOLOGY OF KNOWLEDGE

The normative aspects of society cannot be separated from the cognitive dimension. The sub-discipline that deals with this topic is the sociology of knowledge.[11] The term was coined in Germany in the 1920's. Since then, a number of sociologists have done work under this heading, trying to investigate the general relation between ideas or forms of consciousness and their social contexts. Until recently, the major emphasis of the sociology of knowledge has been to investigate the relationship between intellectuals (that is, the producers and distributors of ideas in society) and the social interests of their particular milieu. A key question in this kind of inquiry has been that of "ideology." The term, originally used by Marx, denotes any set of ideas that directly express the interests of the social group. The question that has greatly concerned most sociologists of knowledge is how to distinguish between ideas that are simply ideology and those that are "more than" ideology.

In English-speaking sociology the best-known representative of this approach has been Karl Mannheim, a European scholar who spent the later years of his life in England. Mannheim thought that he could solve this problem by distinguishing between different types of intellectuals. The group that, according to Mannheim, was most likely to produce ideas untainted by ideology is the one he called the "detached intelligentsia," a group of intellectuals somehow hovering between the different classes and thus unencumbered with the burden of class interests.[12]

[11] For a systematic presentation of the sociology of knowledge, see Peter Berger and Thomas Luckmann, *The Social Construction of Reality* (Garden City, N.Y., Doubleday, 1966).

[12] Karl Mannheim, *Ideology and Utopia* (London, Routledge & Kegan Paul, 1936). For a recent interpretation of the social roles of intellectuals, see Lewis Coser, *Men of Ideas* (New York, Free Press, 1965).

DURKHEIM: *SOCIETY* AS MATRIX OF BOTH NORMS AND INTERESTS

Although the term "sociology of knowledge" was never used by the school, the same basic problem was a central concern of Émile Durkheim and his followers. In Durkheim's own work, the most mature expression of his approach to this problem occurs in *The Elementary Forms of the Religious Life,* the last book published during his lifetime.[13] In this book Durkheim argues that society is the foundation of all "categories," that is, of all ideas by which people organize and explain their experience. This Durkheimian way should not be too readily equated with the kind of sub-structure/super-structure scheme that we mentioned above. For Durkheim, it is not a major concern to trace back ideas to some non-ideal social roots. Rather, society *as a whole* is understood as the matrix of both ideas and practical action, of both norms and interests.

Long before his last book, Durkheim analyzed this relationship with the use of his concepts of *collective representations* and *collective consciousness.* The former term refers to all those ideas (normative or cognitive) that a group of people hold in common. The latter term refers to the sum total of the collective representations —in other words, to whatever coherent view of the world (again, both normative and cognitive) is held by a particular group. Again and again, throughout his work, Durkheim insists that one cannot understand society as a whole, or any particular part of it, except by constant reference to this dimension of consciousness. This understanding is, as it were, the other side of Durkheim's concept of anomie—anomie is precisely the condition in which the coherence of the collective representations breaks down, either for an individual or for a group. Both Durkheim and his followers were, for this reason, extremely interested in the way in which a particular society "categorized" reality. For example, in an early work that Durk-

[13] Émile Durkheim, *The Elementary Forms of the Religious Life* (New York, Collier Books, 1961).

heim wrote together with his student Marcel Mauss, the attempt was made to show some fundamental differences between modern and primitive society by investigating the manner in which the latter categorizes or classifies various phenomena of human experience.[14]

THE DURKHEIM SCHOOL: *DIFFERENT* COLLECTIVE CONSCIOUSNESSES

Even after Durkheim's death, a number of French social scientists influenced by him continued investigation into these problems. Some of these investigations have produced abiding contributions. Maurice Halbwachs, another student of Durkheim's, wrote a number of studies of memory in which both the memory of individuals and of groups is analyzed as a repository of the collective representations of society.[15] Halbwachs emphasized that memory is not a photographic retention of past events but, rather, a continuing *interpretation* of these events, and that this process of interpretation and reinterpretation is inevitably a collective or social one. One of the most interesting application of a Durkheimian perspective is in the work of Marcel Granet.[16] Granet was a historian specializing in the history of China. He tried to show how, in traditional Chinese society, some of the basic categories of human thought (such as time, space or number) were fundamentally different from those prevailing in the West, and how these specifically Chinese modes of interpreting reality were directly related to specific social institutions of China. A very similar procedure was used by Lucien Lévy-Bruhl in his classical analysis of the mental life of primitives.[17] As Granet did in

[14] Émile Durkheim and Marcel Mauss, *Primitive Classification* (Chicago, University of Chicago Press, 1963).

[15] Halbwachs's works on memory are, to date, unavailable in English. See Maurice Halbwachs, *Les cadres sociaux de la mémoire* (Paris, P.U.F., 1952).

[16] Granet's major work on this topic is, to date, also not available in English. See Marcel Granet, *La pensée chinoise* (Paris, Albin Michel, 1950).

[17] See, for example, Lucien Lévy-Bruhl, *Primitive Mentality* (New York, Macmillan, 1923).

the case of China, Lévy-Bruhl tried to show that primitive people think in categories that are fundamentally different from those of modern Westerners, and insisted that one could not understand anything about primitive society without taking cognizance of this difference on the cognitive level.

AN OVERARCHING VIEW OF REALITY: ULTIMATE MEANINGS

There is an overall view that emerges from these Durkheimian approaches. It is a view of society as necessarily containing a set of definitions of reality, both normative and cognitive, which provide the common frame of reference for social action. The further question, though, that concerned the Durkheimians was this: How is this frame of reference maintained? Durkheim, especially in his later work, gave a clear answer to the question: The frame of reference is maintained by an overarching view of reality, a comprehensive explanation of human experience through which both individuals and entire societies could make sense of their lives. This overarching view of reality Durkheim called "religion." [18] It is not too difficult to relate this Durkheimian conception to Weber's approach. As we have seen a number of times, Weber always focused on the meanings of human actions. What Durkheim is talking about under the heading of "religion" is precisely the *ultimate* meanings of human experience and human conduct. In other words, what is at issue here is society's answer to the recurring question, "What is it all about?"

[18] Durkheim, *op. cit.*

COHESIVE VIEWS
OF THE WORLD:
ONCE ALWAYS
RELIGIOUS

It is important to understand that what Durkheim means by religion is considerably more than what most people understand by this term. Sociologists have differed as to the manner in which religion is to be defined for their purposes. Most sociologists continue to follow a narrower definition of religion, one that is closer to common usage, in which religion refers only to those ultimate interpretations of life that contain a belief in God, or gods, or other supernatural entities.[19] Thus, under a Durkheimian definition of religion, such overarching frameworks for human life as Marxism, nationalism or the ethic of sexual liberation would be called "religion" just as Christianity or Judaism would be, because all of these fulfill essentially similar social functions. Under a more conventional definition of religion, of course, the former group of belief systems would be called by some other term to distinguish them from such religions, in the narrower sense, as the Christian or Jewish ones.

For most of human history, this difference in definition is of little significance. Almost all overarching views of reality were religious in the conventional sense of the word. Indeed, it can be plausibly maintained that man's first efforts to provide a cohesive view of the world were invariably religious in content. In primitive and archaic societies, just about every institution and every institutionalized pattern of human activity were directly related to a religious view of the world. The historian Eric Voegelin has called such societies "cosmological," [20] meaning by this that in such societies the ordinary social life of people is directly linked to the fundamental order of the cosmos. Social institutions (for example, the institution of kingship) are regarded as imitations or even emanations of di-

---

[19] For a systematic presentation of key theoretical problems of the sociology of religion, see Peter Berger, *The Sacred Canopy* (Garden City, N.Y., Doubleday, 1967). For a discussion of the definition of religion, see *ibid.*, Appendix I.

[20] Eric Voegelin, *Israel and Revelation* (Baton Rouge, La., Louisiana State University Press, 1956).

vine reality. Social roles (such as the roles of king or priest) are understood as representations or even incarnations of supernatural beings. Similarly, established patterns of human activity (such as sexual relations, agriculture or war) are understood as imitations or repetitions of similar acts performed in the world of the gods.

In such a society, religion provides not only the overarching view of reality that holds the society together but also comprehensive legitimations for every sector of social life. Voegelin tries to show how this unity between society and cosmos was ruptured in Western civilization by Israelite religion, on the one hand, and by the cultural transformation of Greece, on the other. Israel ruptured the cosmological unity by affirming a God who stood outside the world. Greece performed a similar rupture by its discovery of the autonomy of the individual soul, which allowed the individual (in his reason and his freedom) to step out of the old unity that linked every man through his society to the order of the gods. But even after these ruptures had taken place, there continued for a very long time an intimate relation between the sphere of social institutions and the believed order of the universe. Thus, in the Middle Ages, Christian thinkers spoke of an "analogy of being," by which all created things, from inanimate nature to men to the angels, stand in a fixed hierarchy that stretches upward to God. As long as such beliefs prevailed in society, it was relatively easy to endow even the humblest human acts with ultimate meaning. It follows that, in Durkheimian terms, the danger of anomie in such a society is relatively small.

RELIGION: NORMS FOR ACTION IN "THE WORLD"

The central concern of the sub-discipline known as the sociology of religion is the relation of these ultimate meanings to the meanings of everyday life.[21] Weber, in his own work in the sociology of religion, always focused on the relationship of religious beliefs to what he called "the world." [22] He used

[21] For a good recent introduction to the sociology of religion, see Roland Robertson, *The Sociological Interpretation of Religion* (Oxford, Blackwell, 1970).
[22] Max Weber, *The Sociology of Religion* (Boston, Beacon, 1963), pp. 207ff.

this term pretty much the way it was used in the New Testament —"the world" is set against those events and activities that relate to the Kingdom of God. In other words, "the world" is that sphere of human life that is not specifically subsumed under religious meanings.

How does religion relate to "the world"? As should be clear by now, the basic relation is one of providing norms for social action. Weber, as we have seen, was particularly interested in those norms that refer to economic activity, but that was simply because of his original interest in the relation of religion and modern capitalism. A further relation between religion and the social order is that of legitimation. Put simply, religion explains and justifies social institutions and social roles. Through most of human history, legitimation has been mainly undertaken by means of religious definitions of reality. Kings ruled "by the grace of God," wars were fought "for God and country," marriages were solemnized "before God," and even businessmen, until very recently, would write on the first page of their ledgers "with God." It is important to stress, however, that religion has served not only to legitimate but also to *de-legitimate* social institutions. The prophets of ancient Israel serve as paradigmatic figures for this possibility in subsequent Jewish and Christian history. Prophets such as Amos, Isaiah or Jeremiah prophesied "against Israel" in the name of the God of Israel. Under the banner of religion, they dared to challenge the acts of even the mightiest men and to question the institutions of the status quo.

RELIGION: AN EXPLANATION FOR EVIL AND PROSPERITY

Another important relation between religion and "the world" of everyday social life is brought about by religion providing society with a *theodicy*.[23] Once again, Weber brought this term into sociology by slightly modifying its previous usage in theological discourse. The word literally means "the justice of God" and refers to the problem, classically expressed in the Book of Job, of how to reconcile

[23] See *ibid.,* pp. 138ff.

belief in an omnipotent and benevolent God with the presence of suffering and evil in the world.

Weber calls a theodicy any socially established interpretation of human suffering, injustice or inequality. He distinguishes between what he calls the theodicy of suffering and the theodicy of happiness. Those who suffer in the world, be it because of the actions of other men or because of "acts of God," have a natural propensity to ask why they are thus afflicted, especially since other men are not. Religion has always provided answers to this question—though the answers are greatly different in different religious traditions. The theodicy of happiness, on the other hand, satisfies the need of those who are in a more favored condition of life for the comforting reassurance that somehow this condition is what they deserve. Not all, but many, religious traditions have met this need as well. Weber maintained that the most rational and comprehensive theodicy to be found in history is that of classical Hinduism. Hindu theodicy was based on its belief in reincarnation and in *karma* (the doctrine that every human act has inevitable consequences for the actor, some of which extend beyond this present life). This means that every human being is precisely in the condition which he deserves. Those who suffer have no basis on which to complain, and those who are happy have no reason to feel guilty. It is this unique theodicy of Hinduism that explains the astonishing lack of rebellion against the Indian caste system, which, to modern eyes, imposed an intolerably harsh condition upon the lower castes. But since suffering is a universal human condition, even in the most privileged human strata, the need for theodicy is universal. Religion shows most clearly its function of providing ultimate meaning for human life in its ability to integrate the painful and terrifying experiences of life, and even death itself, into a comprehensive explanation of reality and of human destiny.

THE SECULARIZATION OF INSTITUTIONS AND NORMS

The central problem of the sociology of religion in contemporary society is *secularization*.[24] The term, which is widely employed by scholars as well as in common usage, refers to the peculiarly modern process in which religion has become progressively less important in more and more sectors of human life. In Europe there now exists a sizable body of sociological literature, much of it produced under the auspices of the Catholic Church, which studies the declining influence of the Church as an institution and also of religious ideas in general in modern society.[25] American sociologists have also studied the difficulties encountered by the religious institutions in maintaining their traditional pre-eminent position in American society.[26] While, for many historical reasons, there are important differences in the social position of religion in Europe and America, the global process of secularization can be observed equally in both areas. Not only are the religious institutions increasingly relegated to certain margins of social life but, more importantly, religious ideas have become progressively less important in providing meaning for different sectors of social life. For the institutional aspect, the case of education may be taken as an example. Until very recently, this was almost exclusively the preserve of organized religion. Today, it is an overwhelmingly secular enterprise. The area of personal morality may be taken as an example of the same process of secularization on the level of consciousness. It appears that fewer and fewer people take their guidelines for personal conduct from any of the established religious traditions.

[24] See Berger, *op. cit.*, Part II.

[25] For examples of this work in English, see the contributions of F. Boulard, F. A. Isambert and E. Pin in Louis Schneider (ed.), *Religion, Culture and Society* (New York, Wiley, 1964).

[26] An influential study of this situation has been Will Herberg, *Protestant—Catholic—Jew* (Garden City, N.Y., Doubleday, 1955). For recent empirical studies, see, for example, Rodney Stark and Charles Glock, *American Piety* (Berkeley, Calif., University of California Press, 1968), or Jeffrey Hadden, *The Gathering Storm in the Churches* (Garden City, N.Y., Doubleday, 1969).

DOES MAN *NEED* A COMPREHENSIVE ORDER OF MEANING?

At this point, the aforementioned difference in the definition of religion becomes more important. If one takes the narrower, more conventional definition of religion, then one must ask what, in the wake of secularization, has taken the place of the previous religious meanings. If, on the other hand, one operates with the broader, Durkheimian definition of religion, then the term "secularization" is not too helpful. In this approach, society *always* has "religion." The question now becomes: What kind of new "religion" is emerging to take over from the older traditions? [27] But whichever definition one chooses, one must confront the same underlying fact: the breakdown in an overarching view of reality that was formerly provided by the religious traditions of Western civilization.

How one views this state of affairs, and what kind of future development one will then prognosticate, will depend very largely upon one's acceptance or non-acceptance of the fundamental Durkheimian premise that no human society can exist without an overarching view of reality. If the premise is granted, then the contemporary absence of such an overarching view must necessarily be temporary. New comprehensive orders of meanings will necessarily emerge. These could, of course, take quite different forms. Thus, if one assumes that secularization will continue, one will have to look for non-religious definitions of reality. These could be anything from the highly organized doctrines of modern political movements to such diffuse bodies of ideas as the contemporary faith in universal human rights or the new cult of sensitivity in every aspect of physical experience. Alternatively, the overarching unity of meaning for society may once more take religious forms, either through a resurgence or restoration of traditional religious beliefs or, again, through entirely new forms of religious belief, practice and institutionalization.

[27] This viewpoint has been cogently argued by Thomas Luckmann, *The Invisible Religion* (New York, Macmillan, 1967).

If, on the other hand, the Durkheimian premise is not granted, an entirely different scenario is possible. One would then have to argue that modern society is peculiar and not comparable with earlier societies, precisely in that it is *not* in need of an overarching view of reality. It would then be possible to envisage the long duration of a new kind of society marked by pluralism in the most far-reaching sense of the word. Different groups or sectors in the society would have widely discrepant views as to the ultimate meaning of life, and yet would exist side by side. In that case, society *as a whole* would no longer have the solidarity of which Durkheim spoke. The different groups within it would be related to each other contractually, that is, not by a common allegiance to values and ultimate meanings but by rational arrangements that will meet their respective interests. The great majority of sociologists continue to grant the basic Durkheimian premise, and they must therefore choose between prognoses that are based on it.

Durkheim has been given the credit for having most cogently analyzed religion as a social phenomenon. There is nothing wrong with this description of his work. There is, however, a more profound implication to his interpretation of religion—for not only is religion a social phenomenon but, in turn, *society is a religious phenomenon*. What does this mean? It means that, just as every social situation is dependent upon the definitions of the situation that the participants bring to it, so society as a whole is constituted by the definitions of reality that prevail in it. Reality is socially defined, but society is in turn constituted by virtue of these definitions. In the final analysis, society is a community of meaning.

READINGS

For a general discussion of religion in modern society, we suggest: Thomas Luckmann, *The Invisible Religion* (New York, Macmillan, 1967).

For sociological approaches to religion in contemporary American society, we suggest any of the following:

Herberg, Will, *Protestant—Catholic—Jew* (Garden City, N.Y., Doubleday, 1955).

Lenski, Gerhard, *The Religious Factor* (Garden City, N.Y., Doubleday, 1961).

Stark, Rodney, and Charles Glock, *American Piety* (Berkeley, Calif., University of California Press, 1968).

POSTSCRIPT—
WHY
SOCIOLOGY?

THERE ARE, of course, different reasons why students take an introductory course or read an introductory book on sociology. These range all the way from earnest career plans to the tactical requirements of seduction, not to mention the campus reputation and grading habits of sociology instructors. We have no objections to the less than earnest motives. But, optimists by inclination, we assume that having finished the course, and (needless to say) having read this book, at least some students will be more rather than less interested in sociology. In that case the question, "Why sociology?" will also be more interesting to them than it was at the outset.

The question can be asked with two different senses: "What can one actually do with sociology?" And, more searchingly: "Is sociology worthwhile?"

MAKING A LIVING IN THE "KNOWLEDGE INDUSTRY"

One thing that one can obviously do with sociology is to become a sociologist. Only a very small fraction of those who take sociology courses as undergraduates take this direction. For those considering this awesome option, a few words on its practical implications are in order here.

The discipline of sociology is today a well-established and well-organized profession in America. As of late 1969, the membership of the American Sociological Association, the major professional organization of the discipline, was 12,903 if one includes student members and 8,461 if one only counts the fully certified brethren —in either case, a number not be to be sneezed at.[1] The association has an impressive headquarters in Washington and holds conventions in enormous hotels.

The visible output of American sociologists is impressive, too. Large numbers of books are published in sociology every year. There are dozens of journals in the field, more than anyone can possibly read and do anything else besides, so that there is now (as in other disciplines) a journal *about* journals, *Sociological Ab-*

[1] American Sociological Association, *Directory of Members* (Washington, D.C., 1970).

stracts, which classifies and summarizes this vast and rapidly growing body of professional lore.

Sociology constitutes a significant division of what Fritz Machlup, an economist, has called the American "knowledge industry." What is probably more important, sociology occupies, and has occupied for a considerable period of time, a respected place on the American intellectual scene. Naturally, there are also detractors, like the sardonic commentator who said some years ago that a sociologist is a man who will spend ten thousand dollars to discover the local house of ill repute. By and large, though, statements about society by sociologists exercising their professional judgment widely command authority or at least gain a serious hearing. This is true in the mass media, in political debate over current issues, among decision makers in government and business, and in broad segments of the general public. We would not be sociologists if we did not agree that, much of the time, this intellectual status of the discipline is merited. To mention only some of the problems currently troubling American society, sociologists have contributed both important information and clarifying insights to the public discussion of urbanism, of the racial situation, of education, of government measures against crime and against poverty.

American sociology continues to hold a pre-eminent position in the discipline, comparable, say, to the position held by German philosophy and German historical scholarship in the nineteenth century. Sociology in no other country compares with American sociology in terms of academic and intellectual status, the variety and sophistication of theoretical approaches and research technology, both the quantity and quality of output, and the sheer size of the professional establishment. American books and journals throughout the field are necessary reading for foreign sociologists, while the reverse is only true for limited aspects of sociology (as, for example, for sociological theory). Foreign sociology students, if at all possible practically, seek to spend at least some portion of their studies in an American university's sociology department. Not surprisingly, English (one is tempted to add, especially if one looks at the writings of British sociologists, *American* English) has become the lingua franca of sociologists everywhere.

All the same, there has been a quite remarkable upsurge of sociology abroad over the last two decades. Sizable sociological establishments have grown up in Western Europe, particularly in
Germany, France, Britain, Holland and the Scandinavian countries. Although the attitude toward sociology by Communist regimes has vacillated between condemning it as a "bourgeois ideology" and gingerly accepting it as a useful instrument in social
planning, sociology is now a going concern in the Soviet Union and
in the socialist countries of Eastern Europe. The holding of the
1970 World Congress of Sociology in Bulgaria symbolized this new
acceptability of the discipline in the "socialist camp" (at least the
part of it that is within the Soviet orbit). In the countries of the
Third World, sociology is very widely regarded as an important aid
for development planning and policy.[2]

What are American sociologists actually doing? The very great
majority are engaged in teaching at colleges and universities.[3] This
means, quite simply, that anyone planning to become a professional sociologist should reckon with the fact that most jobs in the
field are teaching jobs, and that teaching is very probably what he
will be doing at least much of the time. The most important other
activity of sociologists is research, though for many this is not a
source of continuous employment but rather something that they
do besides teaching or on occasional leaves from teaching jobs. All
the same, there are a good number of full-time research jobs, some
connected with university research programs, others in agencies or
research institutes of the government, business, labor or other organizations (such as churches) with an interest in discerning societal
trends. Thirdly, there is a scattering of sociologists in jobs of the

[2] A good way to obtain an idea of the international scope of recent sociology
is to look at the *Proceedings* of, respectively, the 1966 (Evian, France) and 1970
(Varna, Bulgaria) World Congresses of Sociology, published by the International
Sociological Association. For an interesting discussion of sociology in the Soviet
Union, see George Fischer (ed.), *Science and Ideology in Soviet Society* (New
York, Atherton, 1967). For an overview of the place of sociology in development
planning, see Gayl Ness (ed.), *The Sociology of Economic Development* (New
York, Harper & Row, 1970).

[3] For an excellent overview of the various applications of sociology in America, see Paul Lazarsfeld *et al., The Uses of Sociology* (New York, Basic Books,
1967).

most different sorts, ranging from advertising and personnel management to community action in this country or abroad. Whether interested in teaching or one of the other options, the aspiring sociologist should realize that graduate study, increasingly up to and
including the doctorate, is a prerequisite for jobs that carry professional status (not to mention the pay that one associates with such
status). Different graduate programs emphasize different aspects of
the field, and some thought ought to be given to the choice of
school, especially since the American academic system does not encourage easy transfers from one school to another.[4]

"ESTABLISHMENT" AND "RADICAL" SOCIOLOGY

There has recently been much debate within the profession about its
present condition, the directions it
has been taking and the directions
that it should take in the future.
There are strong differences of opinion among American sociologists both as to diagnosis and prescription.[5] Political radicals in the
field have attacked what they consider to be "establishment sociology" as an ideological tool of the status quo and have demanded a
new conception of sociology as a discipline standing in the service
of radical or even revolutionary politics. Black sociologists have
called for sociological work designed to serve the interests of the
black community, sometimes meaning by this nothing more than
work that would be more sensitive to the black experience in

---

[4] For the student thinking of graduate study in sociology, a logical first step is
to discuss this with a sociology instructor at his undergraduate college. Most college libraries have a fair collection of university catalogues, and it pays to study
their graduate sociology offerings with some care. The American Sociological Association publishes an annual *Guide to Graduate Departments of Sociology,* covering the United States and Canada; although professors do a lot of job-hopping,
this gives a general idea of who teaches where at a given time.

[5] For a broad view of this, see Robert Friedrichs, *A Sociology of Sociology*
(New York, Free Press, 1970). For sharply critical views, see Irving Horowitz,
Professing Sociology (Chicago, Aldine, 1968), and Alvin Gouldner, *The Coming
Crisis in Western Sociology* (New York, Basic Books, 1970). A good source for
what goes on within the profession, in these debates as in other things, is *The
American Sociologist,* one of the journals published by the American Sociological
Association.

America than that of (or so they claim) the work of many white sociologists, sometimes going much further by demanding a distinctively black sociology that would be part of and ideologically attuned to "black consciousness." Various movements concerned with "liberation," most recently (and very audibly so) the Women's Liberation movement, have sought to enroll sociologists and sociology in their ranks. Whatever one may think of these critiques and redefinitions of the field, they have greatly enlivened sociological discourse in recent years. All of this has taken place against the background of a much broader feeling that intellectuals and their disciplines should be involved in the agonies of our time and concerned with the solutions of our most agonizing problems. It is understandable that this feeling has been particularly strong among sociologists, proponents of a discipline that explicitly takes society as its object of inquiry.

Since only a small minority of those who take undergraduate courses in sociology goes on to professional work in the field, a rationale for these courses as nothing but pre-professional education (comparable, say, to a pre-medical curriculum) is hardly persuasive. There ought to be other things that one can do with sociology.

DEALING WITH MEN DIRECTLY: THE HUMAN SCIENCES AND THE HUMANITIES

Information and perspectives provided by sociology have wide applicability to other fields. This is obvious in a variety of practical fields that, in one way or another, must take cognizance of social structures. These range all the way from social work to the law. Sociology, by its very nature, has relevance for most other sciences dealing with man (those that the French, very aptly, call "human sciences"). In many places in this book we have seen the relation of sociology to other social sciences—political science, economics, cultural anthropology and social psychology, to name the major ones. But even in the humanities, where there has been a strongly ingrained animus against sociologists and their "barbarian" incursions into territory where they have no business, the recognition of the usefulness of sociological insights has grown. This is especially true among historians, but it may also be found today among scholars of religion and literature.[6]

But what about the individual who has none of these professional or scholarly ambitions? Is sociology worthwhile for him? We think so. Anyone who wants to live with his eyes open will profit from a better understanding of his society and his own situation in it. But perhaps even more important is the ability to understand the situations and the social worlds of others. Contemporary society needs this ability more than ever.

A PLURALISTIC SOCIETY: IS LOVE *REALLY* ALL YOU NEED?

Good will is not enough. Let us take just one example out of many possible ones. A few years ago a group of white upper-middle-class young people from the New York suburban area decided that, in order to show their concern for the "ghetto" and its people, they would go into some of the black neighborhoods of the city and help in fixing them up. They did so, on one fine weekend, the first and the last of the experiment. They came in full of enthusiasm and started to paint houses, sweep the streets, clean up piles of garbage and engage in other "obviously" desirable activities. Before long they were surrounded by angry black teenagers, and a good many angry black adults, who yelled obscenities at them, threw disagreeable objects and generally interfered with the progress of operation uplift. There is no reason to impugn the good will of the young whites. At worst, they were guilty of naïveté, slightly spiced with self-righteousness. Even a whiff of sociological insight on their part, however, would have avoided the entire debacle. It hardly needs emphasizing that better insight into the social situation, and therefore the motives and meanings, of others can be very useful for blacks as well.

[6] See Lazarsfeld, *op. cit.*, pp. 3ff.

Contemporary society, as we have seen, is becoming increasingly complex and variegated. This is what is commonly called "pluralism." What is more, contemporary society, or any conceivable variation of its present structure, will break down into howling chaos unless a plurality of social groups and social worlds succeeds in existing together with a measure of mutual understanding. Under these circumstances, the insights of sociology are anything but an intellectual luxury. This is especially so if there is a future for democracy in this society. Sociology, as the application of critical intelligence to society, has a particular affinity to democracy, that political form that is based on the assumption that social conflicts can be resolved and social problems alleviated by means of rational persuasion and without recourse to violence. Non-democratic regimes, whether of the "right" or "left," have an instinctive aversion to sociology. Conversely, sociology has developed best in situations where the political structure had some real relationship to democratic ideas.

AWARENESS EXPANSION: A SENSE OF ONE'S POSSIBILITIES

If sociology has a particular affinity for democratic types of government, it has another, more personal relation to liberty.[7] Anyone who seriously immerses himself in the perspective of sociology will find that his awareness of society, and thus his awareness of himself, will have changed considerably. This changed awareness is not always or one-sidedly "liberating," in the sense of expanding the individual's sense of being free and being himself. Sociological insight may lead to a recognition of limitations that one was previously unaware of, and it may further lead to the sad conclusion that courses of action that one had previously regarded as capable of realization are, in fact, illusions and fantasies. Working hard in one's vocation is *not* the sure way to wealth and fame. Participating in a campus riot is *not* a step toward the revolutionary overthrow of the capitalist

[7] For a recent, more detailed discussion of this, see Peter Berger, "Sociology and Freedom," *The American Sociologist,* VI (1971):1.

system. And so on and so forth. Also, sociological insight may lead to an understanding of the great fragility of all the things one holds dear, including one's notions as to who one is, because sociology shows their ongoing dependence on social processes of definition and redefinition. This understanding, more than any other provided by sociology, can be deeply upsetting, as it seems to shake the very ground on which one is standing.

Thus the relation of sociology to the individual's sense of his own liberty is not a simple or easy matter. Still, when all is said and done, the perspective of sociology, correctly understood, leads to a deepening of the sense of liberty. Long ago the Stoics declared that wisdom consists in knowing what I can and what I cannot do, and that freedom is only possible on the basis of such wisdom. There is something of this wisdom in sociologically formed awareness. Precisely because sociology teaches the limitations and the fragility of what the individual can do and be in society, it also gives him a better sense of his possibilities. And, leaving aside philosophical sophistication, perhaps this is as good an operational definition of liberty as any—having a sense of one's possibilities. Politics has been described as the art of the possible. If so, in all modesty, sociology might be described as a *science of the possible*.

It is for these reasons, we think, that sociology has a place in a "liberal arts" curriculum. Whatever may be its uses for professional training or scholarly enterprises, sociology has a bearing on the growth of personal awareness of the world, of others and of self. There is much controversy today over the future of college and university education. Whatever this future may turn out to be, we hope that it will have a place for this "liberal" conception of education, and thus for the peculiarly "liberal" discipline of sociology.

Index

achievement ethos, 31–32; and youth, 224–225
adjustments to organization, 206–207
adolescents, 210–231
affective neutrality, 314–316
affectivity, 314–316
affinities, 33, 86–87, 343
aging, 322–332
alcoholism, 285–286
alienation, 198
American Sociological Association, 357
America, sociology in, 36–40
anomie: in bureaucracies, 198; and deviance, 287; increasing in change, 303; in old age, 327; in *Suicide,* 27
anonymity, 188
asceticism, 338–340
authenticity, and youth, 225
authority, in charismatic movements, 307–311; Weberian typology of, 262
awareness expansion, through sociological study, 363–364
awareness of death, 330

Baltzell, Digby, 274
Becker, Howard, 292–294
Bensman, Joseph, 108
biography: adulthood and work, 233; childhood, 58–65; infancy, 45–58
biological growth, 212
biology: as cause of deviance, 282–283; and change, 300–301; and residues, 341–342
blacks: in caste system, 138–141; etiquette in caste system, 139–141; in stratification system, 131–132
Bloch, H., 290
Borgia, Pope Alexander, 311
Buddha, 324
bureaucracy, 186–209; effect on family, 84–85; as means of revolution, 311; and universalist principles, 315; as fragmented work, 235
business, and power, 268–271

calculability, in a bureaucracy, 193
Calvinsim, predestination and economic success, 338–339
capitalism: and change, 300; a late-capitalist society, 320; and Protestantism, 338–340; as a Weberian problem, 30–34
career: within biography, 11; in illness, 328; and work, 243
caste: American blacks and, 138–141; etiquette of, 139–141; legitimated by Hinduism, 352; as stratification system, 131–132
Castro, Fidel, 308
Catholic Church: and power, 256–257; as rationalized charisma, 310–311; and sociology of religion, 353
change, 298–321; and definitions of reality, 280–282; demographic, 85; technological, 84–85
charisma: as legitimation, 262–263; routinization of, 305–306
charismatic movements, 307–311
Chicago School, 38; on deviance, 285–286; and sociology of occupations, 241–242; of urban sociology, 102–106
childhood, definition of, 58–59
Christendom, de-legitimation of, 18–19
circulation of elites, 265
cities: as urban community, 102–106; and urban ethos, 113; urbanization into, 111–113
class: consciousness, 126–127; differences in feeding practices, 47; families of contrasting, 91–96; and life-chances, 147–154; and mental illness, 288; and opportunity, 147–154; as stratification, 119–124; struggle, 125–127, 267–268; Weberian life-chances, 127; and youth, 227–228
Cloward, R., 288
coerciveness, characteristic of an institution, 72–73